SPEED LIMITS

ALSO BY MARK C. TAYLOR

MARK C. TAYLOR

SPEED LIMITS

Where Time Went and Why We Have So Little Left

Yale UNIVERSITY PRESS

New Haven and London

Published with assistance from the foundation established in memory of James Wesley Cooper of the Class of 1865, Yale College.

Yale University Press books may be purchased in quantity for educational, business, or promotional use. For information, please e-mail sales.press@yale.edu (U.S. office) or sales@yaleup.co.uk (U.K. office).

Designed by Sonia L. Shannon.
Set in Garamond type by Integrated Publishing Solutions.
Printed in the United States of America.

ISBN: 978-0-300-20647-0 (cloth)

Library of Congress Control Number: 2014935570

A catalogue record for this book is available from the British Library.

This paper meets the requirements of ANSI/NISO Z39.48–1992 (Permanence of Paper).

10 9 8 7 6 5 4 3 2 1

For Aaron and Frida, Kirsten and Jonathan

You are running too fast

Now you are tired for the first time

Your happiness can catch up with you.

—Friedrich Nietzsche

Contents

Acknowledgments

Writing is a solitary activity that is impossible without a supportive community. The purportedly proper name of the author is always a pseudonym for others—some known, some unknown, some living, many dead—others who speak through the writer's words, which are never his own. *Speed Limits: Where Time Went and Why We Have So Little Left* grows out of questions I have been pondering since I wrote my first book—*Kierkegaard's Pseudonymous Authorship: A Study of Time and the Self*—more than four decades ago. Over the years, I have developed a philosophy of culture that attempts to understand where we have come from and where we might be heading. Having begun this journey during the tumultuous yet optimistic 1960s, I never could have predicted that the world would be even more fragmented and fragile as I approach the end. Along the way, I have learned lessons and absorbed insights from far too many writers, artists, friends, colleagues, and students to name here. I would, however, like to express my appreciation to a few individuals for their special contributions to this book: Esa Saarinen for his keen critical eye and boundless enthusiasm; Michael LeWitt for helping me decipher financial markets; David Shipley for guidance in unraveling tangled financial news media; Gil Anidjar for always making me look at issues from a different angle; Magnus Bernhardsson, Arnfríður Guðmundsdóttir, and Gunnar Matthíasson for introducing me to Iceland; Richard Robb for his extraordinarily careful reading of the manuscript; Margaret Weyers for her unfailing interest and support; Julie Carlson for her careful editing; Chelsea Ebin for many conversations and her careful attention to detail; Don Fehr for his consistent confidence in this book even when mine wavered; Jennifer Banks and John Donatich for their enthusiastic response to my work; Jack Miles, for too many years of friendship to count; John Chandler without whom I would not have become the teacher and writer I am today; and, finally, my family—Dinny for her patience with obsessions neither of us understands; Aaron, Frida, Kirsten, and Jonathan whose fast-paced lives have made me rethink much of what I once thought I knew; and Selma, Elsa, and Jackson for teaching me that despair is not an option.

December 13, 2013

Introduction

SPEED TRAPS

Call waiting . . . endless conference calls . . . mandatory Skype meetings no matter where you are or what time it is . . . urgent weekend business trips to deal with what could have waited until Monday . . . just-in-time everything . . . sleeping with an iPhone beside the bed . . . checking email all night . . . receiving email while in a cab heading to dinner with a friend and returning to the office . . . longer and longer workdays week after week—seventy, eighty, ninety hours without a break. In "real" time, everything speeds up until time itself seems to disappear, and fast is never fast enough—everything has to be done now, instantly. To pause, to delay, to stop is to miss an opportunity and to give a competitor the edge. Speed has become the measure of success—faster chips, faster computers, faster networks, faster connectivity, faster news, faster communications, faster transactions, faster delivery, faster product cycles, faster brains, faster kids, faster lives. According to the gospel of speed, the quick inherit the earth.

How did this new world of speed emerge, and why does it seem to be inescapable? The most obvious answer is technology. Information, communications, and networking technologies are creating a new world that bends back to transform human life into its own image. Moore's law, according to which the speed of computer chips doubles every eighteen months, now seems to apply to life itself. My life is faster than my father's life, my children's life is faster than my life, and the lives of their children, already hooked on iPhones and iPads, will be faster than theirs. This is not idle speculation but a fact. The examples of speed with which I began these reflections are all taken from the lives of my children and their families. They are young professionals—two lawyers, a financial adviser, and an advertising manager—whose lives are trapped by speed. The speed revolution, it is important to stress, affects different people in different ways; indeed, speed has become a, if not the primary, socioeconomic differentiator. As some people speed up, others slow down; as some people work more than they want, others work less than they want or even not at all; as some people get "ahead," others fall "behind." What "winners" and "losers" in this new fast-paced economy share are the insecurity, anxiety, and discontent that speed creates.

While the ubiquity of high-speed connectivity is changing our lives, technology does not emerge in a vacuum; rather it is driven by social, political, and most important, economic and financial forces, which in turn have been shaped by specific values that have a long, though often unacknowledged, history. The accelerating world of the twenty-first century is inseparable from the new form of capitalism—financial capitalism—that developed during the latter half of the twentieth century. Further, when viewed in the long arc of history, it becomes clear that the specter of Protestantism still haunts the world. Today's high-speed financial capitalism is the culmination of a secularization of the Protestant economy of salvation that began with the Reformation. As we will see, the invisible hand of John Calvin's providential God became the invisible hand of Adam Smith's prudential market. Just as God creates good out of evil and salvation out of sin, so the market transforms the pursuit of self-interest into the common good. The tokens change and the investment strategies vary, but the system of exchange has remained remarkably consistent throughout the centuries. Whereas in previous forms of capitalism wealth was created by selling labor or products, in financial capitalism, wealth is created by exchanging monetary signs and virtual assets that circulate in global networks at the speed of light. The difference between the so-called real economy and this new virtual economy is speed. Since virtual assets compound much faster than real assets, the wealth gap is actually a speed gap that continues to grow at a faster and faster rate. Contrary to expectation, high-speed connectivity deepens old divisions and creates new ones.

There are unavoidable speed limits, however, because the virtual is always bound by the real. The acceleration of life is rapidly approaching the tipping point, where there inevitably will be social, political, economic, financial, physical, psychological, and ecological meltdowns. My sense—or is it a faint hope?—is that many people are beginning to realize that the current trajectory is unsustainable and their present lives unlivable. The price of speed is time, which is of course life itself. With everything in motion and everyone on the move, there is never enough time for anything. The faster we go, the less time we have, and the less time we have, the faster we think we have to go. In the endless effort to save time, we waste what little we have left. As speed increases, losses continue to mount until we realize that once time is lost, it can never be recovered. The most pressing question we face as individuals and a society is whether enough time is left to change before those meltdowns that have already been set in motion occur. If it is not too late to change, it is necessary to slow down long enough to reflect on how the values implicitly and explicitly governing our lives have evolved and how they must be transformed for human life as we know it to survive. The lives of our grandchildren will not be better than ours unless they learn what most of us seem to have forgotten—less is more, and slower is better.

1. Addiction to Speed

Farms, Mines, Trains, Computers

Fast food

Fast fashion

Speed dating

Speed faithing

Instantaneous communication

High-speed networks

High-frequency trading

Flash trade

Flash crash

Acid

Ritalin

Fast signs

Your world in 90 seconds (*CBS This Morning*)

Week of crime in 60 seconds (CNN)

Speed Network (Fox)

Your world in 140 characters (Twitter)

Sleeker, Faster, More Intuitive (*New York Times*)

Welcome to a world where speed is everything. (Verizon Fios)

Speed is God, and time is the devil. (Hitachi Corporation)

"Speed," Milan Kundera writes in his timely novel *Slowness,* "is the form of ecstasy the technical revolution has bestowed on man."[1] We are addicted to speed. In a world the gods seem to have deserted, speed has become the opiate of the people. It's the fix we can't do without. As the pace of acceleration increases, delay and deferral become intolerable— faster is always better. The ecstasy of speed promises to realize the ancient dream of simultaneity in which the present becomes omnipresent. Once not so long ago, this timeless present was called eternity; today it is called real time—24/7/365. In real time, all times, all places, are here and now. But the dream of omnipresence, like the dream of omniscience and omnipotence, is an illusion. When everywhere is anywhere and anywhere is everywhere, the now-here of presence becomes the no-where of absence. Rushing to keep up, we lose ourselves and lose touch with the natural world that sustains us.

Speed. It's always a matter, or increasingly a non-matter, of time. Life is a bet, not Pascal's wager of whether to believe or not to believe, but a different wager. A wager on which the future depends: your money or your life. But what is life other than time? A lifetime. The bet on which everything now turns is how to invest, how to spend the little time we have been loaned. How do we reckon this wager? How do we measure the return on the investment of a lifetime? Does the book of life ever balance? One thing is certain—nothing is ever free; everything has a price, even money. Money and time are the two things no one ever seems to have enough of, and in the new world of extreme finance, the price of money is time. Accounts have become inverted: the less time you have, the more money you have, and the less money you have, the more time you have. The terms of the bet have changed. Your money or your life has become your money or your time.

What is speed's draw? The most obvious answer seems to be technology and economics. In his prescient novel *Prey,* which is about self-replicating and self-organizing microbots that escape into the wild, Michael Crichton writes, "The companies of Silicon Valley are the most intensely competitive in the history of the planet. Everybody works a hundred hours a week. Everybody is racing against milestones. Everybody is cutting development cycles. The cycles were originally three years to a new product, a new version. Then it was two years. Then eighteen months. Now it was twelve months—a new version every year. If you figure beta debugging to golden master takes four months, then you have only eight months to do the actual work. Eight months to revise ten million lines of code, and make sure it all works right."[2] Speed is creating a new world that transforms what we do, what we value, and, more important, who we are. As acceleration accelerates, our very sense of reality morphs. The unquestioned faith in this New Age is that faster is always better and that the quick inherit the earth.

It has not always been thus. The cult of speed is a modern invention. Two of the unfortunate byproducts of the cult of speed are the disappearance of long-range planning and the disintegration of long-term memory. But to understand the contemporary obsession with speed, it is necessary to look beyond the present moment back to the beginning of Western modernity. Within this longer perspective, the story of speed and its relation to time appears to be inseparable from the religious, political, technological, and economic forces that have shaped the modern and postmodern worlds. As we approach the end of a trajectory that began with the Protestant Reformation, the rate of change continues to accelerate until life seems to spin out of control. The question haunting the following pages is whether there is enough time left to slow down processes whose increasing speed threatens the complex social, cultural, political, economic, technological, and natural networks on which life depends.

Always preoccupied with the new new thing, people today tend to forget how recent are the innovations that created today's high-speed world. Most of the decisive changes described in this book have occurred since the time of our grandparents. My father was born and

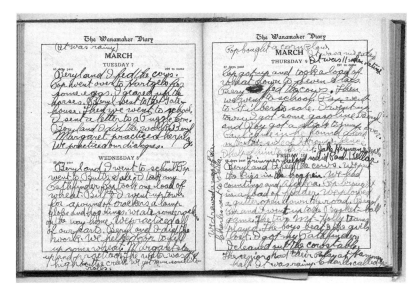

Noel A. Taylor's teenage diary, 1922

raised on a farm near Gettysburg in 1907; his mother, Emma, was born in 1869, and his father, Calvin, in 1871, just a few years after the end of the Civil War. I never knew my grandmother, who died in 1925, but my grandfather lived until 1964. I knew him well and have many fond memories of listening to him tell stories about life in the late 1800s while helping him to weed his garden and tend his beehives, and while hunting with him on the farm where he raised his family. After my father's death, my brother and I found a diary that my father had kept in 1922, when he was fifteen years old.

My father's account offers a fascinating window on rural life in early twentieth-century America. He writes about getting up at 4:00 in the morning and doing chores before walking three miles to a one-room schoolhouse; returning home to trudge behind a horse-drawn plow until dark; beheading chickens and shooting deer, pheasants, and rabbits for family meals; slaughtering hogs to sell to townspeople; harvesting apples and peaches to take to market; riding through the snow on a horse-drawn sleigh; splitting wood to burn on long winter nights; and every evening after the work was done, studying for several hours by gaslight. Tucked in the back of his diary were printed copies of the questions for his final examinations on April 15, 1922, which are included in the Appendix. The subjects covered included arithmetic, spelling, grammar, history, writing, physiology, geography, and reading. The questions were surprisingly difficult; indeed, I would wager that most of today's high-school or even college students could not pass these exams.

My father never idealized his youth; he always said that life was even rougher for him than others because his father was a hundred years behind the times. No telephone, no electricity, no running water, no mechanized tools. Human and animal labor provided the energy that fueled the farm. A year before he died, he recalled these early days in his *Autobiographical Reflections* (1991). I still wonder if he knew that the end was near and if writing was his way of trying to complete his story.

In March, school ended. The spring was a busy time on the farm. We had to get the plowing done early so we could plant the corn. It took a long time to plow a 25-acre field. When I was about 8 or 10, I started plowing. I took pride in plowing. I preferred using mules. Before dad bought the mule, Beryl and I used to work with draft horses. They were big and clumsy, but when you worked with them day after day, you became attached to them even if you did look at their asses all day long. The plow only turned over about 8–10 inches at a time and you don't have to know much arithmetic to know it would take a long time to turn over twenty-five acres. After we had finished plowing, we had to harrow, roll and get the ground ready for planting the corn and oats. We usually tried to have the corn planted by the middle of May. We would sow oats in March and April and would plant potatoes as early as possible. Sometimes it was as early as March, but usually not until April. It depended on the weather.

In these descriptions of a hard life governed by natural rhythms and physical contact with the earth, what comes through most strongly is a love of animals and the land. Today, as we sit sealed in bubbles created by the screens surrounding us, it is worth remembering that even our modern, wired world still depends on the weather, which we are changing.

From grandfather to father to son, there is a direct link to the Civil War. How much has changed so fast! During the final years of his life, my father and I often debated whether he or I would see greater changes in our lifetime. "From the Wright brothers to a man on the moon," he would say, convinced that there was no way I would experience the changes he had. For a long time I agreed with him. In the years following his death, however, I began to change my mind. With the collapse of the Soviet Union and apparent triumph of global capitalism, the pace of change accelerated beyond what either of us could have expected. I wonder if my father would still think he had seen more changes than I as he watched his two-year-old great-granddaughter playing games on her father's iPad and iPhone.

The longer I have pondered my father's world and the world that now is not quite my own, the more I realize how intertwined they remain. Much is written today about the transformative effects of so-called disruptive technologies. While it is obvious that certain technologies have a significant influence on who we are and how we live our lives, exaggerated claims for disruption usually result from a failure of memory, which is symptomatic of a preoccupation with the present in a culture addicted to speed. It has also become customary to distinguish the period commonly known as industrial society from our post-industrial or information society. This distinction is not incorrect, but it should not be overdrawn. Post-industrial society, after all, remains industrial, and the Industrial Revolution was already an information, transportation, communications, and management revolution.

Rather than thinking in terms of the simple binary of industrial versus information, it is more productive to think in terms of changing configurations of capitalism. Capitalism has evolved through five primary forms: agricultural, mercantile, industrial, consumer, and financial. As in any evolutionary process, previous stages are not simply left behind but are taken up into and transformed by later stages. The industrial and information eras are braided together in a way that no simple linear narrative can unravel. The Industrial Revolution was already an information revolution, and the information revolution continues to transform industrial processes. What to the untutored eye appears to be an unexpected disruption is actually a dialectical reversal in which the old gives rise to the new that it inevitably shapes. In history, as in life, the slate can never be wiped clean, and thus there are no absolute beginnings. In a pattern we will see repeated again and again, every system, structure, or network has a condition of its own possibility that which eventually undoes it. When pushed to the limit, a new configuration emerges that disrupts, without completely displacing, previous patterns. Though such changes can be neither anticipated nor predicted, they can be comprehended retrospectively.

As I write these words, the workbench of my maternal grandfather, Mark H. Cooper (1883–1969), after whom I am named, sits beside my desk. He was a small businessman in a coal mining town in Pennsylvania that, strangely enough, bears the same name as the town where I have lived for four decades—Williamstown. He was a jeweler or, as they said in his day, a watchmaker, even though he did not make but only repaired watches.

In the early years of his business, my grandfather had a big clock in his window that kept time very accurately. Most people in town would set their watches by Mark Cooper's clock. His father, Aaron (1853–1916), was the first Cooper to leave the family farm and work for the

Mark H. Cooper's jewelry store, 1930s

coal mining company, not below ground like the eastern European immigrants who had migrated to the mountains of Pennsylvania, but above ground, taking care of the machinery that kept the air and water circulating in the mines. My mother and father met in 1929, when my father took his first job teaching all the sciences and coaching all the sports in the high school where my mother taught English. When they married a few years later, the school board demanded that my mother resign; she refused and won her case. My father quickly discovered that for the sons of miners, football was more important than science because it was the way they hoped to escape a life in the mines.

My grandfather's workbench bears traces of a world in transition. It is filled with the hand tools that he used to repair mechanical watches and sketchbooks in which he developed designs for his elaborate hand engravings. He engraved the pocketwatch he gave me before he died with

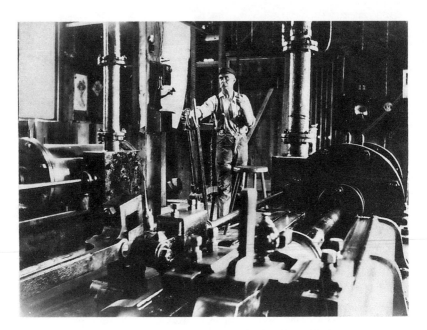

Aaron Cooper working in a Pennsylvania coal mine, later 1800s

his own initials. I have fond memories of visiting his store and sitting on a stool watching him work at his workbench. Tucked away in one of its drawers is his account book with the date, name of the customer, the kind of watch, its identification number, and the repair he made recorded in his elegant and precise handwriting. Another intersection of hand and machine: two other pieces of machinery in the store that I remember were a Burroughs calculating machine and a machine to imprint checks to ensure against forgery. I can still hear the clicking of the calculator as my grandfather sat adding the numbers and recording them in the precise columns of his account book.

Though he never earned more than $3,500 a year, my grandfather was considered one of the town's most successful businessmen. Indeed, for many years he was chairman of the school board and head

Mark H. Cooper's pocketwatch

of the board of directors at the local bank. When visiting my grandparents, every morning I opened the door to discover a copy of the *Wall Street Journal.* I had no idea what this publication was but always diligently brought it to my grandfather, who started his day by studying it. Over the years a mysterious stranger regularly visited my grandfather. They would retire to the parlor and together study the paper and engage in long discussions. Years later I learned that this man was my grandfather's stockbroker. By the time I was about ten, my grandfather decided I was old enough to begin my initiation into the alchemy of finance. He tried to explain to me what a stock market is and told me that the *Wall Street Journal* reported on how well or poorly businesses are doing. Needless to say, I understood none of this but I do remember him saying again and again over the years that his most reliable stock holding was his shares of Pennsylvania Railroad.

Horses, plows, and gaslight . . . mines, watches, railroads, and the stock market. As I have suggested, to understand the changes now occurring, it is necessary to trace an arc of history that dates back to the beginning of modernity—an arc that, as we will see, began with the Protes-

Mark H. Cooper's ledger, 1913

tant Reformation and is now rapidly approaching closure in the world of today's extreme finance. The key to understanding this trajectory is speed. The experience of speed is the creation of the modern world; modernization *is*, in effect, acceleration. One of the first products of speed is the increasing impatience with slowness. What was surprisingly fast yesterday is intolerably slow today. The horse didn't seem slow until the invention of the train and automobile; dial-up modems didn't seem slow until the introduction of Ethernet. From old to new, pre-modern to modern, pre-industrial to industrial, the direction is first from slow to fast, and then from fast to faster.

To avoid confusion, it is important to distinguish modernity, modernization, and modernism. Modernity, like speed, is a modern invention. The word *modern* derives from the Latin *modo,* which means "just now." Modernity is all about the now, the present, rather than the past and, as such, it's all about the new. As the notion of modernity has developed in the West, however, it has not been defined by the simple opposition between the modern (present) and the non-modern (past), but by a more intricate triadic structure that is rooted in the Christian theological tradition: ancient, medieval, modern. Modern philosophers and artists rewrote the medieval narrative of the three ages of the Father, the Son, and the Spirit as the three-part story of the ancient, medieval, and modern periods. What remains constant in this translation is the conviction that the third epoch will be a New Age in which humanity reaches its fullest realization. The worldly or otherworldly Kingdom of God becomes real or virtual in contemporary visions of artistic and technological utopias. Whether religious or secular, such stories are always fantasies because these dreams inevitably have a way of turning into nightmares. While modernity designates a historical period, modernism refers to cultural developments usually, but not exclusively, associated with the arts, architecture, and literature. Modernization, by contrast, is the result of economic, social, political, and technological transformations that have been developing for more than two centuries. So understood, modernization is inseparable from industrialization, which was made possible by a new form of capitalism.

Networking Nations

It has become customary to mark the beginning of the Industrial Revolution in eighteenth-century England. Historians usually identify two or sometimes three phases of the Industrial Revolution, which are associated with different sources of energy and related technologies. In preindustrial Europe, the primary energy sources were human, animal, and natural (wind, water, and fire). By the middle of the eighteenth century, much of Europe had been deforested to supply wood for domestic and industrial consumption. J. R. McNeill points out that the combination of energy sources, machines, and ways of organizing production came together to form "clusters" that determined the course of industrialization and, by extension, shaped economic and social developments. A later cluster did not immediately replace its predecessor; rather, different regimes overlapped, though often they were not integrated. With each new cluster, however, the speed of production increased, leading to differential rates of production. The first phase of the Industrial Revolution began around 1750 with the shift from human and animal labor to machine-based production. This change was brought about by the use of water power and later steam engines in the textile mills of Great Britain. The second phase dates from the 1820s, when there was a shift to fossil fuels—primarily coal. By the middle of the nineteenth century, another cluster emerged from the integration of coal, iron, steel, and railroads. The fossil fuel regime was not, of course, limited to coal. Edwin L. Drake drilled the first commercially successful well in Titusville, Pennsylvania, in 1859 and the big gushers erupted first in the 1870s in Baku on the Caspian Sea and later in Spindeltop, Texas (1901). Oil, however, did not replace coal as the main source of fuel in transportation until the 1930s.[3] Coal, of course, is still widely used in manufacturing today because it remains one of the cheapest sources of energy. Though global consumption of coal has leveled off since 2000, its use continues to increase in China. Indeed, China currently uses almost as much coal as the rest of the world and reliable sources predict that by 2017, India will be importing as much coal as China.[4]

The third phase of the Industrial Revolution began in the closing decades of the nineteenth century. The development of technologies for producing and distributing electricity cheaply and efficiently further transformed industrial processes and created the possibility for new systems of communication as well as the unprecedented capability for the production and dissemination of new forms of entertainment, media, and information. The impact of electrification can be seen in four primary areas. First, the availability of electricity made the assembly line and mass production possible. When Henry Ford adapted technology used in Chicago's meatpacking houses to produce cars (1913), he set in motion changes whose effects are still being felt. Second, the introduction of the incandescent light bulb (1881) transformed private and public space. As early as the late 1880s, electrical lighting was used in homes, factories, and on streets. Assembly lines and lights inevitably led to the acceleration of urbanization. Third, the invention of the telegraph (ca.1840) and telephone (1876) enabled the communication and transmission of information across greater distances at faster rates of speed than ever before. Finally, electronic tabulating machines, invented by Herman Hollerith in 1889, made it possible to collect and manage data in new ways. Though his contributions have not been widely acknowledged, Hollerith actually forms a bridge between the Industrial Revolution and the so-called post-industrial information age. The son of German immigrants, Hollerith graduated from Columbia University's School of Mines and went on to found Tabulating Machine Company (1896). He created the first automatic card-feed mechanism and key-punch system with which an operator using a keyboard could process as many as three hundred cards an hour. Under the direction of Thomas J. Watson, Hollerith's company merged with three others in 1911 to form Computing Tabulating Recording Company. In 1924, the company was renamed International Business Machines Corporation (IBM).

There is much to be learned from such periodizations, but they have serious limitations. The developments I have identified overlap and interact in ways that subvert any simple linear narrative. Instead of thinking merely in terms of resources, products, and periods, it is also important to think in terms of networks and flows. The foundation for today's wired world was laid more than two centuries ago. Beginning in the early nineteenth century, local communities, then states and nations, and finally the entire globe became increasingly connected. Though varying from time to time and place to place, there were two primary forms of networks: those that directed material flows (fuels, commodities, products, people), and those that channeled immaterial flows (communications, information, data, images, and currencies). From the earliest stages of development, these networks were inextricably interconnected. There would have been no telegraph network without railroads and no railroad system without the telegraph network, and neither could have existed without coal and iron. Networks, in other words, are never separate but form networks of networks in which material and immaterial flows circulate. As these networks continued to expand, and became more and more complex, there was a steady increase in the importance of immaterial flows, even for material processes. The combination of expanding connectivity and the growing importance of information technologies led to the acceleration of both material and immaterial flows. This emerging network of networks created positive feedback loops in which the rate of acceleration increased.

While developments in transportation, communications, information, and management were all important, industrialization as we know it is inseparable from the transportation revolution that trains created. In his foreword to Wolfgang Schivelbusch's informative study *The Railway Journey: The Industrialization of Time and Space in the 19th Century*, Alan Trachtenberg writes, "Nothing else in the nineteenth century seemed as vivid and dramatic a sign of modernity as the railroad. Scientists and statesmen joined capitalists in promoting the locomotive as the engine of 'progress,' a promise of imminent Utopia."[5] In England, railway technology developed as an extension of coal mining. The shift from human and natural sources of energy to fossil fuels created a growing demand for coal. While steam engines had been used since the second half of the eighteenth century in British mines to run fans and pumps like those my great-grandfather had operated in the Pennsylvania coalfields, it was not until 1901, when Oliver Evans invented a high-pressure, mobile steam engine, that locomotives were produced. By the beginning of the nineteenth century, the coal mined in the area around

Newcastle was being transported throughout England on rail lines. It did not take long for this new rapid transit system to develop—by the 1820s, railroads had expanded to carry passengers, and half a century later rail networks spanned all of Europe.

What most impressed people about this new transportation network was its speed. The average speed of early railways in England was twenty to thirty miles per hour, which was approximately three times faster than stagecoaches. The increase in speed transformed the experience of time and space. Countless writers from this era use the same words to describe train travel as Karl Marx had used to describe emerging global financial markets. Trains, like capital, "annihilate space with time." Traveling on the recently opened Paris-Rouen-Orléans railway line in 1843, the German poet, journalist, and literary critic Heinrich Heine wrote: "What changes must now occur, in our way of looking at things, in our notions! Even the elementary concepts of time and space have begun to vacillate. Space is killed by the railways, and we are left with time alone. . . . Now you can travel to Orleans in four and a half hours, and it takes no longer to get to Rouen. Just imagine what will happen when the lines to Belgium and Germany are completed and connected up with their railways! I feel as if the mountains and forests of all countries were advancing on Paris. Even now, I can smell the German linden trees; the North Sea's breakers are rolling against my door."[6] This new experience of space and time that speed brought about had profound psychological effects that I will consider later.

Throughout the nineteenth century, the United States lagged behind Great Britain in terms of industrial capacity: in 1869, England was the source of 20 percent of the world's industrial production, while the United States contributed just 7 percent. By the start of World War I, however, America's industrial capacity surpassed that of England: that is, by 1913, the scales had tipped—32 percent came from the United States and only 14 percent from England. While England had a long history before the Industrial Revolution, the history of the United

States effectively begins with the Industrial Revolution. There are other important differences as well. Whereas in Great Britain the transportation revolution grew out of the industrialization of manufacturing primarily, but not exclusively, in textile factories, in the United States mechanization began in agriculture and spread to transportation before it transformed manufacturing. In other words, in Great Britain, the Industrial Revolution in manufacturing came first and the transportation revolution second, while in the United States, this order was reversed.

When the Industrial Revolution began in the United States, most of the country beyond the Eastern Seaboard was largely undeveloped. Settling this uncharted territory required the development of an extensive transportation network. Throughout the early decades of the nineteenth century, the transportation system consisted of a network of rudimentary roads connecting towns and villages with the countryside. New England, Boston, New York, Philadelphia, Baltimore, and Washington were joined by highways suitable for stagecoach travel. Inland travel was largely confined to rivers and waterways. The completion of the Erie Canal (1817–25) marked the first stage in the development of an extensive network linking rivers, lakes, canals, and waterways along which produce and people flowed. Like so much else in America, the railroad system began in Boston. By 1840, only 18,181 miles of track had been laid. During the following decade, however, there was an explosive expansion of the nation's rail system financed by securities and bonds traded on stock markets in America and London. By the 1860s, the railroad network east of the Mississippi River was using routes roughly similar to those employed today.

Where some saw loss, others saw gain. In 1844, inveterate New Englander Ralph Waldo Emerson associated the textile loom with the railroad when he reflected, "Not only is distance annihilated, but when, as now, the locomotive and the steamboat, like enormous shuttles, shoot every day across the thousand various threads of national descent and employment, and bind them fast in one web, an hourly assimilation

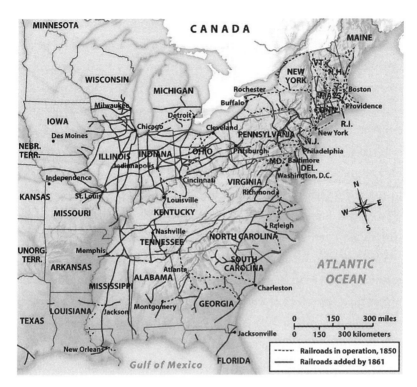

U.S. railroads in operation, 1850, 1861. Reprinted by permission from James A. Henrietta, David Brody, and Lynn Dumenil, *America: A Concise History,* vol. 1: *To 1877,* 3rd ed. (New York: Bedford/St. Martin's, 2006), map 10-3.

goes forward, and there is no danger that local peculiarities and hostilities should be preserved."[7] Gazing at tracks vanishing in the distance, Emerson saw a new world opening that, he believed, would overcome the parochialisms of the past. For many people in the nineteenth century, this new world promising endless resources and endless opportunity was the American West. A transcontinental railroad had been proposed as early as 1820 but was not completed until 1869.

On May 10, 1869, Leland Stanford, who would become the governor of California and, in 1891, founder of Stanford University, drove the final spike in the railroad that joined east and west. Nothing would ever be the same again. This event was not merely local, but also, as Emerson had surmised, global. Like the California gold and Nevada silver spike that Leland had driven to join the rails, the material transportation network and immaterial communication network intersected at that moment to create what Rebecca Solnit correctly identifies as "the first live national media event." The spike "had been wired to connect to the telegraph lines that ran east and west along the railroad tracks. The instant Stanford struck the spike, a signal would go around the nation. . . . The signal set off cannons in San Francisco and New York. In the nation's capital the telegraph signal caused a ball to drop, one of the balls that visibly signaled the exact time in observatories in many places then (of which the ball dropped in New York's Times Square at the stroke of the New Year is a last relic). The joining of the rails would be heard in every city equipped with fire-alarm telegrams, in Philadelphia, Omaha, Buffalo, Chicago, and Sacramento. Celebrations would be held all over the nation."[8] This carefully orchestrated spectacle, which was made possible by the convergence of multiple national networks, was worthy of the future Hollywood and the technological wizards of Silicon Valley whose relentless innovation Stanford's university would later nourish. What most impressed people at the time was the speed of global communication, which now is taken for granted.

Flickering Images—Changing Minds

Industrialization not only changes systems of production and distribution of commodities and products, but also imposes new disciplinary practices that transform bodies and change minds. During the early years of train travel, bodily acceleration had an enormous psychological effect that some people found disorienting and others found exhilarating. The mechanization of movement created what Ann Friedberg describes as the "mobile gaze," which transforms one's surroundings and alters both the content and, more important, the structure, of perception. This mobile gaze takes two forms: the person can move and the surroundings remain immobile (train, bicycle, automobile, airplane, elevator), or the person can remain immobile and the surroundings move (panorama, kinetoscope, film).

When considering the impact of trains on the mobilization of the gaze, it is important to note that different designs for railway passenger cars had different perceptual and psychological effects. Early European passenger cars were modeled on stagecoaches in which individuals had seats in separate compartments; early American passenger cars, by contrast, were modeled on steamboats in which people shared a common space and were free to move around. The European design tended to reinforce social and economic hierarchies that the American design tried to break down. Eventually, American railroads adopted the European model of fixed individual seating but had separate rows facing in the same direction rather than different compartments. As we will see, the resulting compartmentalization of perception anticipates the cellularization of attention that accompanies today's distributed high-speed digital networks.

During the early years, there were numerous accounts of the experience of railway travel by ordinary people, distinguished writers, and even physicians, in which certain themes recur. The most common complaint is the sense of disorientation brought about by the experience of unprecedented speed. There are frequent reports of the dispersion and fragmentation of attention that are remarkably similar to contemporary personal and clinical descriptions of attention-deficit hyperactivity disorder (ADHD).[9] With the landscape incessantly rushing by faster than it could be apprehended, people suffered overstimulation, which created a sense of psychological exhaustion and physical distress. Some physicians went so far as to maintain that the experience of speed caused "neurasthenia, neuralgia, nervous dyspepsia, early tooth decay, and even premature baldness." In 1892, Sir James Crichton-Browne attributed the significant increase in the mortality rate between 1859 and 1888 to "the tension, excitement, and incessant mobility of modern life." Commenting on these statistics, Max Nordau might well be describing the harried pace of life today. "Every line we read or write, every human face we see, every conversation we carry on, every scene we perceive through the window of the flying express, sets in activity our sensory nerves and our brain centers. Even the little shocks of railway travelling, not perceived by consciousness, the perpetual noises and the various sights in the streets of a large town, our suspense pending the sequel of progressing events, the constant expectation of the newspaper, of the postman, of visitors, cost our brains wear and tear."[10] During the years around the turn of the last century, a sense of what Stephen Kern aptly describes as "cultural hypochondria" pervaded society. Like today's parents concerned about the psychological and physical effects of their kids playing video games, nineteenth-century physicians worried about the effect of people sitting in railway cars for hours watching the world rush by in a stream of images that seemed to be detached from real people and actual things.

In addition to the experience of disorientation, dispersion, fragmentation, and fatigue, rapid train travel created a sense of anxiety. People feared that with the increase in speed, machinery would spin out of control, resulting in serious accidents. An 1829 description of a train ride expresses the anxiety that speed created. "It is really flying, and it is impossible to divest yourself of the notion of instant death to all upon the least accident happening." A decade and a half later, an anonymous German explained that the reason for such anxiety is the always "close possibility of an accident, and the inability to exercise any influence on the running of the cars."[11] When several serious accidents actually occurred, anxiety spread like a virus. Anxiety, however, is always a strange experience—it not only repels, it also attracts; danger and the anxiety it brings are always part of speed's draw.

Perhaps this was a reason that not everyone found trains so distressing. For some people, the experience of speed was "dreamlike" and bordered on ecstasy. In 1843, Emerson wrote in his *Journals*, "Dreamlike travelling on the railroad. The towns which I pass between Philadelphia and New York make no distinct impression. They are like pictures on a wall." The movement of the train creates a loss of focus that blurs the mobile gaze. A few years earlier, Victor Hugo's description of train travel sounds like an acid trip as much as a train trip. In either case, the issue is speed. "The flowers by the side of the road are no longer flowers but flecks, or rather streaks, of red or white; there are no longer any points, everything becomes a streak; grain fields are great shocks of yellow hair; fields of alfalfa, long green tresses; the towns, the steeples, and the trees perform a crazy mingling dance on the horizon; from time to time, a shadow, a shape, a specter appears and disappears with lightning speed behind the window; it's a railway guard."[12] The flickering images fleeting past train windows are like a film running too fast to comprehend.

Transportation was not the only thing accelerating in the nineteenth century—the pace of life itself was speeding up as never before. Listening to the whistle of the train headed to Boston in his cabin beside Walden Pond, Thoreau mused, "The startings and arrivals of the cars are now the epochs in the village day. They go and come with such regularity and precision, and their whistle can be heard so far, that the farmers set their clocks by them, and thus one well conducted institution regulates a whole country. Have not men improved somewhat in punctuality since the railroad was invented? Do they not talk and think faster in the depot than they did in the stage office? There is something electrifying in the atmosphere of the former place. I have been astonished by some of the miracles it has wrought."[13] And yet Thoreau, more than others, knew that these changes also had a dark side.

The transition from agricultural to industrial capitalism brought with it a massive migration from the country, where life was slow and governed by natural rhythms, to the city, where life was fast and governed by mechanical, standardized time. The convergence of industrialization, transportation, and electrification made urbanization inevitable. The faster that cities expanded, the more some writers and poets idealized rustic life in the country. Nowhere is such idealization more evident than in the writings of British romantics. The rapid swirl of people, machines, and commodities created a sense of vertigo as disorienting as train travel. Wordsworth writes in *The Prelude,*

> Oh, blank confusion! True epitome
> Of what the mighty City is herself
> To thousands upon thousands of her sons,
> Living among the same perpetual whirl
> Of trivial objects, melted and reduced
> To one identity, by differences
> That have no law, no meaning, no end—.[14]

By 1850, fifteen cities in the United States had a population exceeding 50,000. New York was the largest (1,080,330), followed by Philadelphia (565,529), Baltimore (212,418), and Boston (177,840). Increasing domestic trade that resulted from the railroad and growing foreign trade that accompanied improved ocean travel contributed significantly to this growth. While commerce was prevalent in early cities, manufacturing expanded rapidly during the latter half of the eighteenth century. The most important factor contributing to nineteenth-century urbanization was the rapid development of the money economy. Once again, it is a matter of circulating flows, not merely of human bodies but of mobile commodities. Money and cities formed a positive feedback loop—as the money supply grew, cities expanded, and as cities expanded, the money supply grew.

The fast pace of urban life was as disorienting for many people as the speed of the train. In his seminal essay "The Metropolis and Mental Life," Georg Simmel observes, "The psychological foundation upon which the metropolitan individuality is erected, is the intensification of emotional life due to the swift and continuous shift of external and internal stimuli. Man is a creature whose existence is dependent on differences, i.e., his mind is stimulated by the difference between present impressions and those which have preceded. . . . To the extent that the metropolis creates these psychological conditions—with every crossing of the street, with the tempo and multiplicity of economic, occupational and social life—it creates the sensory foundations of mental life, and in the degree of awareness necessitated by our organization as creatures dependent on differences, a deep contrast with the slower, more habitual, more smooth flowing rhythm of the sensory-mental phase of small town and rural existence." The expansion of the money economy created a fundamental contradiction at the heart of metropolitan life. On the one hand, cities brought together different people from all backgrounds and walks of life, and on the other hand, emerging industrial capitalism leveled these differences by disciplining bodies and programming minds. "Money," Simmel continues, "is concerned only with what is common to all, i.e., with the exchange value which reduces all quality and individuality to a purely quantitative level."[15] The migration from country to city that came with the transition from agricultural to industrial capitalism involved a shift from homogeneous communities to heterogeneous assemblages of different people, qualitative to quantitative methods of assessment and evaluation, as well as concrete to abstract networks of exchange of goods and services, and a slow to fast pace of life. I will consider further aspects of these disciplinary practices in Chapter 3; for now, it is important to understand the implications of the mechanization or industrialization of perception.

I have already noted similarities between the experience of looking through a window on a speeding train to the experience of watching a film that is running too fast. During the latter half of the nineteenth century a remarkable series of inventions transformed not only *what* people experienced in the world but *how* they experienced it: photography (Louis-Jacques-Mandé Daguerre, ca. 1837), the telegraph (Samuel F. B. Morse, ca. 1840), the stock ticker (Thomas Alva Edison, 1869), the telephone (Alexander Graham Bell, 1876), the chronophotographic gun (Étienne-Jules Maney, 1882), the kinetoscope (Edison, 1894), the zoopraxiscope (Eadweard Muybridge, 1893), the phantoscope (Charles Jenkins, 1894), and cinematography (Auguste and Louis Lumière, 1895). The way in which human beings perceive and conceive the world is not hardwired in the brain but changes with new technologies of production and re-production. Just as the screens of today's TVs, computers, video games, and mobile devices are restructuring how we process experience, so too did new technologies at the end of the nineteenth century change the world by transforming how people apprehended it. While each in-novation had a distinctive effect, there is a discernible overall trajec-tory to these developments. Industrial technologies of production and reproduction extended processes of dematerialization that eventually led first to consumer capitalism and then to today's financial capitalism. The crucial variable in these developments is the way in which mate-rial and immaterial networks intersect to produce a progressive detach-ment of images, representations, information, and data from concrete objects and actual events. Marveling at what he regarded as the novelty of photographs, Oliver Wendell Holmes commented, "Form is hence-forth divorced from matter. In fact, matter as a visible object is of no great use any longer, except as the mould on which form is shaped. Give us a few negatives of a thing worth seeing, taken from different points of view, and that is all we want of it. Pull it down or burn it up, if you please. . . . Matter in large masses must always be fixed and dear, form is cheap and transportable. We have got the fruit of creation now, and need not trouble ourselves about the core."[16]

Technologies for the reproduction and transmission of images and information expand the process of abstraction initiated by the money economy to create a play of freely floating signs without anything to ground, certify, or secure them. With new networks made possible by the combination of electrification and the invention of the telegraph, telephone, and stock ticker, communication was liberated from the strictures imposed by physical means of conveyance. In previous energy regimes, messages could be sent no faster than people, horses, carriages, trains, ships, or automobiles could move. Dematerialized words, sounds, information, and eventually images, by contrast, could be transmitted across great distances at high speed. With this dematerialization and acceleration, Marx's prediction—that "everything solid melts into air"—was realized. But this was just the beginning. It would take more than a century for electrical currents to become virtual currencies whose transmission would approach the speed limit.[17]

Aesthetics of Speed

Technological and economic developments are not separate from other currents circulating through societies. Cultural processes shape and are shaped by technological innovations. Throughout the modern period, modernization and modernism have been inseparably related. During the second half of the nineteenth century and first decade of the twentieth century, there was an unusual eruption of artistic creativity. Art historians have long credited the invention of photography with freeing the artistic imagination from the task of representation. While this view is not incorrect, other factors were also important. New technologies transformed art, and artists, in turn, created works that both further transformed human perception and provided ideological justification for technological innovation and economic expansion. Many of the most important artists in this period were fascinated by speed. The challenge they faced was to evoke speed and motion in figures and forms that were for the most part static.

On February 20, 1909, Filippo Marinetti and Umberto Boccioni declared a new aesthetic of speed in their *Futurist Manifesto*. "We say that the world's magnificence has been enriched by a new beauty; the beauty of speed. A racing car whose hood is adorned with great pipes that seem

to ride on grapeshot is more beautiful than the *Victory of Samothrace.*
. . . We cooperate with mechanics in destroying the old property of
distance and wild solitudes, the exquisite nostalgia of parting, for which
we substitute the tragic lyricism of ubiquity and omnipresent speed."[18]
For futurists as well as many other artists working in the early twentieth century, speed bordered on a religious experience that transformed
vision and changed minds. Speed created by mechanical technologies
affected awareness in two contradictory ways—it both fragmented and
blurred perception. On the one hand, acceleration can dissolve discrete
objects and events in a rushing vortex that leaves everything indistinct;
on the other hand, it is possible to speed up so much that time, paradoxically, slows down until it seems to disintegrate into discrete instants
that must be reassembled to create a coherent experience.

When Eadweard Muybridge captured a trotting horse in time-lapsed
images, he effectively stopped time by freezing motion. These images,
which influenced many artists, were the result of new photographic
technology that was funded with Leland Stanford's profits from his
railroad. The first form of photography, the daguerreotype, invented
around 1837 by Louis-Jacques-Mandé Daguerre, was very slow and
could register only immobile people and scenes. A silver-coated copper
plate functioned like a mirror that had to be exposed for as long as ten
minutes. Three-and-a-half decades later, everything had sped up. Muybridge's high-speed photography enabled people to apprehend what
remained imperceptible in the rushing blur of ordinary perception.[19]

What Muybridge had stopped and disintegrated could be animated
and synthesized. By 1834, he had adapted the zootrope, which had
been invented three years earlier, to spin images fast enough to create
the appearance of continuous motion, and by the end of the century,
the Lumière brothers and Edison had invented machinery for producing motion pictures. Muybridge's images disclosed a previously invisible
world that lay hidden within what had been taken-for-granted reality.
The world, people discovered, moves faster than our ability to appre-

hend it. What had appeared to be reality is, in fact, the trace of forms, figures, and forces that are not visible to the naked eye. Reflecting on the impact of railroads and cinema in 1913, the French cubist Fernand Léger commented that life was "more fragmented and faster-moving than in previous periods. . . . A modern man registers a hundred times more sensory impressions than an eighteenth-century artist." Elaborating on Léger's observation, Kern explains: "The view through the door of a moving railroad car or the windshield of an automobile is fragmented, although at high speeds it becomes continuous the way continuity is created out of a series of stills by cinema."[20] Instant/flow, fragmentation/integration, concrete/abstract, analysis/synthesis. The oppositions inherent in Muybridge's images suggest the contrasting rhythms of life at the turn of the last century that leading artists tried to capture in their work.

For the futurist Giacomo Balla, the experience of speed created a sense of dynamism that dissolves discrete forms in a rushing visual flow. His early painting *Dynamism on a Leash* (1912) recalls Muybridge's photographs and is similar to Marcel Duchamp's *Nude Descending a Staircase* (1912). The stereoscopic image of the legs makes it seem that the dog is light enough to float above the surface of the sidewalk. With *Abstract Speed + Sound,* which he painted a year later, forms further dissolve into intersecting shapes and planes that resemble cubist paintings. Here Bella approaches the realization of the dream expressed in the *Futurist Manifesto:* "to express our whirling life of steel, of pride, of fever and of speed." After these experiments, Kern explains, Bella "turned to painting automobiles, but with barely recognizable forms. The speeding windows flash like facets of a turning gem, and spinning wheels spiral into lines of force. The title of one listed the themes: *Speed of an Automobile + Light + Noise.* Toward the end of 1913 he entirely abandoned concrete subject matter and rendered simply *Abstract Speed.* The force lines that formerly eddied about birds and autos now come out of artist forms alone. The arcs of force lines end from movement itself; light reflects along lines of undifferentiable objects, energized by unknown sources."[21] Objects dissolve in a play of light and images that floats across the canvas like traces flickering on a movie screen or computer terminal.

Speed, then, simultaneously blurs and fragments perception and attention. As new technologies caused the world to morph before people's eyes, psychologists, medical doctors, and artists began to investigate problems of perception.[22] If the world as it had been known for centuries is more constructed than discovered, then the question becomes, how is it made? In search of answers, many artists shifted their attention from representing the world to exploring how we perceive and comprehend it. The result was an unprecedented succession of artistic innovations: impressionism, divisionism, pointillism, suprematism, cubism, vorticism. In all of these movements, artists were obsessed with the interplay of fragmentation and integration, fission and fusion, or analysis and synthesis in our ways of world-making.

As acceleration both fragmented attention into a series of isolated instants and blurred the world into an undifferentiated flow, artists explored the ways in which the perceptual apparatus both breaks down and reassembles the surrounding world. They distinguished themselves less by their treatment of the analytic moment than by their presentation of the synthetic moment of world-making. Some argued that whatever coherence the world and our experience of it have is primarily conceptual, some maintained that it is primarily perceptual, and, of course, others insisted that it is a mix of concepts and sensations. Georges Braque succinctly captured the alternating rhythms of fragmentation and integration when he wrote, "The senses deform, the mind forms. Work to perfect the minds. There is no certitude but in what the mind conceives."[23] Artistic innovations both responded to and were shaped by new technologies, and changing perceptual apparatuses were transforming the very sense of reality. In an effort to explain the significance of the changes that cubism eventually would introduce, Albert Gleizes and Jean Metzinger drew a distinction between "superficial realism" and "profound realism." In their influential 1912 work *Du Cubisme,* they maintain that there would have been no cubism without Paul Cézanne. Contrasting the "superficial realism" of Vincent Van Gogh and Claude Monet with the "profound realism" of Cézanne, impressionists, Gleizes and Metzinger argue, are more concerned with registering subjective experience than with representing the objective world. In a manner similar to Muybridge's speed photography, impressionists attempt to capture the fleeting moment in paint. This experience, like the moment it records, is always changing. As if to underscore the primacy of fluctuating perception, some leading impressionist works represent "the same" object at different moments. The classic example of this strategy is, of course, Monet's series of paintings of the *Rouen Cathedral* (1892–94), which appear to be separate slow-motion photographs taken at a fast shutter speed with high-speed film. The preoccupation with momentary sensory impressions creates the appearance of deliberate superficiality. As objects dissolve into fleeting images, depth disappears on surfaces that are nothing more than the play of light.

To move from superficial to "profound realism," it is necessary to begin the journey beneath the surface without leaving behind perception and sensation. From Cézanne's point of view, the impressionists succumbed to what Robert Hughes describes as "the dictatorship of the eye over the mind." Cézanne's art can be understood as an effort to put the mind back into the eye. In an oft-repeated remark recorded in a letter to Emile Bernard, Cézanne insists, "You must see in nature the cylinder, the sphere, the cone."[24] For Cézanne, appearances are not superficial impressions but are traces of profound forms that must be discerned through a process of progressive abstraction.

What Cézanne begins, cubism extends. In a rare comment on his artistic practice, Picasso remarks, "I paint forms as I think them, not as I see them."[25] Analytic cubism follows Cézanne from surface to depth and from exterior to interior. "*Cubism,*" the surrealist Apollinaire explains, "is the art of painting new structures out of elements borrowed not from the reality of sight, but from the reality of insight." Between 1908 and 1911, Georges Braque's and Pablo Picasso's paintings became increasingly abstract until only faint traces of representation remain. Geometric formalism replaced mimetic representation and superficial sensation. As images became more abstract, forms became more complex. Within the shifting perspectives of cubism, the object is never simply one thing. Defending cubist practice from the attacks of hostile critics, Gleizes and Metzinger point out that "an object is not one absolute form; it has many. It has as many as there are planes in the region of perception."[26] The multiplicity of perspectives constitutive of objectivity renders forms on the cubist canvas forever incomplete. This does not mean, however, that every vestige of an encompassing totality has vanished in fragmented forms. Rather, the locus of unity has shifted from individual objects to relationships between and among different entities and perceptions. What once were conceived as discrete objects now appear to be nodes in constantly expanding networks or webs of relations.

Other artists attempted to negotiate the interplay between instant/flow, fragmentation/integration, concrete/abstract, and analysis/synthesis by further immersing themselves in the sensuous presence of the impressionists. Instead of a frozen instant separated from other instants, they discovered porous moments whose distinctiveness was the result of the differential play of light and colors. In works dubbed pointillism by critics, Georges Seurat and Paul Signac appropriated the latest discoveries about color, optical effects, and perception by scientists like Hermann von Helmholtz and Michel Eugène Chevreul, who detected much to their surprise that color is not mixed on the palette but in the eye. The perception of a particular color is a contrast effect produced by the interaction of contiguous colors. Chevreul invented a color wheel consisting of primary colors and intermediary shades to demonstrate that color depends on context. Two colors in proximity appear to be a third color different from either when perceived separately. By testing different combinations, scientists and artists thought it was possible to identify complementary colors that could be used to modulate the emotions of viewers. "Art is Harmony," Seurat writes. "Harmony is the analogy of the contrary and of similar elements of tone, of color and of line, considered according to their dominance and under the influence of light, in gay, calm or sad combinations."[27]

Seurat puts this theory into practice in his signature paintings that effectively integrate fragmentation and synthesis. From a distance, his best-known work, *A Sunday Afternoon on the Island of La Grande Jatte* (1884–86), appears to be more a representational than an abstract work. But at close range, the figures dissolve in a confusing jumble of seemingly disconnected dots. In a manner similar to Chuck Close's signature portraits, as the viewer moves away from the surface of the work, figures gradually appear from the surrounding ground until the tipping point is reached and forms suddenly snap into focus. For anyone initiated in the ways of today's digital world, this experience is completely familiar. Viewing a pointillist painting is exactly like looking at pixels on a video screen or computer monitor.

The artistic experiments of leading modern artists both reflect and expand the perceptual and conceptual changes that resulted from modernization and industrialization. This relationship between art and technology cannot, however, be understood apart from changes in the modern economy. As Andy Warhol always insisted, it is impossible to separate art and finance. Emerging forms of capitalism made possible the industrialization that transformed art, and new forms of art are inseparable from policies and practices that capitalism needs to survive.[28] The establishment of a money economy led to a system in which the currency of exchange became increasingly abstract and immaterial. Since images, data, and code circulate faster than people, material, and things, progressive dematerialization leads to the increasing acceleration of exchange. Whether products are material or immaterial, the rate of exchange must increase for growth to continue. This is the point at which modernism makes its greatest contribution to the ideology of capitalism. Modernism, we have seen, is defined by its commitment to the new and, correlatively, its aversion to the old. So understood, modernism is of the moment, which is here and now. The new, of course, is old as soon it appears and thus must be repeatedly renewed. The motto of modernism is in the words of Ezra Pound—"Make it new!"—and the faster, the better. The aesthetic of speed that is dedicated to the new is, in effect, the aesthetic of planned obsolescence, which is necessary to keep the engines of production running and new products coming off factory assembly lines. This conspiracy between art and finance that began with the intersection of mechanical technology and electrical networks at the turn of the twentieth century imploded with the convergence of digital technologies and high-speed networks at the turn of the twenty-first century.

2. Invisible Hands

....

Redeeming God

When the cover of *Time* magazine asked in bold red letters "Is God Dead?" on April 6, 1966, which was Good Friday, few people realized that the Protestant God whose death had been declared was at that very moment being reborn in a new form that would invisibly dominate the economy and by extension, society and politics, for decades. During the latter half of the twentieth century, money became God in more than a trivial sense. The traditional opposition between liberal and conservative politics as well as liberal and neoliberal economics repeats and extends philosophical and theological disputes that erupted at the end of the Middle Ages and beginning of the modern era. One of the most pressing questions then, as now, concerned the relation of the individual to the group, or the part to the whole. Does participation in the larger social whole make individuals who they are, or is the social group nothing other than an aggregate of independent individuals? The former position represents politically and economically a liberal perspective or, when carried to its logical conclusion, is socialist and perhaps even communist, whereas the latter position is politically conservative and economically neoliberal.

Throughout the postwar period, the two most influential representatives of these alternative positions were John Maynard Keynes and Milton Friedman. Though Keynes suffered through the difficulties of wartime Europe, his view of life was shaped as much by his participation in the influential Bloomsbury group as by economic theory. Unlike so many of his associates, Keynes's involvement with London's bohemian culture did nothing to dampen his enthusiasm for capitalism. In the wake of two world wars and a global depression, it no longer seemed possible to believe in the efficacy of self-regulating free markets. For Keynes, persistent financial instability, especially unemployment, was proof of the failure of the invisible hand. The only way to avoid further disaster was for governments to take a more active role in managing the economy. Sounding a distinctively contemporary note, he argued that the best way to spur economic recovery is by taxing and spending.

Keynes and his followers, like the influential Nobel laureate Paul Krugman, insist that economic problems are best dealt with by managing demand. To increase demand, Keynes supported policies that encourage consumer spending through various forms of stimulus: according to this logic, the more money in circulation, the more people will spend and the more companies can hire—and the more people work, the more money they will have to spend. The resulting growth in demand for production will lead to a drop in unemployment, which will further fuel the economy by increasing both money available for spending and tax revenues for local, state, and federal governments. When these policies are effective, they create a self-reinforcing circuit of exchange that grows the economy. The quickest and most efficient way to increase consumer demand is through government spending. When the government spends or prints money to finance various programs, it pumps more money directly into the system, which, according to the Keynesian multiplier effect, is supposed to lead to an increase in national income that exceeds the original expenditure. Unemployment is a crucial variable in this equation. Unemployment and inflation are inversely related: when employment is high, wages are high and there is inflationary pressure; conversely, when unemployment is high, wages are lower and prices drift downward or at least do not rise with increasing demand, which would stimulate the economy. During the Kennedy and Johnson administrations, Keynesian fiscal policies funded social programs as well as the war in Vietnam. For most of the 1960s, this approach worked well; there was a steady economic expansion and a very strong stock market. By the end of the decade, however, the economy was beginning to falter; spending was out of control, inflation was rising, and there was a growing sense among many people that new policies were needed.

Milton Friedman was one of the most persistent critics of Keynes and his followers. In 1963 he and Anna Schwartz published *Monetary History of the United States, 1867–1960,* in which they presented historical data that they insisted supported a different approach to economic and fiscal policy. Friedman's interpretation of the Depression as having been triggered by a liquidity crisis was crucial for his assessment of Keynesianism. During the 1920s and 1930s, he argues, the crucial variable in the economy was the money supply rather than interest rates. Against Keynes, Friedman insists that what is most important is monetary rather than fiscal policy. His well-known dictum, "money matters," does not ignore unemployment, but stresses the need to control inflation as the key to an orderly economy. Departing from a fundamental tenet of Keynesianism, Friedman contends that this is best accomplished by regulating the money supply instead of manipulating interest rates. The preoccupation with inflation and the money supply leads Friedman to resist what he regards as unnecessary government spending. While Keynesians concentrated on demand, Friedman's followers focused on the supply side of the equation.

The differences between Keynes and Friedman are as much philosophical as economic. Reflecting a general commitment to state-sponsored social welfare programs, Keynes allows the government greater control in running the economy. Friedman, by contrast, believes in the freedom and autonomy of individuals and thus resists centralized authority and governmental interference in social and economic matters. When politicized and popularized, this economic vision translates into the now familiar mantra: less government, lower taxes. Friedman joined the University of Chicago in 1946 and over the next thirty years transformed the economics department into his own image. In the last decades of the twentieth century, his theories and policies became a new orthodoxy for many economists. But his influence extended far beyond the walls of academia. Adviser to political leaders throughout the world, Friedman also was a highly influential public intellectual who relentlessly popularized and promoted his views in various media. When the Soviet Union fell in 1991, many analysts attributed the collapse of communism and the apparent triumph of global capitalism to the Reagan and Thatcher revolution that had been inspired by Friedman's economics. In the past two decades, commitment to the free market has, for many people, gone beyond economic theory to become nothing less than a religious faith. The market, like God for earlier generations, always knows best and any intervention by lowly humans can only do harm. As capitalism spreads across the globe, the market becomes, in effect, omnipotent, omniscient, and omnipresent. For dedicated neoliberal economists and conservative politicians, the continued expansion of the market requires unwavering commitment to the three foundational principles: deregulation, decentralization, and privatization. These developments are the culmination of a long process that began on October 31, 1517, in Wittenberg, Germany.

Economies of Salvation

Nineteenth-century Scottish philosopher Thomas Carlyle claimed, "If Luther had not stuck to his guns at the Diet of Worms, where he stood before the Holy Roman emperor and refused to recant ('Here I stand'), there would have been no French Revolution and no American: the principle that inspired those cataclysmic events would have been killed in the womb."[1] Carlyle echoes Karl Marx's prescient observation that what began as a theological revolution became first a philosophical and then a social, political, and economic revolution that continues to transform the world today.[2] A century later Max Weber extended these insights in his classic analysis of the influence of Protestantism on the distinctive institutions of the modern world—democracy, the nation state, and free-market capitalism.[3] It is, however, necessary to update Weber's argument by extending the analysis to include global capitalism. While Protestantism began as a religious reformation, it was no less an information and communications revolution without which the industrial, information, communications, network, and financial revolutions that continue to sweep across the globe today would have been impossible.

The Reformation actually started as an economic dispute. When Luther nailed his ninety-five theses, entitled *Disputations on the Power and Efficacy of Indulgences,* on the door of the Castle Church in Wittenberg on October 31, 1517, his concern was with both this-worldly and other-worldly economies. The Catholic Church reached the height of its worldly and spiritual power during the high Middle Ages, when the pope declared himself to be the true emperor whose power did not depend on secular authorities. By claiming the title of *pontifex maximus,* the bishop of Rome assumed the imperial mantle that can be traced back to Caesar Augustus. Worldly power, however, depended on spiritual authority. The true power of the Church was "the power of the keys," which, according to Matthew 16:19, Christ gave to Saint Peter and, by extension, his successors who held the office of the papacy. The power of the keys bestowed on the pope and his representatives the authority to include or exclude individuals in the community of the faithful. By the time of the Middle Ages, church membership was confirmed by baptism and participation in the Eucharist. This ecclesiology and doctrine of the salvation rest on philosophical principles that underlie the fundamental differences between Catholicism and Protestantism.

"Nearly all the wisdom we possess, that is to say, true and sound wisdom," John Calvin writes in the opening lines of his monumental *Institutes of the Christian Religion,* "consists of two parts: the knowledge of God and of ourselves."[4] Throughout the history of Western theology, conceptions of God (theology), self (anthropology), and world (cosmology) have been inseparably interrelated. How one conceives of God, for example, influences how one interprets the self, and vice versa. The philosophical and theological revolutions during the late Middle Ages grew out of new ideas about God and self that had an impact far beyond the church. Luther's exploration of faith, rather than Descartes's examination of knowledge, gave birth to the modern subject without which there would be no democracy or free market as we now know them. The emergence of a new notion of human subjectivity that privileges individuality, interiority, and privacy in Protestantism led to the privatization, decentralization, and deregulation of religion, which ran directly counter to the centralization and universalization of authority that the church hierarchy had imposed in the high Middle Ages. These developments, in turn, both promoted and were promoted by the information and communications revolution that began with the invention of the printing press and the creation of new distribution networks throughout Europe.

By the fourteenth century, both the Catholic Church and Europe were in crisis. In the years preceding the Reformation, the papacy had, in effect, reconstituted the empire that Rome had created. The static church hierarchy with its pope, cardinals, bishops, and priests reflected the static social and economic hierarchy of feudalism in which peasants and serfs were bound to manors of nobles and lords, and were forced to labor on behalf of these elites. In this religious, political, and economic structure, order trumped freedom and the individual was subservient to the group. The order of church and world was reflected in the reigning theology of the age.

Thomas Aquinas created what has come to be known as the medieval synthesis by integrating Christian theology with Aristotle's philosophy, which had been rediscovered around that time as a result of the church's expansion into Muslim lands during the Crusades. Aquinas's God is, above all, rational—He is always reasonable and never arbitrary; indeed, for Aquinas, it is unthinkable for God to act in an irrational way. He makes this all-important point concisely in his master work, *Summa Theologica:* "There is will in God, just as there is intellect: since will always follows upon intellect." Because God's will is informed by his reason (intellect), the world is always rational. Aquinas summarizes the basic theological conviction that was the cornerstone of the medieval church in a single sentence: "Providence is the divine reason itself, which seated in the Supreme Ruler, disposes all things."[5] The world created and governed by this God is rationally ordered and hierarchically structured. Man, who is created in God's image, is essentially rational and finds his ultimate fulfillment in the knowledge of God. Since sin weakens humankind's powers, the knowledge of God that can be discovered in the natural world must be supplemented with revealed knowledge, which is available only through participation in Catholic rituals. More specifically, the grace necessary for redemption is mediated to individuals through the channels of the sacraments administered by official representatives of the church. The church, therefore, holds the key to salvation. The sacrament necessary for salvation is baptism, which washes away original sin and prepares the believer for the Eucharist, which allows believers to participate in the ritual repetition of Christ's redemptive sacrifice. The individual's relation to God is never direct but is always mediated by the church hierarchy.

In this scheme, God and believers are bound in an economic relationship: believers invest time and money in God and His church, and God, through intermediaries in the church hierarchy, provides a profitable return on this investment by providing assurance of eternal life. Bread and wine seal the deal. During the Middle Ages and later years, the communion wafer took the form of a stamped coin, which functioned as something like fiat money issued by the priest, whose word magically transformed worthless bread into the priceless body and blood of Christ. By the eighteenth century, the wafer had changed into an actual token that was used in Protestant churches for admission to communion. Though such communion tokens are no longer used, today's currency continues to bear the stamp of its religious past. The dollar sign—$—is derived from the insigne *in hoc signo* (by this sign) that was inscribed on Christian coins.

During the high Middle Ages, the church became a very big business in which the economy of salvation funded an economy that was all too worldly. Expenses grew faster than the church's income; resisting austerity, which became sacrosanct for Protestant reformers, church leaders funded their lavish lifestyle by imposing new taxes and creating new sources of revenue. To justify schemes for raising more money, theologians developed the notion of the Treasury of Merit, according to which Christ's sacrifice on the cross resulted in the accumulation of excess capital that could be tapped for the right price. This doctrine expands the economy of salvation from this life to the next through the sale and purchase of indulgences. Indulgences could not buy redemption but could provide the full or partial remission of temporal punishment for sins the church had forgiven. When the income of the living was not sufficient to fill the church's coffers, the sale of indulgences was extended to benefit the dead. The purchase of indulgences for friends and relatives who had already died was supposed to decrease their time in purgatory. The abuse of this practice finally pushed Luther over the edge and he vehemently objected to the claim that "as soon as money clinks in the chest, the soul flies out of purgatory." His questions about church practices were personal, theological, and institutional. Luther spoke for a growing number of people when he asked, "Why does the pope, whose wealth today is greater than the wealth of the richest Crassus, build the basilica of Saint Peter with the money of poor believers rather than with his own money?"[6] The threat that

Luther's questions posed was as much economic as theological because by the late Middle Ages, the church could not survive without the income that the sale of indulgences provided.

Aquinas's rational and systematic theology seemed perfectly consistent with a static and orderly world and, thus, his theological vision provided a stable framework that lent life meaning and purpose for many people in the high Middle Ages. By the fourteenth century, however, natural, social, and religious factors had intersected to upset the medieval equilibrium and push Europe toward the edge of chaos. In the middle of the fourteenth century, a pandemic of the bubonic plague (or "Black Death") swept across Europe, killing at least twenty-five million people, which, according to the best estimates, was one quarter of the total population. The Black Death offers a cautionary tale about the impact of climate change in an era of globalization. The plague appears to have originated in the Central Asian steppe and spread to Europe with unexpected speed. Historians and scientists now believe that a temperature increase of approximately one degree Celsius resulted in "a series of ecological upheavals—storms, floods and earthquakes—and these disturbances may have forced rodents out of their holes and into contact with humans."[7] The plague traveled by land along trade routes and by sea to ports along the Mediterranean. By 1348 it had reached England, and a year later it extended as far as Scandinavia, bringing extraordinary devastation in its wake. Burgeoning cities were suddenly decimated and the fabric of society began to unravel. Agriculture, manufacturing, and trade were disrupted and universities shut down. As the number of workers decreased, the value of each worker's labor increased. The plague, in other words, created a labor shortage that accelerated the breakdown of feudalism. When manors started competing for serfs, workers were able to sell their services to the highest bidder. Freed from bondage to lord and land, people became mobile. Individuals were no longer members of a secure hierarchical structure but were thrown back on their own resources in a competitive market. By the middle of the fourteenth century, the world no longer seemed as rational, stable, and orderly as Aquinas had believed.

With both society and the church in crisis, people became uncertain and confused and had nowhere to turn for reassurance. What made Luther so influential was his recognition that the critical issues of the day were not merely ecclesiastical and political but, more important, theological. For Luther, however, theological doctrines were always deeply personal rather than merely scholastic abstractions. He did not set out to overthrow the Catholic Church; indeed, he was an exceptionally devout monk who obsessively sought to fulfill his religious and moral obligations. But the more earnestly Luther tried to follow God's law, the more uncertain he became of his ability to do so. As his doubts increased, his anxiety grew until he passed through what Saint John of the Cross described as "the dark night of the soul." Convinced that he was an unredeemable sinner, Luther believed that he was literally condemned to the fires of hell. Then, just at the point of his most profound despair, he experienced what he believed to be a revelation of God through the words of Saint Paul: "He shall gain life who is justified through faith."[8] For Luther, redemption can neither be bought nor be earned through work but is free—it is a gift given by God's free grace. Though every person falls into sin as a result of his or her free actions, God freely chooses to save some through his inscrutable will. In order to provide a justification for this understanding of the dilemma of individuals and its resolution, Luther had to develop an entirely new interpretation of the interrelationship of God, self, and world. His novel vision overturned the medieval theological synthesis and prepared the way for the modern world.

The cornerstone of Reformation theology has always remained the doctrine of salvation by grace rather than by works. Luther found the philosophical resources he needed to develop his religious vision in the writings of the underappreciated philosopher and theologian William of Ockham (1287–1347). By turning to Ockham to formulate his own account of redemption, Luther became involved in a philosophical debate that had started at Oxford and spilled over to the continent. The issue over which Ockham split with his predecessors was the seemingly inconsequential question of the status of universal or general terms. In scholastic theology, the universal idea or essence was considered more real than its individual expression and truer than any particular empirical experience. According to this doctrine, which was known as realism, humanity or any social totality is considered more real than individual human beings, who exist only by virtue of their "participation" in a larger whole. The whole, in other words, is essential and individual members or parts cannot exist apart from their place in the whole. Exercising his fabled razor, Ockham rejects realism and insists that wholes, which he labels essences, are general terms that are merely *names,* referring to nothing real. This position came to be known as nominalism, which derives from the Latin for name (*nomen*). For nominalists, only individuals are real and the empirical experience of individuals validates true knowledge. In the case of human beings, individuals are not constituted or defined by their participation in any group or social totality; rather, they form themselves historically through their own free choices for which they are ultimately responsible. From this point of view every whole—be it religious, political, social, or economic—is nothing more than the sum of the individual parts that make it up.

The interrelated notions of the will and individuality are the two pillars of Ockham's theology. In nominalism, Luther found a view of God and man that emphasized individuality and the importance of the will in both divine and human activity. Ockham insists that God is a radically singular individual who is totally different from the world and human beings; God, in other words, is wholly other and completely mysterious. In contrast to Aquinas for whom God's will is always guided by his reason, Ockham argues that God's will is prior to and determinative of divine reason. With this seemingly simple reversal, Ockham brought about a theological revolution that simultaneously reflected and promoted the dissolution of the medieval society and marked the end of the Catholic Church's claim to universality. If God is radically free, or in theological terms, if God's will is omnipotent, he is bound by nothing, not even his own divine reason. From a human point of view, then, God's actions sometimes seem incomprehensibly arbitrary and, without faith, life often seems to be little more than a random walk that no calculation can plot.

Ockham's anthropology mirrors his theology and, accordingly, has two fundamental tenets: first, priority of the singular individual over the social group; and second, the freedom and responsibility of each individual. His position on these issues forms the foundation of Luther's most devastating critique of medieval theology and ecclesiology. First and foremost, faith, according to Luther, is a private, personal relationship between an individual self and the individual God. The relation to God does not need to be mediated by the church hierarchy of pope, bishops, and priests but can be direct. In contemporary terms drawn from business management, Luther's soteriology does away with the middleman or "disintermediates" the church, thereby undercutting its power and authority. Never subject to ecclesiastical rules and regulations, salvation is a function of the free and absolute will of God, which is grounded in nothing other than itself. Instead of depending on the authority and rituals of the church, God works through His Word, which is present in, but not limited to, scripture and sermon. In contrast to later Protestant fundamentalists, Luther never limits the freedom of God by restricting divine activity to the supposedly literal words of scripture. Bound by neither church nor book, God acts whenever and however He wills. As a result of divine freedom, the priesthood is not limited to the ecclesiastical hierarchy but can be extended to anyone. Luther's doctrine of the priesthood of all believers further erodes the power of the church by decentralizing authority.

Luther's theological challenge to the Catholic Church had a significant economic impact. At the very moment that the church could no longer survive without increased income from taxes and indulgences, Luther was preaching that individuals did not need the church to be saved. In philosophical terms of the time, the Catholic Church tended to be more realist—there was a church universal and an individual could be saved only by interacting with it through the sacraments of baptism and by participating in the Eucharist administered by qualified representatives. For Luther and what became Protestantism, by contrast, every individual can, in principle, have a private, individual relation to God without the mediation of church and clergy. This is not to imply that Protestantism immediately erased all communal aspects of religious belief and practice. But Luther's insistence that the relationship between believers and God is private led to a shift in the understanding of the bond between individuals and community, one that created new interpretations of the church in which individual experience played an increasingly important role. The internalization of faith sowed the seeds for what eventually became the modern notion of the autonomous subject. While some of the radical sects (like Anabaptists, Mennonites, and Shakers) that arose out of Calvinism preserved a stronger sense of community, individualism is as important for Calvin as it was for Luther. Even among radical reformers the personal relationship to God infuses the entire community.[9]

While these seemingly arcane theological debates and religious disagreements might seem irrelevant in our hyperconnected world, the Protestant reformation prepared the way for developments that have resulted in today's financial capitalism, which is pushing speed to its limit. In terms that Milton Friedman made famous, Luther's alternative economy of salvation privatized, deregulated, and decentralized religion and the church. True believers in the virtues of the free market, in turn, have unknowingly redeemed the Protestant God by translating theology into economic theory and practice. The way from Luther's theology to neoliberal economic theology passes through John Calvin and his Scottish protégé, Adam Smith.

Marketing Theodicy

Calvinism not only prepared the way for a flourishing capitalist economy but also provided principles for understanding and justifying market activity. What begins in sixteenth-century Geneva and seventeenth-century Amsterdam ends in the late-twentieth and early twenty-first centuries in New Amsterdam (that is, New York City). The first person to use the image of the invisible hand was not Adam Smith, who is usually credited with developing the modern theory of markets, but John Calvin. For Calvin, God's providence is the invisible hand that sustains the order of the world even when it is not immediately evident to mere mortals. According to common belief, Protestantism's most enduring contribution to capitalism is its work ethic, according to which God rewards people who work hard and save their money. This understanding of the Protestant's original view of salvation is, however, completely wrong. Calvin agrees with Luther's insistence that the most fundamental Reformation principle is that salvation comes by faith rather than works. No matter how hard a person works, he or she can never earn salvation. Uncertainty about one's eternal destiny created great anxiety and people understandably looked for signs of divine grace. As Protestantism evolved, worldly prosperity became a sign that a person had been granted grace. This was, however, a subtle theological point that many believers failed to grasp. Later generations of Protestants reversed Luther and Calvin's point by regarding worldly success as leading to redemption. This debased form of the doctrine led to what was known as the prosperity gospel and its secularized version in which material well-being is the highest good. In its original form, Luther's understanding of grace did not undercut the importance of good works, but it did change the understanding of their significance. Luther actually expanded the importance of worldly works by insisting that religious service was not limited to activity within the church but could be carried out through any earthly vocation. In what Weber famously labeled "inner worldly asceticism," secular work can fulfill a religious calling and worldly prosperity can be a sign of salvation. Within the regime of Calvinism this prosperity cannot express itself in the ostentatious display of wealth because prudent frugality is the measure of religious and moral discipline. In the simplest economic terms, spending damns and saving saves. The inspiration of today's deficit hawks remains thoroughly Protestant even if it is not recognized as such.

Calvin carefully worked out the implications of Luther's interpretation of salvation in a way that systematized, institutionalized, and internationalized Protestant principles. The context that shaped his thought and the people to whom it was addressed differed significantly from Luther's spiritual, intellectual, and social world. Luther's preoccupation with human sinfulness sometimes led him to interpret the world in terms of a cosmic conflict between God and the Devil, who was as real as God for him. Nowhere is the devil more cunning than in his use of money as a seductive lure for those whose faith is weak. "Money," Luther preached, "is the word of the Devil, through which he creates all things the way God created through the true word." What most disturbed Luther about the church of his day was its acceptance of and complicity with the corruption and materialism of nascent capitalism. He went so far as to charge that "the God of the Papists is Mammon." If money is the instrument of the Devil, the Pope is an agent of Satan.[10]

While Luther never lost his peasant roots, Calvin lived in a commercial urban culture where increasing literacy led to growing cultural sophistication. Calvin adapted his message to the growing merchant class in Europe. Trained as a lawyer rather than a monk, Calvin had a greater appreciation for the law than Luther. While Calvin in no way minimized the importance of God's will, he emphasized a side of Ockham's theology that Luther played down. Ockham argues that even though God has absolute power and can do anything that is not self-contradictory, he freely chooses to limit himself by ordaining a particular order for the world and establishing the principles, rules, and laws by which the world operates. On the one hand, there is order in the world that renders it comprehensible, but, on the other hand, this order is contingent and cannot be justified in terms of any rational principles. In different terms, the world system that Ockham proposes is constituted from without and even when seeming to be stable is always subject to unanticipated disruptions. In this world, black swans and fat tails are unavoidable but not predictable.

By embracing Ockham's notion of God's ordained power, Calvin was able to elaborate rational calculations in economic, social, and political areas of life in ways that Luther could not. For many people in Northern Europe in the late sixteenth and early seventeenth centuries, Calvinism provided an effective worldview for navigating the turbulent transition from the Middle Ages to nascent nationalism and capitalism. Rational calculation was critical not only to the changing economy of salvation but also to the emerging capitalist economy. While Luther condemned mercantilism as the work of the Devil, Calvin was much more open to early modern capitalism. When extended beyond religious life, rationalism and legalism created the conditions for the instrumental logic and disciplinary regime without which capitalism could not have flourished. In addition to providing a framework for rationalizing and moralizing life, Calvin made an important decision about money that literally changed the face of the earth by accepting the practice of usury as long as the rate of return was not excessive. Prior to Calvin, both Catholics and Protestants condemned usury and insisted that the only legitimate way to make money was through human labor and the sale of produce and commodities. The issue once again was time or, more precisely, time and money. Usury, which was condemned in the Hebrew Bible (Deuteronomy 23:19–20), was forbidden at the first Council of

Nicea (325). By the Middle Ages, the ban on usury had become more forceful and widespread. The Third Lateran Council (1179) declared that people who charged interest on loans could not receive the sacraments or have a Christian burial. Pope Clement V made usury a heresy and overturned secular laws that permitted it (1311). The theological justification for the prohibition of usury was that since God governs time, man cannot profit from it. Ever the pragmatist, Calvin realized that emerging mercantile capitalism needed usury as much as Protestantism needed merchants, bankers, and businessmen. By accepting this practice, Calvin embraced the principle that money can make money and thereby prepared the way for new investment instruments and financial institutions.

While salvation is the central tenet in Luther's theology, the doctrine of creation is the heart of Calvin's theology. According to Calvin, belief in salvation by grace rather than by works presupposes an all-powerful creator God who is radically free and completely unconstrained by external circumstances. Creation is not a one-time event but is an ongoing process in which God constantly governs the universe. The doctrine of creation, therefore, necessarily entails the doctrine of providence. "To make God a momentary Creator," Calvin writes, "who once and for all finished his work, would be cold and barren, and we must differ from profane men especially in that we see the presence of divine power shining as much in the continuing state of the universe as in its inception. . . . For unless we pass on to his providence . . . we do not yet properly know what it means to say: 'God is Creator.'" For Calvin, providence is not merely general but also extends to each event and every individual. Within this framework, there is no such thing as fortune or chance because everything "is directed by God's ever-present hand." God's hand is not, of course, always visible; on the contrary, since God's plan is "secret," "the true causes of events are hidden to us."[11] The hand of providence is, therefore, invisible. Since this invisible hand is ever active, the logical implication of Calvin's interpretation of providence is the doctrine of predestination according to which God elects some for eternal salvation and condemns others to eternal damnation.

Two implications of the doctrines of providence and predestination are important for the development of capitalism: individualism and dynamism. First, in ways that are not immediately obvious, predestination reinforces the individualism that lies at the heart of Luther's notion of salvation. While God is all-powerful, He has a personal relationship, which can be positive or negative, with each individual. Second, Calvin's insistence on the omnipresence of divine providence led to a dynamism that shattered the static hierarchical universe of the Middle Ages. For some of Calvin's radical followers, the Reformation, like the act of creation, was not a once-and-for-all event but is an ongoing dynamic process. This restlessness, which is both creative and destructive, is not merely spiritual but extends to social, political, and economic relations as well. What Hegel eventually labels "the restlessness of the negative" is a secularized version of divine activity, which Marx reinterprets as the ceaseless circulation and expansion of capital. The negativity inherent in Protestantism's perpetual Reformation unexpectedly reappears in the relentless planned obsolescence of modern capitalism.

The bridge between Calvinism and market capitalism is Adam Smith, who, in effect, divinizes the machinations of the free market by effectively appropriating Calvin's doctrine of providence. Like several other leading eighteenth-century moral philosophers and political economists, he was Scottish, and Scots at the time tended to be implicitly or explicitly Calvinists. Having been trained at the University of Glasgow and having attended the lectures of Anthony Ashley, Third Earl of Shaftesbury and Francis Hutcheson, Smith had been taught to interpret morality in terms of aesthetics rather than reason alone, like the leading German philosophers of the period. Aesthetic sensibilities led Scottish Calvinists to recognize aspects of Calvin's theology that others usually overlook. Calvin sees the world as the theater of God's glory, where "divine power shines brightly"; the world and our activity in it reveal the power and grandeur of the Lord. Contrary to the usual view of Puritanism as suspicious of beauty and hostile to ostentatious display, Calvin recognizes the importance of the nonutilitarian beauty of the natural world. "Did not God," he asks, "so distinguish colors as to make some more lovely than others? What? Did he not endow gold and silver, ivory and marble, with a loveliness that renders them more precious than other metals or stones? Did he not, in short, render many things attractive to us apart from their necessary use?"[12]

Smith first introduces the metaphor of the invisible hand not in his treatise on political economy, *The Wealth of Nations* (1776), but in his study of morality and aesthetics, *The Theory of Moral Sentiments* (1759), where he uses this image to reinscribe Calvin's nonutilitarian notion of beauty within a utilitarian economy. The relevant passage is in a section entitled "Of beauty which the appearance of UTILITY bestows upon all productions of art, and the extensive influence of this species of Beauty."

> They are led by an invisible hand to make nearly the same distribution of the necessities of life, which would have been made, had the earth been divided into equal portions among all its inhabitants, and thus without intending it, without knowing it, advance the interest of the society, and afford the means to the multiplication of the species. When Providence divided the earth among a few lordly masters, it neither forgot nor abandoned those who seemed to have been left out of the partition. . . . The same principle, the love of system, the same regard of order, of art and contrivance, frequently serves to recommend these institutions which tend to promote the public welfare.[13]

In "the beauty of order" Smith discerns a harmony among individuals even when their intentions seem to be in conflict. In *The Wealth of Nations,* he writes, "By pursuing his own interest he frequently promotes that of the society more effectually than when he really intends to promote it. I have never known much good done by those who affected to trade for the public good. It is an affectation, indeed, not very common among merchants, and very few words need be employed in dissuading them from it."[14] It is important to stress that this theory of the market rests on the correlative notions of the individual and free decision first defined by Ockham and later appropriated by Luther. The market, like the social whole for nominalists, is constituted by the aggregate sum of interacting individuals.

With the translation of the Protestant notions of providence and salvation into the economy of markets, the origin of order is no longer external (God's invisible hand), but becomes internal (the market's invisible hand). Far from having been engineered and regulated by an external agent, be it divine or human, the market comes to be interpreted as a self-organizing and self-regulating system or network. So understood, the market, like the erstwhile God, always knows best. Salvation history is rewritten as market history to create a secular theodicy in which "all things work for the good" for those who believe (Romans 8:68). For faithful Christians, the fall is fortunate because God always brings good out of evil; for the faithful economist, greed is good because the omniscient, omnipotent, and omnipresent market always creates profit out of self-interest.

With the shift from external to internal order, the metaphor for the market changes from a mechanical machine, represented by watches and clocks characteristic of industrial capitalism, to an information machine, represented by cybernetic systems characteristic of financial capitalism. F. A. Hayek, who along with Ayn Rand is a great hero of Milton Friedman and today's conservative politicians and neoliberal economists, went so far as to claim that for Smith, the market is, in effect, a cybernetic system that operates by processing information. Hayek had long argued that the triumph over socialism was all but inevitable because of capitalism's "superior capacity to use dispersed knowledge."

When the Soviet Union finally fell, Hayek's prescient prediction echoed the Protestant revolution five centuries earlier. The Soviet Union's collapse, he argues, exposed the inadequacy of socialism's static, hierarchical, regulated, centralized systems, and the superiority of capitalism's dynamic, privatized, deregulated, and decentralized networks.

In the latter half of the twentieth century, communism and the emerging new form of capitalism reenacted the contest between the realists and nominalists during the late Middle Ages. In communism, the social totality has priority over individuals and, thus, social and economic structures should be centralized, hierarchical, and regulated; in neoliberal capitalism, the individual has priority over the social totality and, thus, the social and economic structure should be decentralized, distributed, and deregulated. The authoritarian communist political system bred suspicion of the disruptive effects of new information and communications technologies. With the world changing faster than the communist system could adapt, the Soviet Union remained committed to a form of industrialization whose time had passed. In the United States, by contrast, a neoconservative political agenda and neoliberal economic policies pushed faster and faster technological change, which was seen as the engine of continued economic growth.

3. Time Counts

· ·

Accounting (for) Books

Capitalism would not have developed as it did without the literacy
and numeracy cultivated by Protestantism. There would have been no
Reformation without the printing press and no early printing industry
without the Reformation. While Catholicism is organized around rituals and the sacraments, Protestantism centers on the Word in scripture
and sermon. During the early Middle Ages, literacy was confined almost exclusively to the clergy and the Bible was in Latin. While this
situation began to change during the Renaissance, it was the coemer-
gence of printing and the Reformation that transformed the way in
which information was produced, distributed, and consumed in the
early modern period. This is not to suggest that printing played no role
in the development of Catholicism during this period. Indeed, printing
actually contributed to the crisis that led to the Reformation. With the
introduction of mechanized printing, indulgences could be produced
and sold many times faster than when each indulgence had to be written by hand. As more and more indulgences were sold, Luther turned
up the heat on his reform efforts. During the Counter-Reformation,
the Catholic Church took a page out of the Protestant playbook by
issuing printed copies of foundational creeds and catechisms intended

to guide the faithful. The important point to stress is that contrasting views of religious authority determined the different deployments of print by Catholics and Protestants. While the Catholics insisted that church authorities control access to scripture, Protestants wanted to put information in the hands of the people. Luther jump-started the Western world of personalized print—without Luther, there would be no texting.

According to Myron Gilmore, "The invention and development with moveable type brought about the most radical transformation in the conditions of intellectual life in the history of Western civilization. It opened new horizons in education and in the communication of ideas. Its effects were sooner or later felt in every department of human activity."[1] Paper and printing had been invented centuries earlier in China, but social and cultural events did not create the conditions favorable to their explosive growth until the sixteenth century in Europe, where the Reformation played a decisive role in their rapid expansion. From the beginning, printing and Protestantism were bound in a mutually reinforcing relationship of supply and demand: printing supplied the materials needed to spread the Word, and the spread of the Word created the demand for more printed materials. Lutheranism, Arthur Dickens argues, "was from the first the child of the printed book, and through this vehicle Luther was able to make exact, standardized and ineradicable impressions on the mind of Europe. For the first time in history a great reading public judged the validity of revolutionary ideas through a mass-medium which used the vernacular languages together with the arts of the journalist and the cartoonist."[2] Luther's protest never would have become a world-historical event without the printing press. Indeed, Luther was the first best-selling author and arguably the first media celebrity in the West; between 1517 and 1520, thirty of his works sold an astonishing 300,000 copies.[3] In his informative book *Printing, Propaganda, and Martin Luther,* Mark Edwards calculates: "If we assume conservatively that each printing of a work by Luther numbered one thousand copies, we are talking about an output for Luther alone of 3.1 million copies during the period 1515 to 1546."[4]

This scale of production and distribution required the creation of an unprecedented technological infrastructure. The printing press was the original prototype for the mechanization and standardization of production that eventually made the Industrial Revolution possible. Gutenberg developed a punch-and-mold system in which replaceable letters were arranged in a type tray that could be used to mass-produce printed pages. Early printers were by necessity entrepreneurs eager to find profitable products and to expand markets for them. Bibles, religious pamphlets, prayer books, and self-help books were the most lucrative printed works for much of the sixteenth century. To promote their products, printers developed novel advertising strategies ranging from handbills and book inserts to posters at trade and book fairs. When the Reformation spread to different cities and countries, entrepreneurs developed new trade routes and distribution networks. As markets grew and diversified throughout northern Europe, new lines of communication quickly opened, spreading information and ideas. The faster the ideas proliferated, the greater their influence. Burgeoning transportation and communications networks, then, played a major role in both disseminating Luther's writings and increasing their authority and popularity.

By 1534, when Luther issued the first edition of his Bible translation, there were already eighteen other German editions of the Bible in print—fourteen in High German and four in Low German. The extraordinary success of Luther's translation was due to its style as well as the circumstances in which it appeared. Much of Luther's political success can be attributed to his abiding bond with commoners, which is reflected in his language. As the writings collected in William Hazlitt's 1821 book *Table-Talk* make abundantly clear, Luther's rhetoric is consistently earthy and often vulgar or even obscene. While representatives of the church hierarchy criticized his style, it resonated with ordinary people and contributed to the popularity of his message. The rapid development of printing technology prepared the way for the swift spread of Luther's gospel by creating a growing number of literate consumers. Anticipating the principles of supply-side economics, the increase in the supply of printed material increased the demand for it, which, in turn, led to the further increase in supply. The growth of literacy encouraged the growing privatization and decentralization of religion. The home hearth became the private altar around which the family gathered to read and study what was believed to be good news.

Breaking the church's monopoly on literacy had important consequences that extended far beyond religious life. People who knew how to read were able to make the transition from agrarian to mercantile society, and later to industrialism, much more easily. Printed materials were not, of course, limited to religious texts but also included maps; calendars; schedules; business textbooks; and tables for weights, measures, and currency conversion, all of which contributed to mercantile and industrial development and economic expansion. By encouraging literacy and numeracy, Protestantism helped to create the educated workforce that early capitalism needed.

The Catholic reaction to these developments proved decisive for generations to come. As the Reformation spread, uneasiness about the use of the vernacular and the growth of literacy deepened. At the Lateran Council of 1515, Leo X issued a censorship decree that "applied to all translations from Hebrew, Greek, Arabic and Chaldaic into Latin and from Latin into the vernacular."[5] Protestantism and literacy were so closely associated that the Catholic Church felt that to contain Protestantism, it had to restrict literacy. Additional edicts directed against Bible-printing were issued throughout the 1520s and were backed up by the Inquisition. At the Council of Trent in 1546, the Catholic Church reaffirmed the primacy of the Vulgate (that is, the Latin translation of the Bible), thereby insuring lay ignorance and obedience rather than promoting literacy and education. Pope Pius IV's reaffirmation of the prohibition of Bible printing and reading in his first Papal Index of 1559 put an end to additional translations of the Bible and drastically limited the spread of literacy in Catholic countries for two centuries. One of the most important effects of these developments was to curtail the growth of industrialism and capitalism in Catholic countries. As mercantilism gave way to industrialism, capitalism became much stronger in northern than in southern Europe. The effects of the division between north and south, which were at least in part a result of these religious doctrines and policies, can still today be seen in maps of Europe as well as in cultural distinctions between peoples living in the northern and southern hemispheres.

While these developments proved decisive for later history, the implications of print are even more complicated than these remarks suggest. In ways that are not immediately obvious, print not only individualizes and deregulates, but also standardizes and regulates scripture, creedal codes, and disciplinary practices. The contrasting tendencies to individualize and to standardize correspond to the voluntaristic destabilizing and rationalistic stabilizing sides of Calvinism. The propensity of print to standardize and regulate has economic, linguistic, and political implications. The economic impact of print can be seen in the eventual development of new currencies and the formation of novel disciplinary practices and techniques without which the further development of capitalism would have been impossible. Changes in currencies always presuppose new technologies: just as there could be no metal currencies without the requisite mining and metallurgy technologies, and there can be no virtual currencies without information-processing machines and networks, so there could be no paper currencies apart from technologies for the production of paper and printing. The transition from handwritten (manuscripts and scrolls) to print (pamphlets and books) became the prototype for the transition from agricultural (manual) to industrial (mechanical) society. The use of machines with interchangeable parts increased the speed of production and created the demand for new networks of distribution. Mechanization led to the standardization of the production of printed currencies and materials, which, in turn, vastly increased markets by facilitating trade beyond local markets and fairs.

Paper currency, first introduced in China in 910 CE, was used by Italian goldsmiths during the Middle Ages, but it was the invention of printing that allowed it to spread rapidly. And while the first banknotes were issued by the Bank of Stockholm in 1661 (the Bank of England followed in 1694), paper currency and deposit banking can be traced to the much older practices of Italian goldsmiths. In Florence, Genoa, and Venice, receipts for gold deposits began to circulate and, when signed, functioned as currency. Realizing very early that it was highly unlikely that all deposits would be collected at the same time, goldsmiths began making interest-bearing loans that exceeded their gold reserves. Throughout the high and late Middle Ages, the Genoese developed a sophisticated banking system with a network of merchant banks that served as clearing houses for increasing international transactions. By the end of the sixteenth century, Europe—especially Spain, which was deeply indebted to Genoa—was flooded with silver from America. With this increase in the supply of specie, the Genoese paper empire crumbled.

By the seventeenth and eighteenth centuries, the action had shifted to Amsterdam—mercantile capitalism was thriving and the Amsterdam Stock Exchange had opened. Calvinist Amsterdam quickly became the capital of speculative finance, and its markets governed trade throughout Europe. Printing created the conditions for the standardization and regulation of currencies that further facilitated the development of global networks of exchange. But printing also introduced a subtle yet important change in the nature of money: with paper currency, the token of exchange shifted from valuable material to a sign with no intrinsic worth. As we will see in Chapter 4, once the distinction between stuff and sign had been made, it was all but inevitable that the signifier (sign) and the signified (stuff) would eventually drift apart and the economy would at some point become a groundless play of signs. Describing what might well be twenty-first-century financial markets, Fernand Braudel writes, "Speculation on the Amsterdam Stock Exchange had reached a degree of sophistication and abstraction which made it for many years a very special trading center of Europe, a place where people were not content simply to buy and sell shares, speculating on their possible rise or fall, but where one could by means of various ingenious combinations speculate without having any money or shares at all. . . . The speculator was in fact selling something he did not possess and buying something he never would: it was known as 'blank' buying. The operation would be resolved by a loss or gain. The difference would be settled by a payment one way or the other and the game would go on."[6] With the spread of mercantile capitalism and the emergence of speculative financial markets, the market economy reached a new level of complexity. Not only was it easier to borrow money in Holland in the 1750s than it was in New York in the 1980s, but the Amsterdam exchange of the 1700s was also in many ways surprisingly similar to the financial markets in "New Amsterdam" during the 1980s and 1990s.

Clockwork Universe

Speed. It's always a matter or, increasingly, a non-matter of time. Time and money.

Time: 1936
Place: Any factory, USA

Charlie Chaplin's *Modern Times* begins with music playing and a full-screen shot of a clock with the second hand moving toward 6:00. After the credits roll, words appear superimposed on the clock.

"Modern Times." A story of industry, of individual enterprise— humanity crusading in pursuit of happiness.

The film captures the travails of workers in post-Depression industrial America. The action begins with a herd of pigs rushing to their slaughter, followed by a herd of men emerging from the subway rushing to a factory. Like Lucy and Ethel frantically trying to wrap chocolates faster and faster, workers desperately scramble to keep up with the assembly line, while managers reading newspapers in comfortable offices surrounded by secretaries and calculating machines order their subordinates on the shop floor to keep speeding up production. An elaborate surveillance network of cameras and screens monitors workers even during bathroom breaks. Workers' bodily movements are as automated and mechanized as the production line. Every day begins and ends with workers punching a time clock. When the Little Tramp rushing to keep up gets caught in turning gears, machine literally devours man.

The ancestors of my grandfather, Mark H. Cooper, who was a watchmaker, came from Strasbourg. It is no accident that the famous Strasbourg clock was created in the city with a thriving printing industry to which Calvin had fled to escape persecution. Before the widespread use of mechanical clocks, printed calendars and schedules had already begun the process of rationalizing human behavior in ways that would change work and transform the economy. Just as print had been the *preparatio Evangelica* for Luther, so the standardization and regulation of life prepared the way for industrialization. The emergence of industrial capitalism presupposed not only the development of new technologies and educated workers but also the standardization and regulation of human behavior, which would not have been possible without printing and clocks.

Devices for measuring time are as old as humanity itself. In the West, keeping track of time began as a religious affair and gradually was secularized. The earliest medieval clockmakers were monks whose lives were completely regulated—prayers and rituals followed a strict schedule that required accurate timekeeping. Before the invention of mechanical clocks, hours were measured by devices like sundials and water clocks. When mechanical clocks were introduced, they measured only hours and had no minute or second hands. On special occasions, bells, chimes, and mechanical devices were used to broadcast time to nearby villages. Clock towers gradually spread from monasteries, cathedrals, and churches to town squares but measuring time accurately and uniformly did not become widespread until the modern era. Before the Industrial Revolution, life was governed by the natural rhythms of sunlight and seasons; when time was measured, it was local and varied from village to village and town to town. Space and place mattered more than time. With modernity, modernization, and modernism, this changed. While space dominated premodern experience, time governs modern experience. Time actually changes with modernity—no longer external and natural, time becomes internal and mechanical.

If modernity begins with Luther's transference of the scene of faith from external and objective rituals to internal and subjective experience, modern philosophy begins with René Descartes's inward turn, whereby the locus of truth shifted from the external and objective world to internal and subjective experience and knowledge. Descartes famously doubted everything until he found what he took to be indubitable—his own mind in the act of doubting. Truth and certainty, in other words, became inseparable from individual self-consciousness. The more that Descartes and his successors probed consciousness and self-consciousness, the more complex these ideas became. Since self and world are inextricably related, changes in the interpretation of self-consciousness led to changes in the understanding of the world.

Nothing would seem to be more external and objective than space and time. By the end of the eighteenth century, however, self-reflection had recast the world in its own image. In his monumental *Critique of Pure Reason* (1781), Immanuel Kant argues that space and time are part of human beings' perceptual and cognitive apparatus rather than characteristics of the outer world. Far from a blank slate, the mind is hardwired with twelve categories of understanding (unity, plurality, totality, reality, negation, limitation, subsistence, causality, reciprocity, possibility, existence, and necessity), as well as two forms of intuition (space and time). The forms of intuition and categories of understanding are the glasses or goggles through which we see the world. In different terms, they function like programs that process the data of experience or like filters that separate noise from information, thereby creating order out of chaos. These forms and categories do not depend on experience, and thus are universal. *What* people experience differs from person to person, but *how* they order experience is the same for everyone. Space and time, therefore, are homogeneous and thus standardized.

In retrospect, it is clear that Kant's insistence on the universality and homogeneity of space and time was to a significant degree a function of new forms of industrial production that were emerging at the time. Anticipating developments that would become widespread a century later, Kant effectively industrializes perception and thinking. Within his scheme, space and time are not only uniform and homogenous but also linear: space consists of a rectilinear grid that connects discrete points, and time consists of a straight line that connects separate points. It is important to stress that segmentation, separation, and disassembly (analysis) do not preclude integration, connection, assembly (synthesis). To the contrary, these are two complementary processes that create uniformity and homogeneity by first breaking down processes and activities and then connecting the dots.

As the locus of production shifts from heaven to earth, man creates the world in his own image and the world, in turn, recreates man in its image. The process of standardization, I have argued, began with the invention of the printing press, which in turn regularized language and laws. Industrialization on the one hand, and standardization and routinization on the other, form a paradoxical relationship: industrialization creates the standardization and routinization, which makes industrialization possible. In other words, industrialization is at once the cause and the effect of standardization and routinization, and vice versa. A classic chicken-and-egg problem if there ever were one. For industrialization to spread, standardization and routinization had to be extended to other modes of production, reproduction, and distribution as well as to everything from weights, currencies, measures, prices, credit, and even packaging. None of this would have been possible without the standardization of space and time.

The standardization of time, which led to the standardization of space, was the result of new technologies for sea and land transportation. As is often the case, what appears to be rational has an irrational origin. The rationalization and standardization of both space and time began with two accidents in which speed played a critical role. Temporal standardization grew out of spatial acceleration on sea and land. In 1707, Admiral Cloudesley Shovell was the commander of a fleet of British ships when they ran into a heavy fog. "For eleven days," Edward Casey reports, "the fleet drifted, increasingly uncertain as to where it was located. On the twelfth day navigators thought the fleet was safely west of Brittany but later that night the ships crashed into the Sicily Islands to the southwest of England. Two thousand men, including Admiral Shovell, were killed and four ships sank. The only way to avoid such disasters in the future was, paradoxically, through the administration of time."[7]

It took seven years for the British parliament to establish the Board of Longitude, which offered "a publick reward for such person or persons as shall discover the Longitude."[8] The solution to Admiral Shovell's navigation problem required the invention of a device that accurately measured longitude by determining the precise position east or west of the prime meridian in Greenwich, England. This device was the marine chronometer, invented by the Englishman John Harrison (1693–1776). A self-educated clockmaker, Harrison realized that it is necessary to use time to determine spatial location. "For longitude is not merely a matter of spatial position. It is a matter of where one is *at a certain time*—'mean' or 'local' time—relative to the time it then is at the prime meridian."[9] In 1735, Harrison built a chronometer that proved to be very accurate for maritime navigation. After five more maritime clocks and countless trials, the Board of Longitude awarded the prize to Harrison, who was then eighty years old. It was not until 1884, however, that the International Meridian Conference adopted the Greenwich meridian as the Universal Prime Meridian, or zero point of longitude.

On land, synchronization of train schedules required the standardization of time. For trains as for ships, an accident proved decisive. On October 5, 1841, two Western Railroad passenger trains collided on the country's first intersectional rail link between Albany, New York, and Worcester, Massachusetts. Two people were killed and eight injured, provoking a public outcry that led to an investigation by the Massachusetts legislature. Once again, speed was deemed the culprit. In his informative book *The Control Revolution: Technological and Economic Origins of the Information Society,* James R. Beniger writes, "People were not yet used to traveling at the speed of inanimate energy—certainly not to the Western's operating speeds of up to thirty miles per hour." The company was trying to manage six trains running simultaneously on 150 miles of track without the information necessary to do so safely. As rail travel became more common, accidents became more frequent. "Without the technologies of centralized bureaucratic control," Beniger explains, such as "telegraphic communication and formalized operating procedures along the line . . . and lacking even standardized signals, timetables, and synchronized watches, many accidents did occur."[10]

In the United States, all time was local until the end of the nineteenth century. In Great Britain, by contrast, British railways standardized time on December 11, 1847, by adopting Greenwich Mean Time (GMT) as the national standard, which years later was still called "railway time." By 1855, all public clocks in Great Britain conformed to GMT, while in the United States, railroads continued to determine their own time until 1883. This practice made it virtually impossible to operate the safe and efficient national rail network that industrialization required. To address this growing problem, Charles F. Dowd, who was the principal of the Temple Grove Ladies Seminary, which is now Skidmore College, proposed four national time zones for American railroads based on the meridian that passed through Washington, D.C. Though the need for standardization was obvious, squabbles among different railway companies concerned that the new system would hurt their business prevented final approval of a nationally uniform system until the passage of the Standard Time Act in 1918.[11] Standardization facilitated the rationalization of transportation but the price was centralization and even nationalization, which increased and reinforced bureaucratic control.

It is important to note that the standardization of space and time involves competing tendencies that both reflect and reinforce the contradictions of industrial as well as post-industrial society. From Adam Smith's pin factory to cell phones and wireless networks, modes of production and reproduction simultaneously segregate and integrate, separate and connect. Modern time and space are both homogeneous and divided, unified and fragmented. We will see in Chapter 7 that these tensions have important social, political, and economic implications.

With standardization, transportation as well as everything else speeds up. Just as the standardized time and schedules were necessary for trains and ships to run safely and smoothly, so too the standardization of time and schedules was a prerequisite for factories to run efficiently. With the spread of railroads and factories, time was privatized, even if not personalized. In order to keep trains running on time, every station master had to have his own pocketwatch, which was synchronized with the watches of other station masters. Wristwatches were introduced in England around 1900, but remained fashion accessories until they were used to synchronize troop movements first in the Second Boer War (1899–1902) and then in World War I. The standardization and privatization of time both coordinated the activities of people and synchronized man and machine. The pocketwatch and wristwatch were to industrial society what the Blackberry and iPhone are to information society—personal technologies that bind individuals to ever-accelerating engines of production and reproduction.

It was not only *that* time was measured but *how* it was measured that changed lives. We have seen that industrialization was coterminous with the emergence of the linearity of perception in which separate points are connected in grids to form a sense of space, and sequential moments are strung together in series to create a sense of time. Space as well as time became a matter of punctuality. The rectilinear grid of Midwestern farmland and towns as well as the practice of punching a time clock are the effects of the mechanization and modernization of space and time. Factories, like trains, required punctuality. Workers no longer could follow natural cycles and rhythms but had to conform to the logic and pace of machines. Standardization required the correlative processes of abstraction and quantification. As quality gave way to quantity, what could not be measured by standardized procedures, norms, and values was considered insignificant or even unreal. The organizational structure of workers' days became as abstract, quantifiable, and repeatable as the products they produced and the currency with which they were paid.

Standardization, abstraction, and quantification exponentially increased the speed of production in a relentless search for efficiency. "Efficiency, an American gospel in the twentieth century," Daniel Boorstin writes, "meant packaging work into units of time. In a nation where labor was often scarce and always costly, efficiency was measured less by 'quality' or 'competency' than by the speed with which an acceptable job was accomplished. Time entered into every calculation. An effective America was a speedy America. Time became a series of homogeneous—precisely measured and precisely repeatable—units. The working day was no longer measured by daylight, and electric lights kept factories going 'round the clock.' Refrigeration and central heating and air conditioning units had begun to abolish nature's seasons. One unit of work became more like another."[12]

As workers migrated from country to city, employers offered them a deal: our money for your time. In industrial society, time counts because time is money. Captains of industry counted minutes and hours like the quarters and dollars they actually were. Workers, who did not own the means of production, had nothing else to sell than their time, which was, of course, their life. If time is to be bought and sold on a market that is far from free, it must be measured accurately and used efficiently. Critics of early industrial capitalism exposed how factories destroyed individual lives and tore apart both families and society. At the end of the eighteenth century, the German philosopher and poet Friedrich Schiller wrote in what would become the manifesto for the modern artistic avant-garde, *On the Aesthetic Education of Man in a Series of Letters:* "Everlastingly chained to a single little fragment of the whole, man himself develops into nothing but a fragment; everlastingly in his ear the monotonous sound of the wheel that he turns, he never develops the harmony of his being, and instead of putting the stamp of humanity on his own nature, he becomes nothing more than the imprint of his occupation or of his specialized knowledge."[13] Schiller could never have imagined how far personal and social fragmentation would be carried a century later.

No one did more to accelerate and fragment human activity, and by extension, life, than Frederick Winslow Taylor. As early as 1895, Taylor presented a paper to the American Mechanical Engineers developing what he eventually labeled "the principles of scientific management" in his 1911 book bearing that title. The goal of this investigation, he explains, is to insure "maximum prosperity" by developing procedures to determine "the maximum efficiency" of workers. Taylor's analysis is based on his assessment of the importance of speed in the production process. "The most important object of both the workmen and the management," he writes, "should be the training and development of each individual in the establishment, so that he can do (at the fastest pace and with the maximum of efficiency) the highest class of work for which his natural abilities fit him."[14] To accomplish this goal, Taylor develops what is, in effect, the analytic equivalent of Muybridge's time-lapsed photography, which breaks down the activity of individual workers into a fragmented series of steps or moments. The key to his method is the stopwatch. Describing his procedure, Taylor explains that he finds ten to fifteen different men from different factories who are skilled in the particular activity he is studying. The second, third, and fourth steps are decisive for his analysis.

> *Second.* Study the exact series of elementary operations or motions which each of these men uses in doing the work which is being investigated, as well as the implements each man uses.
>
> *Third.* Study with a stop-watch the time required to make each of these elementary movements and then select the quickest way of doing each element of the work.
>
> *Fourth.* Eliminate all false movements, slow movements, and useless movements.[15]

The goal of the principles of scientific management is to develop a disciplinary regime that reprograms workers' bodies to conform to the logic and pace of mechanical machines.

It is important to stress that Taylor is most interested in *management.* His method of scientific management effectively reinscribes the Cartesian opposition between body, which is mechanically determined, and mind, which is free. In Taylor's scheme, workers represent the body and managers represent the mind. This relationship is not reciprocal— mind controls body but the body cannot influence the mind. Taylor replaces Descartes's infamous pineal gland, which is supposed to connect mind and body, with the principles of scientific management as they are codified in rational rules, procedures, and codes. Since time is money, faster is always better. "The work of every workman is fully planned out by the management at least one day in advance, and each man receives in most cases complete written instructions, describing in detail the task which he is to accomplish, as well as the means to be used doing the work. . . . This task specifies not only what is to be done but how it is to be done and the exact time allowed for doing it. And whenever the workman succeeds in doing his task right, and within the time limit specified, he receives an addition of from 30 percent to 100 percent." Taylor leaves no doubt about his disdain for workers when he applies his principles to laborers handling pig-iron. "This work is so crude and elementary in its nature that the writer firmly believes that it would be possible to train an intelligent gorilla so as to become a more efficient pig-iron handler than any man can be."[16]

Taylor's written procedures replaced the oral tradition of rules of thumb and anecdotal advice that had been handed on from master to apprentice in pre-industrial society. The formalization of these practices made the individuals who carried them out as replaceable as parts of the machines they operated. Boorstin correctly points out that "scientific management, which made the worker into a labor unit and judged his effectiveness by his ability to keep the technology flowing, had made the worker himself into an interchangeable part."[17] For Taylor, institutional memory is depersonalized and downloaded in the written files controlled by management. By substituting the impersonal for the personal, Taylor gives priority to system over individual. Like Charlie Chaplin's managers sending messages to workers ordering the acceleration of the assembly lines on TV screens, Taylor's quest for speed eventually spins out of control and workers are consumed by machines.

Industrialism's "mechanism of management" disciplined minds as well as bodies. While industrialization both fragments and integrates labor and production, industrialized perception simultaneously distracts and concentrates attention. On the one hand, new transportation technologies like trains, automobiles, and airplanes, as well as new technologies of reproduction like panoramas, kinetoscopes, and cinemato-graphs, created distraction by blurring perception in a continuous flow of superficial images. Jonathan Crary points out that this mobilization of the gaze is not accidental but is actually required by the logic of capitalism. "Capitalism, as accelerated exchange and circulation," he writes, "necessarily produced this kind of human perceptual adaptability and became a regimen of reciprocal attentiveness and distraction." On the other hand, telescopes, microscopes, and photographic devices concentrated attention by focusing on an isolated object or freezing a particular moment. The impact of these technologies is more a function of *how* perception occurs than of *what* is perceived. The industrialization of perception and conception brought about by new transportation, production, and reproduction technologies resulted in contradictory tendencies that anticipated the perceptual and psychological tensions created by today's electronic media and digital technologies.

Though Taylor emphasizes physical rather than mental discipline, effective scientific management requires a rewiring of human attention. Workers in factories and on assembly lines had to maintain sustained concentration while repeating the same limited action for many hours. Losing focus or becoming distracted not only resulted in inefficiencies, but also could cause accidents that might result in serious injury or even death. Like Monet painting the Rouen Cathedral or Muybridge photographing Leland Stanford's horses, the factory worker had to immerse himself in the fragmentary instant of an endless linear series without any regard for the total process of which it was a part. In what Crary aptly describes as "modern disciplinary and spectacular culture," "what is important to institutional power, since the late nineteenth century, is simply that perception function in a way that insures a subject is productive, manageable, and predictable, and is able to be socially integrated and adaptive."[18]

Punctuality is important in other ways for industrial society. Like trains, factories, and assembly lines, workers must operate on a strictly regulated schedule. During the early Industrial Revolution, factory workers often labored from ten to sixteen hours a day, six days a week. The standardization and regulation of working hours began as a labor movement in the early nineteenth century. In 1810, Robert Owen raised the demand for a ten-hour work day in England. A few years later, the goal had become an eight-hour day and workers marched to the slogan "eight hours labor, eight hours recreation, eight hours rest." The United States lagged behind other industrializing countries. Even though excessive working hours created labor unrest throughout the latter half of the nineteenth century, it was not until 1884 that the Federation of Organized Trades and Labor Unions demanded the legalization of an eight-hour work day. This movement received a significant boost on January 5, 1915, when the Ford Motor Company cut the work day from nine to eight hours and doubled pay to five dollars a day. One year later, in the wake of continuing labor unrest, Congress passed the Adamson Act, which established the eight-hour day with the guarantee of extra pay for overtime work for all railroad workers. This law, which was the first time the federal government regulated working hours for private companies, testified to the growing power of organized labor. In 1917, the U.S. Supreme Court upheld the law, thereby guaranteeing its extension to all workers.[19] In anticipation of issues to be considered in later chapters, two points related to these developments must be emphasized. First, while the privatization of time made the increasing regulation of personal life possible, the establishment of the eight-hour work day placed limits on the demands that managers could make on workers. Factory owners and managers might be able to insist that people work faster while on the job, but they could not legally make them work longer hours without paying them more. Second, the standardization of the day into three parts consisting of labor, recreation, and rest was a legal acknowledgment of the importance of leisure for all people. In today's post-industrial 24/7/365 society, both the limitation of work hours and the acknowledgment of the importance of leisure have disappeared.

The different phases of industrialization, I have noted, are correlated with different sources of energy. The shift from human, animal, and natural energy sources to fossil fuels resulted in a previously unprecedented acceleration of life. From the twelfth to the nineteenth centuries, processing and production rates remained quite slow. With the use of coal, steam, and iron, the pace quickly picked up. The next phase shift in the speed of production, and by extension, life, came with the widespread introduction of electricity. For electricity to be useful, it must be produced and distributed efficiently. Even today most electricity is still generated by electro-magnetic generators driven by fossil fuels, which were introduced in the late nineteenth century. In the following years, the development of the electrical transformer created the possibility of transmitting more voltage with less current. While Edison promoted direct current (DC), European engineers favored alternating current (AC). When the Serbian-American electrical engineer, physicist, futurist, and showman Nikola Tesla introduced alternating current generators at the 1893 Chicago World's Fair, people took notice. By the late 1880s, the British electrical firm Ferranti had installed an AC generating station in London and had successfully transmitted electricity to Paris. George Westinghouse was so impressed with this technology on his visit to London in 1885 that he put his company's development of AC technology on the fast track. One year later an AC distribution system was installed in Great Barrington, Massachusetts, a few miles down the road from where I am writing these words, and all the pieces were in place for establishment of electrical power grids that started locally and quickly became national: "by allowing multiple generating plants to be interconnected over a wide area, electricity production cost was reduced. The most efficient available plants could be used to supply varying loads during the day. Reliability was improved and capital investment cost was reduced, since stand-by generating capacity could be shared over many more customers and a wider geographic area." The electrification of households began in cities and areas served by electric railways in 1905. By 1930, approximately 70 percent of households had electricity; in rural areas, however, the situation was different: only 10 percent of farms had it.[20]

Neither modern assembly lines nor postmodern financial markets would be possible without electricity. Henry Ford introduced his assembly line in Highland Park, Michigan, in 1913. While the idea for this new form of mass production came from Gustavus Swift's Chicago meatpacking plant, which was made famous, or more precisely, infamous, in Upton Sinclair's 1906 novel *The Jungle,* Ford's comment in 1930 makes it clear that the ultimate source of his inspiration was Adam Smith's pin factory. " 'To make automobiles,' he explained, 'is to make one automobile like another automobile, to make them all alike, to make them come through the factory just alike; just as one pin is like another pin when it comes from a pin factory, or one match is like another when it comes from a match factory.' "[21] Ford realized that economies of scale made it necessary to extend control beyond the factory floor. That is, "much as Swift, Philip Armour, and other meatpackers sought to integrate the flow of meat from range to consumer using the railroads, disassembly lines, refrigerated cars, and warehouses, so too did Henry Ford dream of nonstop flow—never quite achieved—from raw materials to finished product."[22] He expanded his network of production from Michigan to rubber plantations in Brazil. Though the experiment in rubber production ultimately failed, the efforts in Michigan proved to be a spectacular success. Ford's innovation depended on the coordination of standardized and interchangeable parts on a continuously moving assembly line with standardized and interchangeable workers regulated by the principles of scientific management. By 1927, there were 1.3 million Model T cars on the road and 15 million new cars rolling off the assembly line. The production of each car required

Calvin and Emma Taylor in their Model T Ford at Devil's Den on the Gettysburg battlefield, June 23, 1912

workers to perform 7,882 separate tasks.[23] One my most cherished possessions is a photograph of my paternal grandfather and grandmother, dated June 23, 1912, posed in their Sunday best sitting in a Model T in front of Devil's Den on the Gettysburg battlefield.

Technologies of Control

The combination of increasing complexity and accelerating speed of production required the development of more effective and efficient technologies and strategies of control. The organizational and operational principles of industrialization and standardization that grew from this need involve a series of transfers that proved decisive for all later developments:

From person to machine
From individual to system
From oral to written
From ad hoc to standardized
From decentralized to centralized
From distributed to hierarchical
From personal to organizational memory

Beniger argues persuasively that what has traditionally been called the Industrial Revolution was actually a "control revolution." Though his approach is historical rather than philosophical, the developments he charts represent the translation of what Nietzsche described as the will to power into the will to control. Throughout the Industrial Revolution, material and immaterial flows remained inseparably interrelated. As communication and information technologies became more sophisticated, production processes accelerated. During the latter half of the nineteenth century, a burst of new technologies changed the ways that people did business and lived their lives. These inventions included, among many others, blotting paper (1856), pencil with an eraser and steel pen (1858), telegraph ticker (1867), carbon paper (1869), stock ticker (1870), typewriter with modern keyboard (1873), modern calculating machine (1887), and punch-card tabulator (1889). Beniger points out that "other major components of the generalized information processor that the modern office and—by aggregation—emerging bureaucratic structure would become also appeared in the early decades of industrialization. Recording or information storage capabilities increased with the systematization of shorthand, including the first professional shorthand journal (1848), the systematizing of office record keeping (early 1870s), and the dictating machine (1885)."[24] Taken together, these technologies and others created a revolution in the production, reproduction, storage, and searching of data and information that was every bit as transformative as the changes taking place in workshops and on factory floors.

The extension of the print revolution from press to the desktop led to novel possibilities for producing and processing information. Between 1827 and 1893, "printing speed increased three-hundred fold. . . . The Columbian press, manufactured in Philadelphia in 1816 . . . differed little from the hand-press used by Gutenberg three centuries earlier. . . . By 1893 octuplet rotary power presses could print up to 96,000 eight-page copies per hour."[25] Though the typewriter was operated manually, it was actually a significant innovation in digital desktop publishing. Christopher Latham Sholes, Carlos Glidden, and Samuel Soule patented the typewriter in 1868, but it was not until the Remingtons, who had manufactured sewing machines and firearms, entered the business that production became commercially viable. Between 1874 and 1878, only 4,000 machines were sold; by 1900, however, when other companies like Underwood had emerged, 144,873 typewriters had been purchased.[26] New technologies created the demand for new workers. From 1880 to 1900, thousands of stenographers and typists, many of whom were women, entered the workforce. With the introduction of keyboard calculators and punch-card tabulating machines, the demand for a new class of workers known as "computers" arose. Another easily overlooked invention made it possible to reproduce information quickly, easily, and accurately—carbon paper. Before mechanical means of reproduction, documents had to be copied by hand, which was slow and resulted in a lack of uniformity as well as many errors. When typewriters and carbon paper removed the human hand from the process of document production, speed and accuracy greatly increased. By 1887 Edison had invented the rotary mimeograph machine, and a little more than a decade later the first photocopying machine, which was the prototype for what eventually became the Xerox machine (1960), was introduced.

As documents accumulated faster than ever before, new methods for storing and retrieving information were required. In her informative study *Control through Communication: The Rise of System in American Management,* JoAnne Yates points out that "the significance of turn-of-the-century innovations in storage systems for documents is much less acknowledged now than the typewriter, carbon paper, and duplicators. Yet files of correspondence and other documents played an increasingly important role in the management of firms by the turn of the century. And while written documents were far from easily accessible in the latter half of the nineteenth century . . . that situation worsened as the other technologies supported growth in internal and external correspondence triggered by firm growth and systematization."[27] While this amount of data may seem insignificant by today's standards, the flood of information and rate of its flow were as disorienting for people at the turn of the twentieth century as the speed of trains hurtling through the countryside. Industry could not continue to grow without new search engines that enabled managers to bring order out of the chaos created by the flood of new data and information and to find what they needed quickly. Among the many inventions during this period, two stand out as particularly significant—the Dewey Decimal System and vertical files.

The Dewey Decimal System was invented by American librarian, educator, and entrepreneur Melvil Dewey. A graduate of Amherst College, Dewey was head librarian at Columbia University from 1888 to 1906. While still in college, he founded the Library Bureau, which "sold high quality index cards and filing cabinets and established the standard dimension for catalog cards."[28] The code Dewey established is based on ten—the classification is made up of ten categories, each of which is divided into ten divisions, which, in turn, are divided yet again ten times. The system is hierarchical with books cataloged in ascending numerical order with further subdivision arranged alphabetically. This method requires vertical files for cards. Dewey also invented hanging vertical files, which were first introduced in 1893 at the Chicago World's Fair, also known as the World's Columbian Exhibition.

It is difficult today to appreciate the importance of vertical filing when it replaced flat filing in letterboxes in the 1890s. Previous filing systems took up lots of space and did not permit easy organization. This changed with the invention of a new search engine—file drawers and cabinets took up less space than boxes and could store up to ten times more documents than previous horizontal systems. Most important, this new search technology allowed rapidly accumulating information to be accessed quickly. Though multiple ordering principles were possible, three became widely used: alphabetic, chronological, and subject. The combination of new duplication and filing technologies made it possible to produce multiple copies of data and documents that could be filed in different ways. Cards and folders with tabs and dividers allowed faster access and the possibility of easy rearrangement. When the proliferation of information made it clear that scientific management required the control and distribution of information, management principles were identified and organized in systematic theories. Just as managers overseeing industrial production flows formalized oral rules of thumb that standardized factory work in written rules, so too did people struggling to manage information flows develop written procedures that standardized office work. These rules were codified in everything from calendars, time cards, forms, memos, and circulars to pamphlets, manuals, and books—all of which regularized production and management across departments, companies, firms, and even industries. These developments resulted in what was, in effect, the programming of industrial labor and information processes. Standardized rules and procedures were codes that function like algorithms for managing material, labor, data, and information. It is no accident that when computing moved from the mainframe to the desktop, the metaphor for organizing information was the file folder.

Then, as now, more complex codes and new search engines created the demand for new forms of education. Beginning in the 1840s, business schools emerged to complement vocational and technical schools, a process that led in 1881 to the founding of Wharton, which was the first university business school. Once again, the print revolution and the Industrial Revolution were inextricably interrelated in directing the interaction of material and immaterial flows. The Cartesian body-mind dualism was reinscribed in the growing gap separating physical laborers and information workers. And the belief in systematic management of work and the workplace extended the modern struggle between the individual and the system that had begun with Luther's reformation of the Catholic Church.

Whether it was used for controlling industrial production or for reproducing information, systematic, scientific management was based on principles that Henry Metcalfe already had summarized as early as 1885 in an article entitled "Shop-Order System."

The proposed system of shop accounts is based on two compensating principles.

1. The radiating from a central source, let us say the office, of all authority for expenditure of labor or material. These being, however they may be disguised, the elemental forms of all internal expenditure.
2. The conveying toward the office of the circumferential points, of independent records of work done and expenses made by virtue of that authority.[29]

Within this regime, the industrial management of material and immaterial flows involves a centralized and hierarchical system of command and control that is regulated through feedback mechanisms. Power flows from the center to the periphery and from the top down. This understanding of management structure discloses unexpected organizational similarities among bureaucracies in the Catholic Church, industrial capitalism, socialism, and even communism. In anticipation of analyses developed in later chapters, it is important to note that this centralized, top-down systematic structure breaks down with the emergence of decentralized, distributed technologies in the consumer and financial capitalism of postmodern network culture, in ways that are reminiscent of Protestant organizational structures.

Throughout the Industrial Revolution and even down to the present day, what drives the engine of production and reproduction is the relentless search for efficiency. Yates reports that from at least 1910, "System, efficiency and scientific become catchwords in the business world and beyond. . . . By the beginning of World War I, efficiency was a widely-accepted goal and business systems were accepted methods of achieving that goal."[30] Efficiency was not only a concern of private business but became a preoccupation of government from the municipal to the federal levels. In 1910, President William Howard Taft appointed the Commission on Economy and Efficiency to consider reforms to improve the efficiency of government. The commission was headed by Frederick Cleveland, who had created one of the first municipal budgets for New York City. Cleveland and his colleagues studied everything from paper clips, envelopes, folders, and carbon copying to mechanical modes of printing, reproducing, and distributing documents. By this time, information technologies included dictographs, adding machines, telephones, telegraphs, and even pneumatic tube systems for the rapid distribution of memos and instructions in offices, and for the circulation of credit and sales receipts in stores.[31] The commission's recommendation for the establishment of a national budget was ignored, but the report's summary of the importance of emerging technologies for the rationalization and standardization of management procedures had a lasting effect.

The extraordinary preoccupation with efficiency was actually a function of the obsession with speed. The primary aim of his study, Taylor acknowledged, was "to point out, through a series of simple illustrations, the great loss which the whole country is suffering through inefficiency in almost all our daily acts." Scientific management promised to increase efficiency by decreasing production time. To make more money, it is necessary to save time by programming employees to work faster. Following the logic, "maximum productivity" equals "maximum prosperity," Taylor concludes: "If the above reasoning is correct, it follows that the most important object of both the workmen and the management should be the training and development of each individual in the establishment, so that he can do (at his fastest pace and with the maximum of efficiency) the highest class of work for which his natural abilities fit him."[32] The influence of Taylor's system has not decreased over the years; indeed, scientific and systematic production and management are, if anything, more powerful today than ever before. Faster is always better, and the best way to become more efficient and get faster is by cutting out the "fat."

4. Windows Shopping

Wearing Thin

Slow . . . Fast. Country . . . City. I live in the country and the city. In the city, my thirteenth-floor apartment overlooks the Cathedral of Saint John the Divine. My apartment is on a short block midway between Broadway and housing projects. On the corner of Broadway and 103rd Street, there is a Starbucks—at latest count, one of ten on Broadway, one of 255 in Manhattan, one of 12,781 in the United States, and one of 19,435 worldwide in fifty-eight countries. People do not come together in Starbucks; they are, in Sherry Turkle's fine phrase, "alone together," congregating without communicating. Though it is located only a block from the projects, with very few exceptions the only people of color I have ever seen there are behind the counter. There is little conversation, chatter, or banter; no laughter; and mostly repetitious music. The most commonly heard sounds are the endless noise of commerce and the relentless clicking of keyboards. Each person is locked into a fast computer or iPad on a high-speed wireless network with earbuds blocking out all sound that is not his or her personalized playlist. The only people talking are speaking into the void to people who are not there. Everyone is cut off from the surrounding world, cut off from other people, cut off even from themselves. Cells within cells within cells, metastasizing in clouds floating above the earth threatening to turn toxic. I pass Starbucks every day but have never been inside.

Three blocks north on the corner of Broadway and 106th Street, there is a Kentucky Fried Chicken store—one of only nine in Manhattan and one of 18,000 worldwide in 120 countries. I go to this local KFC often and am frequently the only white person there. People are almost never working or playing on computers and few talk on their cell phones. Most people are usually in small groups, conversing while they eat or wait to pick up their orders. Mayor Bloomberg's calorie count listed in big figures on a sign above the counter is ignored. In the inverted economy of food, the more you pay, the less food you get, and the less you pay, the more food you get. A colleague once took me to Per Se for lunch. The bill for the twelve-course meal with wine was $980 and when we left the restaurant, I was still hungry. At KFC, I get a bucket of twelve pieces of chicken, a side of macaroni and cheese, and four biscuits for twenty bucks. Almost all the people in the store are overweight. When I confess to friends and colleagues that I frequent KFC, they invariably are appalled but I tell them not to worry because I run every day.

Thin . . . Fat. Thin is cool, fat is not. But it was not always thus; think of Peter Paul Rubens's voluptuous nudes. Not long ago fat was the mark of success, luxury, and freely chosen leisure, whereas now it is for many the mark of failure, poverty, and forced unemployment or underemployment. Far from prestigious, fat has become a disease and obesity an epidemic. But not all fat is the same—there are different kinds of fat: football player fat, farmer fat, peasant fat, hard-hat fat, white-collar fat, food-stamp fat, couch-potato fat, sumo fat, Buddha fat, video game fat, fast-food fat. Lifestyle is embodied in flesh. Athletes gain weight to gain leverage; tight t-shirts over tight guts of hard-hat workers are macho; flabby stomachs hanging over belts of office workers and executives are an embarrassment that must be hidden under loose shirts and blouses; farmers' big arms and big chests display strength; fat arms, legs, and trunk are the price of high carbohydrate diets of the poor; roly-poly fat is the luxury of the jolly; drinking too much beer and eating too many wings while watching the NFL on TV leads to the lethargy of couch-potato fat.

Thin . . . Fat. Thin is cool, fat is not. But lean can also be mean. Not all thin is the same—there are different kinds of thin. There is stylish thin, streamlined thin, athletic thin, model thin, sickly thin, anorexic thin, deadly thin. By the time of Steve Jobs's untimely death, Apple had become the Calvin Klein of tech, and he was the Kate Moss of thin. The astonishing popularity of Apple is as much a matter (or non-matter) of style as of substance. No company has done more to make thin stylish than Apple, and no entrepreneur had a better sense of style and showmanship than Jobs. His fashion was always the same: black turtleneck, jeans, running shoes, and rimless glasses. This was an un-likely twist for a person who showed up for an interview for his first job at Atari wearing sandals. When his boss, Al Alcorn, sent the young Jobs to Munich to solve a problem with one of the early computers, Walter Isaacson reports, "he flummoxed the dark-suited German managers. They complained to Alcorn that he dressed and smelled like a bum and behaved badly."[1]

But beneath the ragged clothes and offensive smell, Jobs always had a sense of style or, rather, a savvy aesthetic that was at once supremely modernist and superficially spiritual. This aesthetic is formal and minimalist—strip away excessive ornament to reveal pure form. Sleek, slender, streamlined. Not heavy but light—pure light. Jobs's aesthetic was actually a vestige of his youthful spiritual quest; in his early years his spiritual yearnings led him to India, where he studied Hinduism and Zen Buddhism. Long after returning to Palo Alto, he reflected on his time in the East, "Zen has been a deep influence in my life ever since. At one point I was thinking about going to Japan and trying to get into the Eihei-ji monastery, but my spiritual advisor urged me to stay here. He said that there is nothing over there that isn't here, and he was correct. I learned the truth of the Zen saying that if you are willing to travel around the world to meet a teacher, one will appear next door."[2] From the mechanical to the digital: Zen and the art of the iPhone.

While Jobs was a devotee of Zen, he was no less a follower of Andy Warhol. The philosophy of Andy Warhol is virtually the same as the philosophy of Steve Jobs. "Business art is the step that comes after Art. I started as a commercial artist," Warhol writes, "and I want to finish as a business artist. After I did the thing called 'art' or whatever it's called, I went into business art. I wanted to be an Art Businessman or a Business Artist. Being good in business is the most fascinating kind of art. During the hippie era people put down the idea of business— they'd say, 'Money is bad,' and 'Working is bad,' but making money is art and working is art and good business is the best art."[3] The hippie Jobs already had an eye for both style and money. In his business aesthetic, thinner is always better than fatter, and faster is always better than slower. The most successful entrepreneurs are the stylish and fashionable ones who know the value of wearing thin. Markets grow with faster chips, faster processors, faster machines, faster networks, faster workers, and faster managers. The preoccupation with speed leads to the obsession with thinness.

Anorexia is a disease that is symptomatic of a society consumed by speed and where thinness is big business. Indeed, thin has become so fashionable that Swedish modeling agencies have been recruiting new talent from the country's largest eating-disorder recovery clinic. Ana-Maria af Sandeberg, the head doctor at the facility, reports that talent scouts "have been standing outside our clinic and trying to pick up our girls because they know that they are skinny. It absolutely sends the wrong signals when what the girls need is treatment."[4] Anorexia is most common among girls and young women, who are bombarded with images of svelte feminine beauty into which they struggle to transform their often resistant bodies. The condition is particularly prevalent among women distance runners, who lose excessive amounts of weight so they can run faster. This sets up a destructive feedback loop—the more weight they lose, the faster they run, and the faster they run, the more weight they lose. As acceleration increases, bodies of all kinds virtually melt away.

At the same time that some people are getting thinner and faster, others are getting fatter and slower. The culture of speed that produces excessive thinness also produces excessive fatness. It hardly seems a coincidence that the two countries in the world with the greatest obesity problem are the two countries most dedicated to the principles of neoliberal economics—the United States and Great Britain. According to the Centers for Disease Control and Prevention, 35.7 percent of adults in the United States are obese. The rate is highest among non-Hispanic blacks (49.5 percent), as compared to Mexican Americans (40.4 percent), Hispanics (39.1 percent), and non-Hispanic whites (34.3 percent). The percentage of children ages 6–11 years in the United States who were obese increased from 7 percent in 1980 to nearly 18 percent in 2010. Similarly, the percentage of adolescents ages 12–19 years who were obese increased from 5 percent to 18 percent over the same period.[5] Until recently, the United States led the industrialized world in the rate of obesity, but Great Britain has caught up. An article entitled "Britain's Weight Crisis Almost Hits U.S. Proportions" reports that "latest figures showed two thirds of British adults are overweight and one quarter are obese. One in three British children is obese. More than one million are morbidly obese—basically, so fat you're about to explode in a hail of fat globules and soda-stream."[6] A pleasant thought, indeed!

While it is impossible to identify a single cause for this obesity epidemic, surely one of the most important contributing factors is the sedentary lifestyle that the culture of speed promotes. This problem is exacerbated by changing eating habits. With people more rushed because they are working longer hours, they have less time to prepare meals at home. Today, even in difficult economic times, Americans eat out four to eight times a week on average.[7] Though not everyone eats at fast-food restaurants, many adults and far too many children eat on the run. When they are not eating out, they are heating up prepared foods with too much sugar and salt in microwaves because doing so is quick and easy. Children and young people are particularly vulnerable to the short- and long-term health effects of fast food. The appeal of this sort of food, however, is enhanced by the ubiquitous fast computers that run video games and wireless phones that have countless apps. Playing *World of Warcraft*, *Angry Birds*, or *Farmville* while eating chips and pizza and drinking a super-sized sugary soda is tempting, culturally acceptable, and a prescription for disaster. Fast computers and fast food set up another destructive feedback loop—the more kids sit in front of a computer screen eating junk food, the more weight they gain and the slower they run; the slower they run, the more weight they gain and the more they are inclined to sit around playing video games—and the more weight they gain.

Fat . . . Thin. Thin . . . Fat. Slow . . . Fast. Fast . . . Slow. Further paradoxes of speed: dematerialization leads to materialization—thinner, faster machines create fatter, slower bodies and, perhaps, slower minds.

Departmentalization

Neither modernity nor modernism would have been possible without plate glass and windows, which prefigure the screens and Windows now surrounding us. From the glass of train stations and department store windows to the glass of optical fiber cables, modern architecture began in 1851 with the Crystal Palace, designed by John Paxton for the Great Exhibition in Hyde Park, London. Writing at the turn of the twentieth century, Expressionist architect Paul Scheerbart articulated the view of many artists and architects, who saw glass as the symbol for a new age:

Happiness without glass—
What an absurdity!

Brick pass away
Glass colors stay.
The joy of color
Is only in glass-culture.
Larger than a diamond
Is the glass-house's double wall.
Glass brings a new age—
Brick buildings are depressing.[8]

People were drawn to what came to be known as *Glasarchitektur* for its thinness, lightness, transparency, and effervescence. In 1907, Alfred Gotthold Meyer identified the ambition informing the new architecture: "The striving for lightness is one of the main motivating forces in the developmental history of interior space." As anyone who has seen Ludwig Mies van der Rohe's Barcelona Pavilion or the glass house in New Canaan, Connecticut, created by his epigone, Philip Johnson, knows, such glass buildings seem to dematerialize and disappear before one's eyes in a play of light that leaves only spaces for reflection.

Paxton's concerns were less ambitious and more pedestrian. Before designing the Crystal Palace he had specialized in building greenhouses, but when the architects commissioned to create the grand hall for the 1851 London exhibition failed to deliver, the authorities brought in Paxton to save the day. The result was a building that literally changed the world. The transportation revolution and the commercial revolution intersect in unexpected ways in the iron, steel, and glass of the modern architecture that Paxton introduced. Other architects and builders quickly appropriated his design to create three transformative types of structures: train stations, arcades, and department stores. Railway stations both reconfigured urban design and rewired human perception. Wolfgang Schivelbusch records the German immigrant Lothar Bucher's response to the startling effect of Paxton's glass architecture: "If we let our gaze slowly move downward again, it encounters the filigreed girders, painted blue, far apart from each other at first, then moving ever closer, then superimposed on each other, then interrupted by a shining band of light, and finally dissolving in a remote background in which everything corporeal, even the lines themselves, disappears and only the color remains."[9] The disappearance of the railway station in a play of light extended the sense of dematerialization that train passengers experienced when they saw objects and landscapes disappear through the windows as the countryside rushed by.

In the years immediately preceding the completion of the Crystal Palace, plate glass started to be used for display windows in stores and shops along dark and winding urban streets. Glass transformed the exchange relationship in ways that were not immediately evident. From the earliest days of the market economy, the site of production and the site of sale often had been the same. Exchange involved a face-to-face relationship in which producer and consumer engaged in bargaining about the price of the commodity. Plate glass, however, allowed merchants to create and preserve increasingly elaborate visual displays to lure customers even when the merchants were unavailable. Windows filled with commodities began to appear in the United States as early as the 1840s, but it was not until after the turn of the century that window display became an art. From 1897 to 1902, L. Frank Baum, who published *The Wonderful Wizard of Oz* in 1900, edited a highly influential monthly journal entitled *The Show Window*, whose primary purpose was to advance the "arts of decoration and display." Using mechanical devices and electrical technology, Baum sought to create spectacular displays that, in his own words, would "arouse in the observer the cupidity and the longing to possess the goods."[10] Just as fleeting images in train windows dissolved the real countryside in momentary images, so too advertising displays in shop windows dissolved the real product into a contrived scene. Window shopping began a long process of disengaging image from product, one that eventually became online "Windows" shopping.

The bridge between railway stations and shop windows on the one hand, and department stores on the other, was the arcade. The transformation of clusters of shops enclosed by the iron-and-glass architecture of the arcades into department stores created what Walter Benjamin, following Louis Philippe, labeled "temples of commodity capital." For Benjamin, the arcades were to modernity what cathedrals were to the Middle Ages—"Dream Houses: arcade as nave with side chapels."[11] The Paris opening of Bon Marché, designed by L. C. Boileu and Gustave Eiffel in 1852, marked a new chapter in the economic history of the West. Five years later, Macy's opened in New York and other department stores quickly followed, most notably Wanamaker's in Philadelphia (1861) and Gimbels, also in New York (1887). Since mail-order business was essential for department stores, it is not insignificant that John Wanamaker served as postmaster general from 1889 to 1893. In 1856, Marshall Field left his native Pittsfield, Massachusetts, and moved to Chicago, where he found work in a dry goods firm. An energetic entrepreneur, he negotiated a series of deals that led to the opening of the Marshall Field's Department Store, which in 1868 came to be known fondly as the Marble Palace.

Recalling the discussion of the relationship between industrialization and modernism in Chapter 1 and in anticipation of the following discussion of the relationship between post-industrialism and postmodernism, it is important to note that from Wanamaker's to Barneys, there has always been a close relationship between department stores and contemporary art and architecture. Andy Warhol, whose first real job was as a window designer and whose first real exhibition was in the Bonwit Teller's display window in 1961, predicted that "all department stores will become museums and all museums will become department stores."[12] William Leach's survey of shopping suggests that Warhol's comment is actually more of a historical observation than a prediction: "it was in department stores, not museums[,] that modern art and American art found their first true patrons." He continues: "The Gimbel brothers, inspired by the Armory Show of 1913, became among the most ardent supporters of modern art, buying up Cézannes, Picassos, and Barques, and displaying them in store galleries in Cincinnati, New York, Cleveland, and Philadelphia. . . . John Wanamaker, the man most apt to advertise his stores as 'public institutions,' was, not surprisingly, also the most innovative merchant of all in his display of art. He deplored the way museums jumbled pictures together 'on walls, destroying the effects of the finest things,' and month after month, to sustain customer interest, rotated his personal collection for the 'studio' in Philadelphia—a Constable here, a Reynolds there, to say nothing of a Titian or a Turner, a Wanamaker favorite—to his New York store and back again."[13] In the latest twist in this ongoing relationship, many of today's museums are completing what Warhol anticipated by using the most fashionable architecture that can be bought to turn museums into department stores and online shopping malls.

The invention of department stores was a response to the demand created by the industrialization of production. To sell mass-produced commodities, marketers had to produce mass consumption. The increase in the speed and efficiency of production created the problem of excess supply. The design of department stores reflects the structure of the assembly line. Just as mass production breaks down machines into interchangeable parts and systematic management breaks down labor into homogeneous units, so too does the scientific marketing of department stores separate items for sale into different departments with homogeneous products and fixed prices. In other words, specialization in production leads to departmentalization in consumption. When such departmentalization is combined with the introduction of fixed pricing, the result is the further abstraction, quantification, and depersonalization of exchange. Instead of producer and consumer engaging in face-to-face bargaining, the site of consumption is separated from the site of production and the price, like products, is standardized. While arcades and department stores created a new kind of public space where flaneurs and especially women were free to roam, they afforded little op-portunity for personal interactions. In standardized spaces, exchange became as mechanized as the machines that produced both products and architectural spaces. The effect of these spaces was nonetheless dazzling. In his 1883 novel *Au Bonheur des Dames,* Émile Zola captures the visual effect of the proliferation of commodities in department stores at the dawn of what by the 1960s had become "the society of the spectacle." "Mme. Desforges saw everywhere only the great big signs with enormous numerals whose garish colors contrasted with the bright calico, the radiant silk, the muted wool materials. People's heads almost disappeared behind piles of ribbons; a wall of flannel protruded like a headland; every-where around, mirrors made the salesrooms seem even more huge, re-flecting displays and parts of the public, appraising heads, half-glimpsed shoulders and arms; while to the right and left, the side corridors al-lowed glimpses of the snowy bays of white goods, the mottled deeps of knitted things of remote worlds illuminated by a beam of light from some part of the glass roof, where the crowd became merely human motes of dust."[14]

If people buy only what they need, the wheels of production grind to a halt. The necessity of creating mass consumption to absorb the excess produced by mass production led to the invention of a new industry —advertising. One of the most important purposes of advertising is to create desire where there is not necessarily need. In 1841, Volney B. Palmer opened the first advertising agency in Philadelphia and by 1849, his American Newspaper Subscription and Advertising agency claimed to represent 1,300 of the two thousand newspapers published at the time.[15] From their earliest days until their recent demise, newspapers and advertising have always enjoyed a symbiotic relationship. By taking advantage of faster printing technologies, advertising moved merchan-dising beyond display windows. Paradoxically, the uniformity of mass-produced commodities created the need for product differentiation. Until the turn of the twentieth century, consumer products like crackers, cookies, flour, and bread were sold in bulk without individual packaging or brand identification. Though some merchants experimented with labeled packages, nothing really changed until 1899, when the National Biscuit Company "launched the first million-dollar advertising campaign intended to establish a new brand-labeled consumer product, the Uneeda Biscuit. By 1913 National Biscuit ranked seventy-sixth in assets among U.S. Industrials. . . . It also provided an early model for other companies of how trademarks, consumer packaging, and national advertising could be used to attain bureaucratic control of a market, even for an industry in crisis." The Uneeda Biscuit promotional campaign jump-started the advertising industry. In 1880 annual advertising expenditures totaled $200 million, by 1904, this amount had risen to $821 million, and in 1917 it had reached $1.6 billion. By this time most advertising was handled by specialized agencies.[16]

As the success of branding and advertising spread, department stores tried to get a piece of the action by printing catalogs to promote their products. As early as 1894, Sears Roebuck was distributing a catalog of more than five hundred pages; and, by 1897, circulation had reached 318,000. A decade later, circulation was an impressive 3 million. Sears's main competitor, Montgomery Ward, produced a 540-page catalog promoting 24,000 items. By 1927, Sears was mailing 75 million catalogs, which was approximately one for every person in the country.[17] While not all marketing campaigns were so ambitious, many companies and stores developed mail-order programs that expanded their business beyond store walls. Obviously, this entire distribution network depended on reliable rail and road transportation as well as the increasing efficiency of the U.S. Postal Service. The first postage stamp was issued in 1847, but a truly national postal network had to await the introduction of Rural Free Delivery in 1898. Formally approved by Congress in 1901, by 1910 the Rural Free Delivery area covered 993,068 miles and was served by 40,997 carriers. Parcel post delivery began in 1913 and within twelve months, 300 million packages were being shipped every year. The integration of production, marketing, sales, and distributions networks ignited an explosion in mail-order business that lasted until it ended abruptly with the Depression.[18]

Two other developments that began during this period have contributed to many of the problems we still face today: consumer research and consumer debt. Then, as now, advertisers would stop at nothing to get inside consumers' heads. New technologies developed in the early twentieth century made it possible to collect and process data about customers' preferences and choices. As early as 1879, Beniger reports, "N. W. Ayer & Son advertising agency had a prospective client asking for market research. . . . In three days, based on telegrams to state government officials and publishers throughout the grain belt, Ayer compiled a survey of the thresher market, which it gave to Nichols-Shepard free in exchange for the advertising account." In the following two decades, feedback technologies were developed that permitted advertisers to collect information that their clients could use in their marketing campaigns. The origin of today's much ballyhooed "big data," which I will consider in Chapter 7, can be traced to 1910, when the Harvard Bureau of Business Research and the National Retail Dry Goods Association started to collect sales statistics. Six years later the *Chicago Tribune* began house-to-house interviewing, which benefited not only its own sales but also those of its potential advertisers.[19] Armed with this data, advertisers tried to persuade consumers to buy what they did not need by spending money they did not have.

To spend money they don't have, consumers need credit. Credit dates back to ancient times. While in the early modern period the use of credit by local merchants and in company stores was widespread, industrialization brought radical changes to both credit and money. Credit cards as we know them today did not appear until the 1950s, when they started with fee-based cards like Diners Club, American Express, and Carte Blanche. They quickly became a national industry. By 1970, there were two major credit cards: National BankAmerica (later Visa) and

Master Charge/Interbank (later MasterCard). Yet not until the 1980 Monetary Control Act and the 1982 Garn–St. Germaine Depository Institutions Act extended deregulation did plastic become ubiquitous in America.

As early as the 1800s, however, merchants and consumers had developed ad hoc forms of credit by using credit coins and charge plates as currency. By 1900, oil companies and some department stores had begun using proprietary credit cards for purchasing from the designated company or in the store that issued the card.[20] Stores had also introduced lay-away purchasing plans that eased the burden of buying expensive items by dividing payments into regular installments. As the use of credit spread, finance companies had emerged to meet the growing demand. In 1904, the Fidelity Credit Company was founded to buy installment contracts from companies and stores. The credit business was driven by purchases of large appliances and especially automobiles. In "1917 there were 40 sizeable automobile-sales-finance companies; in 1923 they numbered 1,000, and by 1925 the number of such companies exceeded 17,000."[21] General Motors entered the credit business in 1919 and Ford followed in 1925 by establishing the Universal Credit Corporation. On the eve of the Depression in 1929, car loans totaled $1.3 billion, which was 20 percent of all consumer debt.[22]

The use of residential mortgages was slower to develop. The word "mortgage" derives from the French phrase *mort gage,* which means "death contract." Such agreements end or die when the loan is repaid or the property is seized through foreclosure. Early settlers brought the practice of mortgage lending with them from England, where it dated back to the twelfth century. Puritans were always wary of borrowing and spending. This caution resulted in restrictive lending practices throughout the early years of the country, when it was not uncommon for a mortgage to require a 50 percent down payment for a limited five-year loan. By the time of the Depression, homeowners still had to come up with a down payment of 30 percent of the purchase price for loans of only five to ten years at an annual rate of 8 percent. During the Depression, the housing market, like everything else, collapsed and it did not begin to recover until President Roosevelt and Congress passed the Home Owners' Loan Act in 1933. The establishment of the Home Owners' Loan Corporation provided loans at much more generous conditions: up to 80 percent of the purchase price at 5 percent interest for as long as twenty-five years.

Though lending and borrowing have a long history, industrialization and mass production created a need to accelerate economic growth that took these practices to an entirely different level. For the generation that had lived through the Depression, debt was to be avoided at all cost; indeed, for many erstwhile Protestants, debt was a moral or even religious matter. The ethical weight of debt is suggested by the German word *Schuld,* which means both debt and guilt.[23] Today such beliefs and practices have become a distant memory. Nothing has contributed more to the excesses of today's consumer and financial capitalism than changed attitudes toward debt. This issue is not limited to personal finances but extends to the economy as a whole. If people, states, nations, companies, and institutions do not borrow and spend beyond their means, the economy suffers. At a certain point, however, the process reverses itself and the excessive borrowing and spending that had been fueling economic growth cause its collapse.

Losing Weight

It was not just attitudes toward money that were changing during the first half of the twentieth century; with the emergence of widespread credit and debt, money itself was undergoing a transformation. During the 1980s and 1990s, I was drawn into prolonged conversations with a group of leading architects—Frank Gehry, Rem Koolhaas, Peter Eisenman, Daniel Libeskind, Steven Holl, and Bernard Tschumi, among others. It was a particularly lively period for architectural theory and practice. These conversations exposed me to a new world, where I learned a great deal both about how creative architects use philosophical ideas and about the complex relationship between art and money. By the 1970s and early 1980s, electronic and digital communications technologies had created a culture of images that had come to be known as postmodernism or "pomo" for short. In contrast to modernism, which reflected and informed industrial society, postmodernism grew out of and shaped post-industrial consumer and information society. Postmodernism, in the strict sense of the term, began in architecture with a 1968 seminar at the Yale School of Architecture and the subsequent publication of the book *Learning from Las Vegas,* which was based on the class by Robert Venturi, Denise Scott Brown, and Steven Izenour. But it quickly became clear that these experts' insights were not limited to architecture but instead revealed important aspects of all postwar American society and culture. Venturi and his colleagues saw the ways in which new media and communication technologies were transforming industrial society. The Vegas Strip, they argued, is where modern industrial automobile culture meets postmodern post-industrial media and the culture of information. The result was not only a new social and economic system but also the transformation of our very sense of reality.

In 1948, the population of Las Vegas was 4,800; by the late decades of the twentieth century, it was the fastest-growing city in the country year after year. What began in the Paris arcades and New York department stores came to fruition on the Vegas Strip. Along the Strip, you could see reality morphing before your eyes. What had once seemed to be matters of substance now were revealed to be an incessant flow of images in an infinite play of recycled signs along the main drag of casino capitalism. Though Venturi's interests were broad, his focus was always on architecture. Along the Strip, architectural foundations and structures disappear in images and signs that create the space where we increasingly dwell. Surveying the Vegas Strip, Venturi observes: "Symbol dominates space. Architecture is not enough. Because the spatial relationships are made by symbols more than by forms, architecture in this landscape becomes symbol in space rather than form in space. Architecture defines very little: The big sign and the little building is the rule along Route 66. The sign is more important than the architecture."[24] While modernism had labeled ornament a crime and developed an architecture of seemingly pure form, Venturi and his colleagues called for an architecture of excessive signs in which decorative surfaces absorb structural foundations. The signs that are important to postmodernists are not original but are recycled from earlier times and previous architects; they are, in other words, signs of other signs. In the postmodern world emerging in the 1970s, there seemed to be no escape from the endless loops of recycled signs.

In 1966, Robert Venturi carried the rebellion to the heart of glass architecture by responding to Mies's foundational dictum "less is more" with a resounding "less is a bore." Recalling Protestant Puritanism in a book entitled, significantly, *Complexity and Contradiction in Architecture,* Venturi writes, "Architects can no longer afford to be intimidated by the puritanically moral language of orthodox Modern architecture. I like elements which are hybrid rather than 'pure,' compromising rather than 'clean,' distorted rather than 'straightforward,' ambiguous rather than 'articulated,' perverse as well as impersonal, boring as well as 'interesting,' conventional rather than 'designed,' accommodating rather than excluding, redundant rather than simple, vestigial as well as innovating, inconsistent and equivocal rather than direct and clear. I am for messy vitality over obvious unity. . . . More is not less."[25] Venturi's manifesto hit a nerve that extended beyond architecture. He had taken the pulse of the late 1960s and early 1970s and had discovered rhythms that had turned irregular. Other architects quickly followed him—Robert Stern, Charles Moore, Michael Graves, James Stirling, Stanley Tigerman—

and started creating buildings that looked more like billboards or Warhol silkscreens than functional grids and transparent structures. Having given up the modernist dream of originality, postmodern architects ripped off signs and images wherever they could find them and stuck them on the façades of buildings that seemed to be deliberately built not to last. As signs were piled on signs and images were layered on images, clarity gave way to obscurity and order devolved into chaos.

The more deeply immersed I became in these debates, the more convinced I became that just as there is an inextricable relationship between modern industrialism and modern architecture, so too there is a close connection between postmodern media and our information society, on the one hand, and postmodern art and architecture, on the other. When the stock market crashed on October 19, 1987, I thought these suspicions had been confirmed. In recent years, the frequent gyrations of the financial markets have made us somewhat immune to market shocks, but in 1987 the precipitous drop in the market jarred people into the awareness that something had really changed. On that memorable October day—which since then has been known as Black Monday, echoing 1929's Black Tuesday—the Dow Jones Industrial Average dropped what was then a shocking 508 points to 1,738.74 (a decline of 22.61 percent). The cascade effects of the crash (Hong Kong's market fell 45.5 percent, Australia's 41.8 percent, Spain's 31 percent, and the United Kingdom's 26.45 percent) revealed that the global financial networks had become much more volatile as they had become more closely connected. The day following the crash, I said over the dinner table to my son, Aaron, who was fifteen at the time and now works in finance, "Yesterday was an amazing day." "Why?" he asked. "Because billions and billions of dollars disappeared in an instant." He responded, "Where did they go?" As is so often the case, seemingly simple questions turn out to be the most difficult. Pausing, I realized I had no answer. After stuttering and stammering, I lamely answered,

"Well, I guess they sorta weren't there in the first place." "Then what's the problem?" Aaron replied.

Exactly two months later, my questions deepened when Oliver Stone's film *Wall Street* was released. Though Michael Douglas will always be remembered for his paean to greed ("Greed is good, greed is right, greed works"), later in the film the character he plays, Gordon Gekko, presents a more suggestive analysis of the market frenzy of the 1980s. Two silent actors frame the action: architecture and art. Gekko's office and house, which look like classically white and austere Richard Meier structures, are filled with ostentatiously colorful paintings. The film's decisive scene is set when Bud Fox, Gekko's young protégé played by Charlie Sheen, confronts Gekko about his plans to take over and then break up and sell off the airline for which Bud's father had long worked. In a desperate effort to become a player in the world of high rollers, Bud had betrayed his blue-collar father by giving Gekko inside information he could use to manipulate the price of the airline's stock. Feeling guilty about his disloyalty to his father and outraged by Gekko's duplicity, Bud charges into his boss's office and interrupts an important meeting with Japanese investors. After a heated exchange, Gekko responds to Bud's challenge by presenting his take on the world that he and other so-called masters of the universe had created.

> "It's all about the bucks, kid; the rest is conversation. Hey, buddy, you're still going to be president, all right? And when the time comes, you're going to parachute out a rich man. With the money you're going to make, your dad's never going to have to work another day in his life."
>
> "So tell me, Gordon, when does it all end? How many yachts can you water ski behind? How much is enough?"
>
> "It's not a question of enough, pal. It's a zero-sum game. Somebody wins, somebody loses. Money itself isn't made or lost, it's simply transferred from one perception to another. Like

magic. This painting here, I bought it ten years ago for $60,000. I could sell it today for $600,000. The illusion has become real and the more real it becomes, the more desperately they want it. Capitalism at its finest."

"How much is enough, Gordon?"

"The richest 1% of this country own half our country's wealth—$5,000,000,000,000. One third of that comes from hard work, two thirds from inheritance—interest on interest accumulating to widows' idiot sons, and what I do—stock and real estate speculation. It's bullshit. You got 90% of the American public out there with little or no net worth. I create nothing; I own. We make the rules, pal; the news, war, peace, famine, upheaval, price of paper clips. We pick the rabbit out of the hat while everybody sits out there wondering how the hell we did it. Now you're not naïve enough to think we're living in a democracy are you, buddy? It's the free market and you're part of it."[26]

In a world where more is not less, enough is never enough. By 1987, what passed for the free market would have been unrecognizable to early twentieth-century titans of industry.

I was not alone in misreading the signs that fateful October day. The week following the crash, a group of thirty-three leading economists from different nations gathered in Washington and confidently predicted that "the next few years could be the most troubled since the 1930s."[27] But while I thought that the axis of the world had shifted, everything returned to what seemed to be normal with unexpected speed. The Dow, which had started 1987 at 1,897, ended the year at 1,939, though it did not regain its August high of 2,722 for almost two years. It turned out that Aaron was right and the experts and I were wrong—there wasn't really anything to worry about. The longer I thought about these baffling developments, the more I became convinced that what was really important was not what had happened but the fact that nothing seemed to have happened. Aaron's questions lingered; I realized that I no longer knew either what money is or where it is in the economy. What I did know was that money was also dematerializing; it too was losing weight and thus wearing thin.

It turns out that money had been dematerializing throughout its long and surprising history, which began in Greek temples and ends in today's temples of finance, where believers in omniscient, omnipotent, and omnipresent markets worship their virtual currencies. The trajectory of this history is characterized by the progressive dematerialization of tokens of exchange: people → animals → commodities → precious metals → paper → electrical current → data, information → e-money → virtual currencies. The word "money" derives from the epithet for Jupiter's sister and wife, Juno Moneta, who was best known for her monitory (cautionary) tales. Roman coins were first minted in the Temple of Juno Moneta, thereby beginning the practice of associating money-making with temples. Other etymological clues suggest a link between money and ritual sacrifice. The German word *Geld* (money), Horst Kurnitzky points out, "means more or less 'sacrifice' [*Opfer,* whence the English offering]. . . . In the eighth century, the verb *gelten* meant to sacrifice."[28] The Greek word *drachma,* which is the name of a common coin once used to designate a handful of sacrificial meat (*oblos*), and the Latin word *pecunia* (English, "pecuniary"), derives from *pecus* meaning cattle, which served as offerings to the gods. These linguistic clues suggest that in many of its forms, religion involves an economy of sacrifice in which the relationship between the believer and the god is established by the currency they exchange.

Within this sacrificial economy, the current flows in two directions: from worshipper to god, and from god to worshipper. Ritual practices establish a system of exchange in which devotees offer sacrifices to secure protection and benefits from the gods. In the early stages of religious development, these offerings tended to be human or animal sacrifices. In time, however, substitutions were introduced. At first, small figures of the sacrificial animals, which usually were made out of precious metals, and, later, coins bearing the images of the animals, were offered to the gods. As the rituals were formalized, priests and other religious and political leaders prescribed the terms of the exchange. The communion tokens shaped like coins and bearing inscriptions discussed in Chapter 2 derive from these early practices.

The use of especially gold and silver as money can be found in Mesopotamia as early as the twentieth-fourth century BCE, when the king and religious authorities determined standardized weights and established the value of commodities in silver. Records of trade provide evidence of a similar system in Egypt. But the scarcity of precious metals led to the use of a string of substitutes that have become increasingly immaterial. Looking back from the perspective of today's electronic currencies, it is instructive to note that from earliest times, there was a strange association between money and electricity. The most common substitute was an alloy of gold and silver with traces of copper that was called electrum. The color of electrum is light yellow and the name is a Latin translation of the Greek word *electron,* which was also used for amber because of its similar color. The English words "electron" and "electricity" derive from "electrum." Electrum, commonly known as white gold, was used to make coins as early as the third millennium BCE.[29]

In the earliest use of precious metals for money, value was measured by weight. But this practice proved impractical because of the difficulty of securing and transporting significant quantities of metal. Thus it eventually gave way to the practice of imprinting symbols and seals on the coins and insuring the value with the signature of the issuing authority. Value was no longer determined by the actual quantity of a substance but, rather, by symbols and signs. While this practice continues today, metallic money has other disadvantages that led to the use of paper currency. Paper currency, I have noted, originated in China during the Tang dynasty in the seventh century, but did not appear in Europe until the fourteenth century, when Italian merchants introduced bills of exchange to facilitate increasingly international trade. In Genoa and Venice, receipts for gold deposits began to circulate and, when signed, functioned as currency. Around the fourteenth century, there was an explosive expansion of banking and credit in Florence. As trade expanded, the use of bills of exchange spread, thereby creating increasingly integrated international markets. During the Middle Ages, bills of exchange were used in ways that anticipate today's futures and options. In the most elementary transaction, for example, a merchant might buy a farmer's crop before it is harvested and then sell the bill of exchange to another merchant on a different market. The seller, like the farmer, would receive his money immediately and the buyer would receive payment for the produce at its market value when the contract came due. As European markets and fairs grew and became more centralized, bills of exchange facilitated international financial payments within increasingly integrated European markets. And as the weight of currencies decreased, the speed of exchange increased.

The history of money in the United States is complex. The Massachusetts Bay Colony was the first to issue banknotes in the early 1690s, and throughout much of the eighteenth century each of the thirteen colonies issued its own banknotes. The use of precious metals did not disappear with the invention of paper currency; to the contrary, the value of paper currency was determined by its relation to gold and silver. The Coinage Act of 1792 authorized the issuance of the dollars and established its value based on precise amounts of gold. Unlike the Spanish dollar on which the American dollar was modeled, Congress established a decimal system for monetary units. As we will see in Chapter 8, Spanish currency was valued on a base-eight system, which was used by financial exchanges like the New York Stock Exchange until a few years ago. Within the new U.S. monetary scheme, paper currency functioned like a linguistic sign or signifier whose value was determined by its relation to a substance or a signified (a thing). The link between any sign and its signified stuff, however, is always tenuous, and throughout history, whenever the need for more money has arisen, this link has been weakened or broken. For example, wars are very expensive and they have primarily been financed either by borrowing or by taking off the brakes of gold and silver and letting the printing presses run faster. When more money was needed to finance the Revolutionary War, the Continental Congress first issued paper money, which was called Continental currency. The funding of the recent wars in Iraq and Afghanistan is the latest chapter in this long story.

A national banking system was also slow to evolve in the United States. Congress authorized the Bank of the United States in 1791 and gave it a charter to operate until 1811, when the Second Bank of the United States was established. Though these banks were private, the government authorized them to print paper banknotes. Federal banks proved to be very unpopular and, bowing to western and agrarian interests, Andrew Jackson revoked the bank's charter in 1832. This action led to the "Free Banking Era," and by 1860, approximately eight thousand state banks were issuing "wildcat" or "broken" banknotes in denominations ranging from half a cent to $20,000. When the Civil War broke out, Congress once again authorized the printing of money that was not backed by gold or silver. These notes were known as greenbacks. At the same time, the Confederacy was issuing its own currency. Using economic warfare to advance its military cause, the Union tried to undercut Confederate currency by printing counterfeit notes. A national banking system was not created until 1863, when President Lincoln persuaded Congress to pass the National Banking Act, which established a uniform national currency that was issued by new national banks. Just as the gold standard was reinstituted after the Revolutionary War, so too was the link between paper currency and precious metals reestablished after the Civil War.

Today's paper currency takes the form of Federal Reserve Notes. In 1913, the Federal Reserve Act "created the Federal Reserve System as the nation's central bank to regulate the flow of money and credit for economic stability and growth. In 1914, Federal Reserve Notes were issued by Federal Reserve Banks as direct obligations of the Federal Reserve System. They replaced National Bank Notes as the dominant form of paper money."[30] Once again paper currency was linked to gold, and once again this link was broken to finance World War I and World War II.

Whether in office management or in bank transactions, paper is the bridge between the industrial and the post-industrial ages. For more than two centuries, Crane & Company, located in Dalton, Massachusetts, has printed paper currencies. Stephen Crane started the company in 1770 and sold paper to Paul Revere, who was an engraver and printed the American colonies' first paper money at the time of the Revolutionary War. In 1806, Crane began printing currency on paper for local and regional banks, and eventually for the federal government. The U.S. Bureau of Engraving and Printing awarded Crane a contract to produce currency paper in 1879 and the company has been the sole provider of paper for money ever since.[31] In 2002, Crane purchased the Swedish company Tumba Bruk from the Bank of Sweden. Tumba Bruk was founded in 1755 to produce Swedish banknotes, which is still its primary business. The first European banknotes were issued by the predecessor of the Bank of Sweden, Stockholms Banco, in 1661.

Revolution after revolution after revolution. From Paul Revere to Karl Marx to Abraham Lincoln to Jack Kemp to Ronald Reagan, all by way of paper currency. It is hard to imagine Kemp and Reagan agreeing with Marx about anything, but they all share worries about fiat money and are attracted to gold. Gold, they believe, provides a secure anchor that can serve as the foundation of a stable economy. Marx always feared that the disappearance of gold and money's loss of weight could have a destabilizing effect on the economy. He observes that "the natural tendency of circulation to convert coins into a mere semblance of what they profess to be, into a symbol of the weight of metal they are officially supposed to contain, is recognized by modern legislation, which fixes the loss of weight sufficient to demonetize a gold coin, or to make it no longer legal tender." The separation of nominal value and real weight creates a distinction between coins as "mere pieces of metal on the one hand, and as coins with a definite function on the other." This development, Marx cautions, "implies the possibility of replacing metallic coins by tokens of some other material, by symbols serving the same purpose as coins."[32] When gold gives way to symbols, there is nothing to prevent monetary authorities from freely printing money until it becomes as worthless as the paper it is printed on.

Nietzsche shares Marx's concern about money's loss of weight but realizes that insubstantial signs have consequences far beyond the economic realm. Nothing less than truth is at stake in the currency of exchange. "What, then, is truth?" Nietzsche asks. "A mobile army of metaphors, metonyms, and anthropomorphisms—in short, a sum of human relations, which have been enhanced, transposed, and embellished poetically and rhetorically . . . ; truths are illusions about which one has forgotten that this is what they are; metaphors, which are worn out and without sensuous power; coins, which have lost their pictures and now matter only as metal, no longer as coins."[33] Nietzsche, who came from a long line of Lutheran pastors, is of course best known for his famous declaration of the death of God. What usually goes unnoticed is that the phrase "God himself is dead" is first used in the Lutheran Good Friday hymn, "Oh Sorrow Dread," written by Johann von Rist (1607–67). G. W. F. Hegel, too, appropriated the phrase in his monumental *Phenomenology of Spirit* (1807). Nietzsche's musing on truth and money suggests that his understanding of the death of God can be translated into economic terms. For true believers, going off the gold standard was the economic equivalent of the death of God. Gold, like God, is an illusion created to provide certainty and security in a world from which they have disappeared. In linguistic terms, gold and God are signs constructed to deny their status as signs and thereby ground the meaning and value of all other signs. These foundations, however, are specious because the value that gold and God are grounded in is really nothing other than the expression of an act of faith. God and gold are valuable only because of the ungrounded confidence that people have in them. In matters of economics as well as religion, in the beginning is faith. It's all a confidence game.

The years after the outbreak of the Civil War were marked by heated controversies between backers of gold (known as gold bugs) and backers of silver (silverites). This dispute, which came to a head in the 1896 election that pitted William Jennings Bryan against William McKinley, was not settled until the 1900 Gold Standard Act that decided the issue in favor of the backers of gold. Once established, the gold standard did not permanently collapse until 1973. The financial exigencies created by World War I forced most countries to suspend the gold standard—and in 1931, the Bank of England was without sufficient gold reserves to maintain convertibility and was forced to let the pound float, a move that created turmoil in international financial markets. But the United States remained committed to the gold standard until 1933, when President Roosevelt was forced to suspend it until the end of World War II.

Before the end of World War II, it was already clear that the international monetary system was in hopeless disarray. Beginning in 1941, the Allies held a series of meetings to develop an economic plan for the postwar period. These discussions culminated in the 1944 Bretton Woods agreement, which was conceived by John Maynard Keynes, representing Great Britain, and Harry Dexter White from the United States. In addition to establishing the International Monetary Fund and the World Bank, the Bretton Woods accord reinstated a modified gold standard. Participating countries were committed to accepting exchange rates set at an agreed-on ratio against the dollar, whose value was determined given a price for gold of $35 per ounce. (The price of gold today is well over $1,000 per ounce.) The United States assumed the responsibility for exchanging dollars for gold at this fixed rate whenever any foreign country wanted to do so.

This system maintained relative stability in global markets for almost three decades. By the late 1960s, however, economic and political problems in the United States combined with a changing international scene made the dollar an unreliable anchor for the world economy. While European economies were prospering, the United States, bogged down in the Vietnam War and struggling to fund the social programs of President Lyndon B. Johnson's "Great Society" at home, was facing mounting economic problems. These difficulties were compounded by the growing oil crisis in the early 1970s. Billions of dollars—called Eurodollars—accumulated offshore and quickly became an alternative source of investment capital on global markets. By 1971, foreign institutions were holding dollars worth more than twice the gold reserves that the United States had available. At this point, gold convertibility, which had been the foundation of the international economy established at Bretton Woods, was effectively dead. On August 15, 1971, President Nixon suspended the gold standard and devalued the dollar. Secretary of the Treasury John Connally and Paul Volcker, treasury undersecretary for monetary policy, devised a plan to manage exchange rates. By 1973, the United States had to devalue the dollar again and the system of fixed exchange rates broke down. Currencies were allowed to float freely and for the first time in history all the currencies in the world were fiat money.

As Marx and Nietzsche anticipated, economic developments like these have important implications for how meaning and value are determined. As I have argued, the gold standard presupposes a referential notion of value in which the value of money or the monetary sign is determined by its relation to the real substance of gold. Once the dollar or the sign is unlinked from gold, signs no longer represent anything substantial or real. By suspending fixed exchange rates as well as the gold standard, Nixon instituted a new regime in which currencies are allowed to float. With this development, the value of monetary signs is determined by their relation to other monetary signs. Signs, in other words, do not signify anything real, but are signs of other signs. At this point, the economy, like postmodern architecture and art, becomes an infinite play of signs grounded in nothing beyond themselves. In 1973, the year the gold standard was finally suspended, Reuters, provider of news and financial data, installed the first electronic system for international currency trading. Currency completely dematerialized and became actual current, that is, a flow of electrical charge. With the suspension of the gold standard and the introduction of international electronic trading systems, the pieces were in place for the next phase of capitalism—financial capitalism. But first the world had to be wired.

5. Net Working

· ·

Wiring the Globe

Today's network revolution began in the nineteenth century with the invention of the electrical telegraph and the wiring of the world. My wife, Dinny, and I spent the 1971–72 academic year in Copenhagen, Denmark, where I was writing my first doctoral dissertation on Søren Kierkegaard. I used a small portable typewriter and carbon paper because we could not afford the cost of photocopying the five-hundred-page manuscript. Throughout the year, we communicated with our families in the United States by letter. We wrote only what would fit on blue lightweight aerograms, which usually took about a week to arrive. That was a considerable improvement over mail service in the nineteenth century, when letters were sent by ship overseas and took six or more weeks to get to their destinations. We talked on the phone with our parents in the States only twice all year—once when my father called to tell me that my mother had suffered a stroke, and once when I called my father to give him flight information for our return home. We had no private phone to make calls so we went to the local post office, where we gave the number to someone who placed the call and then notified us when we could talk using a phone in a small booth. Though it was not obvious at the time, in the early 1970s, the world was on the brink of a network revolution that would spread with astonishing speed and quickly change everything.

In his thorough and informative book *Network Nation: Inventing American Telecommunications,* Richard John records the early history of wiring the country. "The United States," he explains, "has long boasted an impressive array of facilities for circulating information regularly and reliably over vast distances and at high speed. By 1840, the mail linked thousands of localities in a single countrywide network, while line-of-sight optical, or optical, telegraphs hastened ship-to-shore communications in several of the country's largest seaports. By 1920, the United States had become integrated into a global telegraph network and boasted the world's largest and most intensively patronized federation of telephone exchanges."[1] Not everyone saw networking the nation as a sign of progress. Just as Thoreau had questions about the effect of speed on human conversation, so too he worried about the impact of the telegraph. Sounding like a parent worrying about his teenager's incessant tweeting, he observes, "Our inventions are wont to be pretty toys, which distract attention from serious things. They are but improved means to an unimproved end. . . . We are in great haste to construct a magnetic telegraph from Maine to Texas; but Maine and Texas, it may be, have nothing important to communicate. As if the main object were to talk fast rather than sensibly."[2]

Telegraph wires strung along train tracks were used to transmit messages and information that enabled trains to run on schedule at ever-faster rates of speed. William Cooke and Charles Wheatstone patented the first commercial telegraph in May 1837 and one month later successfully demonstrated it in London. A year earlier, Samuel Morse and Alfred Vail had developed the electrical telegraph that proved to be superior to this five-needle device, which was restricted to the use of twenty characters and, thus, had to eliminate six letters. To overcome this limitation, Morse devised a code consisting of dots and dashes that was designed for maximum efficiency and speed of transmission. In

1842, Morse persuaded Congress to appropriate $30,000 to fund an experimental telegraph line from Washington, D.C., to Baltimore. Two years later, he publicly demonstrated his telegraph for the first time by sending a message from the U.S. Supreme Court to the Baltimore & Ohio Depot that read, "What hath God wrought!" (Numbers 23:23). To some the telegraph initially seemed little more than a useless toy, and to others nothing less than the Devil's black magic. But its practical value soon became apparent as it revolutionized not only transportation and communication but also news gathering and dissemination, business, and finance.

The telegraph system developed differently in Europe than in the United States. In Europe the telegraph functioned more like today's social networks. It was regarded as a public utility and by 1869 had been incorporated into the post office system. In the United States, by contrast, Western Union had a virtual monopoly on the telegraph business by 1870. Tom Standage cites one nineteenth-century commentator who described the American telegraph system as "peculiarly a business system; eighty percent of the messages are on business matters. . . . The managers of the telegraph know that their business customers want the quickest and best service, and care more for dispatch than low tariffs. Thus the great difference between the telegraph systems of Europe and America is that [in Europe], the telegraph is used principally for social correspondence, here by businessmen for business purposes."[3] Whether used for personal or business purposes, the telegraph inspired utopian dreams for many people. Technophiles of the day sounded like Marshall McLuhan declaring that the spread of electronic technology would bring about the Global Village. In 1858, the later British ambassador to the United States, Edward Thornton, waxed eloquent about the millenarian possibilities the telegraph had brought. "What can be more likely to effect [peace] than a constant and complete intercourse between all nations and individuals in the world? . . . Steam [power] was the first olive branch offered us by science. Then came a still more effective olive branch—this wonderful electric telegraph, which enables any man who happens to be within reach of a wire to communicate instantaneously with his fellow men all over the world." "The telegraph wire," he concludes, is "the nerve of international life, transmitting knowledge of events, removing causes of misunderstanding, and promoting peace and harmony throughout the world."[4]

In the following years, the globe was networked and the telegraph system became the central nervous system of business, finance, and increasingly, personal communication. By 1907, the year my father was born and Pablo Picasso painted *Les Demoiselles d'Avignon,* a writer for the *Wall Street Journal,* commenting on the telephone rather than the telegraph, actually looked forward to a day when people would have something like iPhones. "The time may come when the telephone will be a walking companion, will be carried in the pocket like a note book, and while walking the crowded avenue or by the shaded brook, or lying on the sands of the sea, one may be able to communicate with princes or command the work of multitudes thousands of miles away."[5]

By the early 1870s, what Standage aptly labels "the Victorian internet" was taking shape. The first transatlantic submarine cables were laid between 1857 and 1858, thereby creating a link that a century and a half later would become the World Wide Web. Cyrus West Field, who was born in Stockbridge, Massachusetts, and Morse laid a four-hundred-mile telegraph line between St. John's, Newfoundland, and Nova Scotia, where they connected with lines from the United States. One year later they formed the America Telegraph Company and began developing plans for a transatlantic cable, which would run between Newfoundland and Ireland. Nine years before the Central Pacific and Union Pacific railroads met in Promontory Summit, Utah Territory, creating the first transcontinental railroad, the sailing vessels *Agamemnon* and *Niagara* met in the middle of the Atlantic on June 28, 1858, and crewmen spliced the two halves of the cable to create the first transatlantic telegraph link. This cable broke on the first day and had to be repaired several times before the first message was transmitted on August 16, 1859. With this connection, faith in the utopian possibilities of technology went global. The first message transmitted on this cable read, "Glory to God in the highest; on earth, peace and good will toward men." Queen Victoria responded by sending a telegram to President James Buchanan expressing the hope that this new technology would provide "an additional link between the nations whose friendship is founded on their common interest and reciprocal esteem." President Buchanan replied, "It is a triumph more glorious, because far more useful to mankind than was ever won by conqueror on the field of battle. May the Atlantic telegraph, under blessing of Heaven, prove to be a bond of perpetual peace and friendship between the kindred nations and an instrument destined by Divine Providence to diffuse religion, civilization, liberty and law throughout the world."[6] The immediate triumph was short-lived because the cable proved fragile and had to be replaced. After solving significant technological problems, a more reliable cable was completed on August 28, 1866.

Before the telegraph, communication between the United States and Europe was unreliable and could take months. The first cable message in 1858 took seventeen hours to transmit, but the new cable was a significant improvement and could relay messages and information at a rate of eight words a minute. With the proven success of transoceanic telegraph transmission, London became the center of the burgeoning telecommunications industry. Cables linking London and the rest of the world quickly proliferated: Malta to Alexandria (1868); France to Newfoundland (1869); London to India, Hong Kong, China, and Japan (all in 1870); London to Australia (1871); and London to South America (1874). The expansion of the cable system allowed for the centralization and regulation of telecommunications networks, which made the management of the expanding British Empire more effective and efficient. By the 1870s, "there were over 650,000 miles of wire, 30,000 miles of submarine cable, and 20,000 towns and villages were

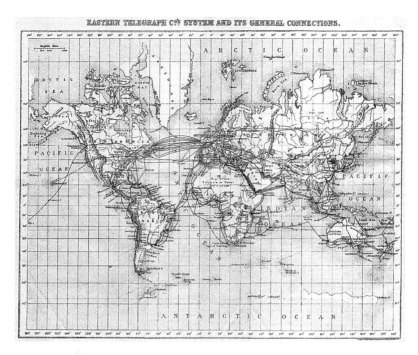

Telegraph connections, 1891. From *Stielers Hand-Atlas (World Map in Mercators Projection)*, plate 5 (Courtesy the Commons, available at www.flickr/commons).

on-line—and messages could be telegraphed from London to Bombay and back in as little as four minutes."[7]

Since telecommunications was a private business rather than a public utility in the United States, it developed somewhat differently. In the years after the invention of the telegraph, firms competed fiercely for market share within the new industry. "By 1851, ten separate firms ran lines into New York City. There were three competing lines between New York and Philadelphia, three between New York and Buffalo. In addition, two lines operated between Philadelphia and Pittsburgh, two between Buffalo and Chicago, three points between the Midwest and New Orleans, and entrepreneurs erected lines between many Midwestern cities. In all, in 1851, the Bureau of the Census reported 75 companies with 21,147 miles of wire." With competing networks expanding, redundancies created inefficiencies and in 1856, several major companies called a truce and signed what came to be known as the "Treaty of Six Nations." This agreement divided markets among the six largest regional telecommunication firms. By 1864, only two of the original six, Western Union and the American Telegraph Company, remained and less than two decades later, Western Union controlled 80 percent of the market. While sending telegraph messages was expensive, improving technology resulted in a cost reduction during the latter half of the nineteenth century. That is, a decline in competition led to increased volume and lower prices. From 1867 to 1900, the number of messages grew from 5.8 million annually to 63.2 million, and the cost per message dropped from an average of $1.09 to thirty cents.[8]

The communications and information revolution created by the telegraph would not have been possible without the invention of codes and a new class of information workers. The high cost of sending messages put a premium on brevity. The earliest and most common code was, of course, the Morse code, which was invented in 1836 and transmitted information by using electrical pulses and the silence between them. Morse initially planned to send only numbers, but his colleague Alfred Vail figured out a way to send letters by first calculating the frequency of the use of letters in English and then correlating them with dots and dashes. The more common the letter, the shorter was the sequence of dots and dashes. In the network of networks that emerged in the nineteenth century, messages were not transmitted directly from point to point but passed through a series of relays. Once again there was a premium placed on speed—"the fastest operators were known as bonus men, because a bonus was offered to operators who could exceed the normal quota for sending and receiving messages. So-called first-class operators could handle about sixty messages an hour—a rate of twenty-five to thirty words per minute—but the bonus men could handle even more without a loss of accuracy, sometimes reaching speeds of forty words per minute or more."[9] Like today's tweeters and texters fingering messages at lightning speed with a limited number of characters, telegraph operators sent messages digitally with limited codes. The fastest operators gravitated to the city, where the pay was better and life was faster, and slower operators stayed in the country, where the pay was lower but the pace of life more leisurely. Even in urban centers, the rate of message traffic varied from time to time and day to day. During slow periods, telegraph lines functioned something like today's online chat rooms. Operators gossiped with each other and even devised ways to play games like checkers and chess online. In some cases, romantic relationships developed and there is at least one report of an online wedding with the bride in Boston and the groom in New York. The disapproving father unsuccessfully challenged the legality of the wedding in court.[10]

Coding was not limited to telegraph companies. Then as now, concerns about security led to a booming business in cryptography. Companies hired specialists to devise secret codes that could be used to transmit valuable messages as well as money and securities. Since the telegraph industry was private rather than public, competing companies created their own codes. In many cases, however, the disadvantages of privacy proved to outweigh the advantages because confusion created by the difficulty of transmitting and translating these communications was costly. To address this growing problem the International Telegraph Union was established in 1865 and charged with establishing standards for international telecommunication.

The global telecommunications network in the nineteenth century prepared the way for the high-speed global financial networks in the twenty-first century. The impact of telecommunications on business was immediate and far-reaching. Standage goes so far as to suggest that "the information supplied by the telegraph was like a drug to businessmen, who swiftly became addicted."[11] Telecommunications transformed everything in business from manufacturing and marketing to finance and investment. With the establishment of regional, national, and international transportation and communications networks, markets quickly expanded. The telegraph and commerce formed a symbiotic relationship in which each profited from the other. As with any new technology, some people benefited and others did not. One of the most immediate effects of the telegraph was a version of what today is called "disintermediation." As Luther had cut out the church by establishing a direct relation between God and the individual, so did producers—be they farmers, retailers, or manufacturers—cut out the middleman and go straight to individual customers. Greater knowledge about supply and demand on local and distant markets enabled producers to move toward what by the twentieth century became just-in-time production. With better information about widely dispersed markets quickly and easily available, retailers could anticipate demand and monitor inventory more effectively and, in many cases, decrease both carrying costs and the need to borrow money to stock inventory. In this way, improved communications information technologies enabled producers and merchants to adapt to demand faster and more efficiently.

The most enduring effect of nineteenth-century telecommunications networks, however, was the transformation of the financial markets. The telegraph and related technologies changed both how financial transactions took place and, more important, what speculative investors traded. The era of big business with trusts, mergers, and early versions of today's mega-corporations, which began in the 1870s, was in no small measure the result of the telegraph network. Three years after Morse transmitted the first message from Washington, D.C., to Baltimore, a telegraph operator named Edward A. Callahan invented the electric stock ticker. This device connected investment firms directly to stock exchanges and produced a continuous record of stock prices by printing a tape with abbreviated company names indicated by letter symbols, followed by a numerical record of the price and volume of transactions. This was the first mechanical means of transmitting stock prices quickly over long distances. Prior to the invention of the telegraphic stock ticker, prices had been sent either orally or written on paper and delivered by messengers. In 1869, Edison introduced an improved machine named the Universal Stock Ticker, which used alphanumeric characters and ran at a speed of one character per second. The increased transmission speed led to more accurate information and faster trades. Furthermore, since tickers ran continuously, minute-by-minute movements of securities could be tracked more accurately. This increase in speed made time an even more important variable in transactions. As early as the 1850s, half of all telegraph messages involved stock exchanges and another one-third were related to business.[12] For wired firms, transmission speed became more important than physical location. This trading network created the possibility for what today is called real-time trading for the first time. The electronic ticker was used in financial markets until the 1960s, when it was replaced first by television and later by computers. Even today, however, stock prices coded in a variation of Edison's system are displayed on a continuous electronic ribbon that runs around the Morgan Stanley building in Times Square.[13]

More than stock prices were transmitted electronically. The expansion of markets created the demand for faster and more efficient ways to transfer money. In 1872, Western Union developed the prototype for PayPal and Bitcoin when it introduced a system that allowed customers to transfer up to a hundred dollars securely among several hundred towns in its network. Standage explains that "the system worked by dividing the company's network into twenty districts, each of which had its own superintendent. A telegram from the sender's office to the district superintendent confirmed that the money had been deposited; the superintendent would then send another telegram to the recipient's office authorizing the payment. Both of these messages used a code book based on numbered code books. . . . Only the district superintendents had copies of each office's uniquely numbered book."[14] This manual cryptography system served the same purpose as today's extraordinarily complicated digital and electronic cryptography systems.

Electronic telecommunications technology also introduced changes in financial instruments that were as important as the changes in how transactions occurred and how money was transferred. The ability to transfer money swiftly and securely greatly expanded both domestic and international markets. In an instructive article entitled "The Telegraph's Effect on Nineteenth-Century Markets and Firms," JoAnne Yates points out that "before the railroads made them readily transportable, such commodities were still more or less site-specific (depending on their location vis-à-vis available waterways), but by the 1850s and 1860s they could be transported fairly easily and reasonably inexpensively."[15] Increased business resulting from the improvement in transport and sale of commodities created new investment opportunities in options and futures markets. Options and futures, we have seen, are not new; indeed, there is evidence of an instrument resembling an option in the 3,800-year-old Babylonian Code of Hammurabi. Twelve hundred years later, the Greek philosopher Thales invented an option contract that enabled him to purchase crops before they were planted. In today's markets, an option is *"a right without an obligation.* More precisely, the holder of an option has a right without an obligation but the writer (or seller) of the option has an absolute obligation. For the right that the option provides, the option purchaser pays the option writer an upfront one-time fee called the option premium."[16] Options and futures serve different purposes for different sellers and buyers. For some, they provide opportunities to hedge investments, while for others, options and futures make it possible to manage volatility in commodities and currencies as well as stocks and bonds by limiting downside risk while not necessarily losing upside possibilities.[17] Economic historian Richard DuBoff explains that "organized futures markets took shape between 1848 and 1875, as 'to arrive' contracts began to displace the older system of making advanced or 'certified' inspection of representative lots. The telegraph was making it possible to negotiate future delivery contracts instantaneously, at the very point of production." Between 1848 and 1871, commodity exchanges and futures trading began in Buffalo, Chicago, Toledo, New York, St. Louis, Philadelphia, Milwaukee, Kansas City, Duluth, and New Orleans.[18] More important, these exchanges were all wired together, creating a national market that quickly became global. "Elaborate schemes were even devised to flash European commodity and money market quotations from arriving ships, or to send them via carrier pigeon, to telegraph operators waiting on shore before the ships docked at Halifax, Boston, and New York. Investment in telegraph facilities boomed from 1846 to 1857 (a recession year), then continued climbing until the Civil War."[19] This consolidation led to the standardization of these financial instruments, which made it possible to use options and futures to hedge other investments and broaden markets. The origin of today's hedge funds can be traced to nineteenth-century telegraph networks.

While commodities and futures exchanges were expanding, other exchanges were also emerging. In 1867, for example, the Gold & Stock Telegraph Company was founded to provide telegraph service to banks and brokerage houses in New York. Sustained growth during the following decade led to their partnership with Western Electric to provide more than 1,200 miles of private lines to financial firms in New York City and its suburbs.[20] With these developments, New York was emerging as the financial capital of the country, if not of the world. Throughout the first half of the nineteenth century, stock exchanges were local or regional. DuBoff points out that with the advent of the telegraph, "centralization of the securities market in New York City was accomplished between 1850 and 1880."[21] As markets were wired and centralized, transaction times were cut from days or even a week to minutes and sometimes seconds.

Print also played an important role in the telegraphic network revolution that transformed nineteenth-century financial markets and prepared the way for today's global capitalism. Between 1867 and 1880, the printing press that Gutenberg had invented went high-tech. The stock ticker was redesigned and high-speed automatic printing of both letters and numerals became possible. This innovation transformed the news business and led to now familiar dire predictions about the imminent demise of newspapers. The Associated Press, which had been founded in New York City in 1848, became increasingly influential with high-speed transmission and printing. Furthermore, high-speed printing and high-speed financial markets entered into complex feedback loops that continue to this day. Over the decade of the 1850s, "specialized reporting services were created, and, by 1865, *The Commercial and Financial Chronicle* in New York began publishing weekly and monthly information about commodity and money markets."[22] During the next several decades, news and information services diversified and expanded and by 1870, publications were delivering price information and credit ratings to more than 400,000 businessmen. These extraordinary developments had contradictory effects. On the one hand, the rapid distribution of information led to a decrease in price differentials, thereby making markets more efficient; on the other hand, the concentration of commodities, futures, and security exchanges in urban areas gave financial firms located in major cities a significant advantage over firms in the country, making markets less efficient. Paradoxically, when speed "annihilates space and time," place matters more than ever. This too, we will see, is the story of our own time.

What began in the commodities, options, and futures markets of the first half of the nineteenth century culminated in Chicago in the 1970s. On April 27, 1973, the Chicago Board of Trade Options Exchange opened and other exchanges quickly followed. This exchange used state-of-the art digital and electronic technology to create what was then regarded as extremely high-speed trading, but was actually only a faint foreshadowing of what would come by the beginning of the twenty-first century. In the early 1970s, traders were buying and selling options and futures and all kinds of commodities on markets throughout the world. As the trading of real things or options on real things increasingly gave way to exchanging money and buying and selling intangible options and currency futures on secondary and tertiary markets, the nature of the investment game changed. Exchanges began to resemble high-stakes casinos more than agricultural or traditional stock markets. According to Thomas Bass, Las Vegas actually provided the model for the Chicago Board of Trade's new venture. "Borrowing the idea from Las Vegas, where the game was first played, the Chicago Board of Trade opened a pit in the early 1970s for betting on the price of individual stocks like IBM and Texaco. Then it opened another pit for betting on the aggregate value of America's five hundred leading stocks. . . . [In these pits,] the action is a fast-ball series of round-robin plays in which brokers buy options on stocks and sell futures contracts on the stock index."[23] With the shift from betting on stuff to first betting on stocks and then on indexes, options on stock, and futures contracts, gambling turns back on itself and investing becomes a postmodern game of betting on bets on virtual assets that are nothing more than signs of other signs.

From Spectacle to Speculation

While the Las Vegas Strip displays the out-of-control spectacle of consumer culture, Times Square illuminates the out-of-control speculation of financial capitalism. Always ahead of the curve, Vegas saw it coming when, on January 3, 1997, investors tried to forestall the displacement of the society of spectacle by the society of speculation with the opening of New York–New York Hotel and Casino on the Strip. This multimillion-dollar fantasy palace is a simulacrum of New York, featuring a forty-seven-story knockoff of the Empire State Building and replicas of other New York City attractions. One thing that is missing is the New York Stock Exchange, which by this time had become the world's largest casino.

The link connecting the telegraphic markets of the nineteenth century with the wired markets of the twentieth and twenty-first centuries is Reuters. As we have seen, the combination of the suspension of the gold standard and the installation of the first electronic global currency trading system in 1973 created the conditions for the emergence of high-speed financial capitalism in the closing decades of the twentieth century. In 1851, Paul Julius Reuter established the Reuter news agency in London. Born in Germany and working in France as a book publisher, Reuter created a news service in 1848 that used carrier pigeons. With the advent of the electric telegraph and the link between France and England in 1851, Reuter switched from pigeons to the telegraph and moved his operation to London. Reuter's genius was to recognize the value that businessmen placed on receiving timely news. During the 1840s, he created a network of correspondents across Europe. "Each day, after the afternoon close of the stock markets, Reuter's representative in each town would take the latest prices of bonds, stocks, and shares, copy them onto tissue paper, and place them in a silken bag, which was taken by homing pigeon to Reuter's headquarters" where Reuter "compiled summaries and delivered them to his subscribers, and he was soon supplying rudimentary news reports too."[24]

Fast-forward from Victorian England to today's Times Square. Many of the most important fibers constituting the complex network economy intersect here in what might be described as the finance-entertainment complex. All three major television networks have a presence there: ABC, which is owned by the Disney Corporation, has a studio and televises from the middle of Times Square; the headquarters of the media conglomerate Viacom is located at Broadway and 44th Street; and NBC regularly broadcasts from the top of One Times Square. Under the direction of Robert Pittman, who later became AOL's chief pitchman

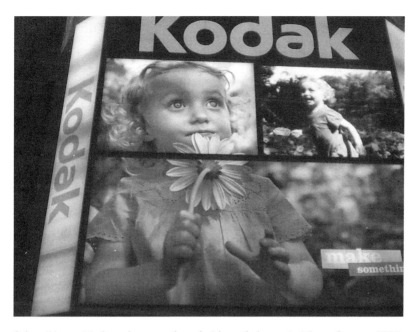

Selma Linnea Taylor, photograph and video ad shown in Times Square, 2008

and remained so until his ouster in the aftermath of the Time Warner debacle, MTV was launched in 1981 and quickly transformed the music business and television. Today the network televises from its second-story studio, which is open to Broadway. Farther south, on the corner of 42nd Street, which Disney revitalized in the 1980s, ESPN has one of its major studios. Farther up Broadway, on the Marquis Hotel, there is a huge sign for the company that invented the digital camera only to go bankrupt when other companies developed it and put film cameras out of business—Kodak. From July to November 2008, a huge photograph and video of my granddaughter Selma looked down from the Kodak sign on Times Square.

Most important in this context, however, is the fact that "the crossroads of the world" is framed by buildings housing the current or former financial institutions that are running the global economy into what once was thought to be the ground. Morgan Stanley and the previous headquarters of Lehman Brothers border the north and on the south are NASDAQ and Reuters: Instinet. Taking a page from the Vegas Strip, the most distinctive characteristics of all of these buildings is not their architecture but their signs. The erstwhile Lehman Brothers building is circled by a multistory video screen that transmits a fast-moving stream of images, and the Morgan Stanley building displays an electronic version of the traditional running paper tape reporting stock prices in real time. The Reuters: Instinet building, designed by Fox and Fowle, stands directly across the street from NASDAQ, and its sign, which features 8,200 panels capable of displaying 16.7 million distinct colors, is still the most spectacular in Times Square. The National Association of Securities Dealers (NASDAQ) was founded in 1971 and was the world's first electronic stock market. Unlike the New York Stock Exchange, which, until recently, had a real trading floor with real people, from the beginning NASDAQ has been a computer network linking sellers and buyers through something like a bulletin-board system. The building on Times Square has nothing to do with stock trading but was constructed to serve as a broadcast studio that would supply real-time video to burgeoning financial news television and later online networks like CNBC, CNN Headline news, CNNfn, and Bloomberg. The signature sign on the Reuters: Instinet building, which is directly across from NASDAQ, is a huge news thermometer that monitors the news 24/7 and measures its importance by gauging the rising or falling temperature in different colors. NASDAQ and Reuters form a positive feedback loop in which the news transmitted by Reuters to NASDAQ influences the stock prices on financial markets (up or down), and the movement of stock prices transmitted by NASDAQ to Reuters increases or decreases the heat of events reported in the news.

During the years when NASDAQ was emerging, other trading networks were also being developed. As early as the late 1960s, some major brokerage houses were establishing electronic communications networks (ECNs), which enabled them to trade with each other directly, eliminating all third parties or financial intermediaries. One of the most successful ECNs was Instinet, founded in 1969. In addition to displaying bids and offers, Instinet enabled member institutions but not individuals to execute transactions electronically. The initial attraction of ECNs was that they allowed major institutional investors to trade large blocks of stock when markets were closed. But there were also disadvantages—the information on these networks was proprietary and trading was limited to participating institutions.

Recognizing the increasing significance of automated trading, the British media conglomerate Reuters purchased Instinet in 1987. In spite of the market crash that year and a price-fixing scandal in the early 1990s, Instinet continued to grow and by the middle of the 1990s, five thousand brokers were subscribers. As the most successful ECN, Instinet was handling 20 percent of all NASDAQ trades in stocks and was also linked to fifteen other markets. The rapid growth of Instinet and other ECNs introduced greater transparency and distributed information faster for those who were able and willing to pay for it. The market crash of 1987 made it clear to both business interests and federal regulators that reforms were necessary to ensure more equal access to the information necessary for investors to execute trades when they wanted to do so. In an effort to level the playing field, the U.S. Securities and Exchange Commission instituted regulations doing away with proprietary networks and requiring open access to prices and order sizes, which previously had been restricted to market specialists and institutional investors. It was not long before new trading networks for individual investors sprang up. Just as the telegraph had disintermediated middlemen by allowing producers to go directly to consumers, computerized day trading disintermediated financial firms by allowing individual investors to go directly to stock exchanges.

By the late 1990s, NASDAQ's growth had become exponential. The number of shares traded grew to 1.7 billion per day, more than twice the number of shares traded on the New York Stock Exchange. In addition, 4,800 companies were listed on NASDAQ, double the number listed on the New York Stock Exchange. Many of the companies fueling NASDAQ's expansion were the companies driving the media, information, and communications revolution. From 1990 to 1999, the NASDAQ composite index rose from 500 to 3,500. With plans to expand to Europe and Japan, NASDAQ became the most important web portal for online trading, linking 5,400 brokerage firms, 88,000 trading offices, 670,000 brokers, and approximately 10,000,000 online investors. The dematerialization of currencies and proliferation of financial instruments combined with the wiring of global financial networks led to a new form of virtual capitalism that more closely resembles the postmodern art world than the world of traditional banking and markets.

Artful Finance

As finance was becoming a play of insubstantial signs and images circulating at the speed of light, art was becoming a high-stakes financial game played on a global scale. Developments in the art world during the late twentieth and early twenty-first centuries both reflect and illuminate seismic shifts that were occurring in financial markets. The new form of this emerging art market extended and transformed the network of galleries, auction houses, museums, and collectors that had controlled the art market since the end of World War II.

Andy Warhol is to late industrial and consumer capitalism what Jeff Koons is to financial capitalism. Once again the trajectories of modernity, modernization, and modernism intersect. In the years after World War II, the center of the art world, like the center of the financial universe, shifted to New York City. During the war, many leading European artists had fled to the United States. As American artists mingled with European masters, they gradually overcame the anxiety of influence and began to stake out a distinctively modern American art, whose guiding principle was a deep commitment to human freedom and individual expression. The search for artistic identity received unexpected support from the federal government. Concerned about the spread of communism, the U.S. Information Agency, which from 1953 to 1999 was also known as Propaganda Agency of the United States, enlisted the support of artists by subsidizing their work and sponsoring exhibitions throughout the world. In ways that were rarely obvious, art and culture were enlisted to promote "the American way of life." Art became an extension of the government's expansionist policies by serving to extend America's financial and military global power.

The economy of art was changing in other ways as well. The postwar economic boom quickly raised the standard of living for the American middle class. With social distinctions becoming harder to draw, intellectuals and leftists formed an unexpected alliance with the so-called upper middle class by turning to the works of the artistic avant-garde for cultural markers that would set them apart from the supposedly unsophisticated masses. Advertisements in fashionable publications like *Partisan Review* transformed high art into an unmistakable sign of a particular lifestyle. Commenting on an ad for engravings by Jackson Pollock, Serge Guilbaut writes, "In the eyes of the public and the company that paid for the ads, the unusual stood for escape, for access to a higher rung of the social hierarchy. For example, a Pollock engraving became identified with the social position of the people for whom the homes being advertised were intended. These were exclusive homes for those who sought to distinguish themselves from the mass of 'housing developments' . . . then burgeoning in the suburbs to accommodate the growing middle class."[25]

The increasing demand for art led to the emergence of the New York gallery system whose glitz and glamour further increased the demand for art. Works of art became commodities that were marketed with sophisticated advertising campaigns, and artists became celebrities who appeared on the pages of glossy magazines and the screens of ever-more-universally owned televisions. While artists became famous for what they produced, gallery owners became famous for what they sold, and collectors became famous for what they bought. Many artists were ambivalent about these developments—some thought that commodification destroyed true art, whereas others eagerly embraced the art market and started turning out works and watching their once nonexistent bank accounts grow.

There had never been a celebrity artist like Andy Warhol. He understood the new art market better than any other artist as well as most gallery owners and collectors, and he played the media better than movie stars and politicians. But unlike the work of many other artists at the time, Warhol's art is ambiguous—it is never clear whether Warhol is embracing or criticizing consumer culture. His consistently ironic persona creates an uncertainty that makes his work intriguing. Warhol bridges the industrial era, which culminates in the expansion of consumerism through brands, and the world of captivating images used for expensive marketing campaigns. He called his studio The Factory and consistently praised mechanical means of reproduction. Instead of pursuing the romantic dream of originality and idealization of individual works of art created by the hand, Warhol declares, "I think everybody should be a machine. I think everybody should be like everybody."[26] In Warhol's Factory, artworks roll off the assembly line with minimal human intervention. He even erased the traditional mark of the artist's hand—the signature—by inventing a machine to sign his works. The value of the machine is that it is faster than the hand and, thus, more commodities can be produced for the market in a shorter time. "In my art work," he explains, "hand painting would take much too long and anyway that's not the age we're living in. Mechanical means are today."[27] The products that roll off Warhol's assembly line are images or, more precisely, images of images that are signs of signs. Warhol and his fellow Pop artists appropriated signs of consumer culture—Coke bottles, Brillo boxes,

Campbell's soup cans, newspapers, comic books, magazines, police reports, and most telling of all, dollar bills.

During the late 1950s and early 1960s, the machines that artists imagined were industrial; by the end of the decade, information-processing machines were beginning to appear. Though still working with industrial metaphors, Warhol's fellow Pop artist Roy Lichtenstein pointed toward the technological, social, and economic transformation that was already under way: "I want my painting to look as if it had been programmed," he writes. "I want to hide the record of my hand."[28] When the idea producing the work becomes a program, art enters the information age in which financial capitalism displaces—but does not replace—industrial and consumer capitalism.

Even Andy Warhol could not have anticipated the explosion of the art market by the turn of the twenty-first century. According to reliable estimates, by 2006 the private art market had reached $25 to $30 billion.[29] Christie's and Sotheby's, the two leading auction houses, reported combined sales of $12 billion and more than two dozen galleries were doing $100 million in sales annually. This phenomenal growth in the art market was not limited to the United States. Global capitalism created a global art market. Between 2002 and 2006, the global art market grew 95 percent, from $25.3 to $54.9 billion. This unprecedented growth was fueled by emerging markets in Russia, China, India, and the Middle East. The price of individual works escalated as quickly as the purported value of the financial securities with whose profits they were being purchased. In 2004, cosmetics magnate and chairman of the board of the Museum of Modern Art, Ronald Lauder, purchased Gustav Klimt's *Portrait of Adele Bloch-Bauer I* for $135 million, which at the time was the highest price ever paid for a single painting. No artist was better positioned to take advantage of this booming market than erstwhile commodities trader and stockbroker Jeff Koons. Three years after Lauder's excessive expenditure, Koons's *Hanging Heart,* which looks more like a carnival prize than a work of fine art, sold at auction for almost $27 million. At the time this was the highest price ever paid for a work by a living artist.

Koons, like Warhol, is more a manager than a creator. He too has a factory where he oversees an army of workers who produce works according to his specifications. But there the similarities end. Whereas Warhol's ironic distance from his work creates a critical edge, there is not an ounce of irony or criticism in Koons. Trying to reassure rather than question, he goes so far as to confess, "I realized you don't have to know anything and I think my work always lets the viewer know that. I just try to do work that makes people feel good about themselves, their history, and their potential. . . . I think art takes you outside yourself, takes you past yourself. I believe that my journey has really been to remove my own anxiety. That's the key. The more anxiety you can remove, the more free you are to make that gesture, whatever the gesture is. The dialogue is first with the artist, but then it goes outward, and is shared with other people. And if the anxiety is removed everything is so close, everything is available, and it's just this little bit of confidence, or trust, that people have to delve into."[30] Feel good, be happy, buy my art. The confidence that Koons seeks to instill is intended to remove anxiety about the confidence game being played by the Wall Street moguls, who use their obscene profits to buy art at prices as inflated as their virtual assets. In the high-speed 24/7/365 Wall Street world of the early twenty-first century, money, as Oliver Stone once again perceptively suggests, never sleeps; it just keeps circulating faster and faster, requiring new investment instruments and strategies to maximize opportunities for additional profits. (I will examine some of these new financial instruments in Chapter 6.)

At this point, it is helpful to consider how the art market's appropriation of Wall Street's investment strategies illuminates financial markets. Wealthy hedge-fund managers and private equity investors have taken celebrity collecting to another whole level. The most prominent representatives of the new model for the art market are Damien Hirst and his hedge-fund patron Steven A. Cohen. Hirst, like Koons, produces works of art that are designed specifically to serve as financial instruments for wealthy investors, but Hirst ups the ante. An article published in the *International Herald Tribune* in 2007 observes that Hirst "has gone from being an artist to being what you might call the manager of the hedge fund of Damien Hirst's art." The most ostentatious example of his strategy was the production and marketing of his $100 million diamond-studded skull ironically entitled *For the Love of God.* The financial machinations surrounding the sale of this work were as complex and mysterious as a high-stakes private equity deal. One year after the sale of this work, Hirst decided to disintermediate the entire gallery system and he held his own two-day art sale at Sotheby's in September 2008—at the precise moment that global financial markets were collapsing. With the Dow plummeting, investors decided it was time to hedge their bets by diversifying their investment portfolios with art purchases. The auction brought a total of $200.7 million, which exceeded Sotheby's high estimate of $177.6 million.

As new investors brought their financial models and strategies to the art market, auction houses as well as traditional galleries were cut out of deals. The most disruptive investing strategy so far has been the creation of private equity funds for buying and selling art. London financer Philip Hoffman, for example, has established Fine Art Management Services, Ltd., which speculates in art rather than stocks. In his article "Picasso Lures Hedge-Fund-Type Investors to the Art Market," Deepak Gopinath explains Hoffman's strategy:

> Melding art and finance, art funds aim to trade Picassos and Rembrandts the way hedge funds trade U.S. Treasuries or gold—and collect hedge-fund-like fees in the process. Hoffman's Fine Art Fund, for example, charges an annual management fee equal to 2 percent of its assets and takes a 20 percent cut of profits once the fund clears a minimum hurdle.

Hoffman, a former finance director at London-based auction house Christie's International PLC, says his fund isn't about beauty, truth and passion; it's about making money.

"We take a completely cold view," Hoffman says.

Hoffman's investors need cool heads too. He requires a minimum investment of $250,000, and investors can't withdraw their money for three years.[31]

This strategy securitizes works of art in the same way that collateralized mortgage obligations (CMOs) securitize mortgages. Just as mortgages are bundled and sold as bonds, so works of art are bundled and sold as shares of a hedge fund. In other words, rather than owning an individual work of art, or several works of art, an investor owns an undivided interest in a group of artworks. In these schemes, what is important is not the real value of the company, commodity, or artwork but the statistical probability of its price performance within a specified timeframe relative to other portfolio holdings. Furthermore, insofar as investors hedge bets, the value of any particular work of art is determined by its risk quotient relative to other works of art held by the fund. Like investors in CMOs, who know nothing about the actual real estate holdings whose mortgages they own, investors in art hedge and private equity funds know nothing about the actual artworks in which they are investing. Indeed, they never even see the works of art they partially own. In addition, there is nothing to prevent investors in art funds from selling their shares to other investors, so secondary and tertiary markets have emerged. As trading accelerates, derivatives (fund shares) and underlying assets (artworks) are once again decoupled, creating a quasi-autonomous sphere of circulating signs in which value constantly fluctuates. These funds are marketed to the highest-end investors as a new opportunity for asset diversification in their investment portfolios.

By early 2013, concerns were growing that the art market might be imitating financial markets by permitting a lack of transparency that could open the door to insider trading and market manipulation. With projected sales approaching $8 billion a year, some lawmakers started calling for regulation of the art market. In an article entitled "As Art Values Rise, so Do Concerns about Market Oversight," by Robin Pogrebin and Kevin Flynn, James R. Hedges IV, a New York collector and financier, explained that "the art world feels like the private equity market of the '80s and the hedge funds of the 90s. . . . It's got practically no oversight or regulation."[32] These fears were reinforced when news of yet another financial scandal broke. In a devastating article "The Hunt for Steve Cohen," Bryan Burrough and Bethany McLean write that twenty-five years after the downfall of junk bond pitchman Michael Milken, featured in Oliver Stone's original 1987 film *Wall Street,* it's happening all over again, this time with characters who could be drawn from the 2010 sequel *Wall Street: Money Never Sleeps.* "Once more a relentless U.S. attorney, this time forty-four-year-old Preet Bharara, has seemingly targeted the billionaire investor Steve Cohen, founder of SAC Capital Advisors, the $14 billion hedge fund based in Stamford, Connecticut. One by one, Bharara has picked off onetime SAC traders and analysts, confronting them at their homes, pulling them before grand juries, bringing criminal cases, and pressing them for evidence that Cohen has broken insider-trading laws. . . . 'If Steve Cohen gets off,' one hedge-fund manager observes, 'he will be the O. J. Simpson of insider trading.'" Cohen, like Milken, is more than just any player; he has become the symbol for an era when financial markets are spinning out of control. "Steve Cohen," Burrough and McLean point out, "isn't just another hedge-fund billionaire; he is *the* hedge-fund billionaire. He doesn't live in just another Greenwich, Connecticut, mansion; he lives in the largest of them all, complete with its own two-hole golf course and Jeff Koons's *Balloon Dog* sculpture adorning the driveway. Inside, the walls are festooned with paintings from his fabled collection of Impressionist and contemporary art, which includes Francis Bacon's *Screaming Pope,* hanging just outside his bedroom." While insisting that his traders had done nothing illegal or improper, Cohen nonetheless agreed to a $616 million settlement, which is the largest fine in the history of the Securities Exchange Commission. But questions still remain and the investigation is ongoing. With investigators closing in, Cohen has responded by flaunting his wealth, as if daring the government to come after him personally. "A week after the settlement, news broke that he had paid casino owner Steve Wynn an astounding $155 million—a record sum for a U.S. collector—to buy Picasso's *Le Rêve* (which Wynn had accidentally put his elbow through in 2006)."[33]

In the new wired world of global financial markets, material and immaterial flows intersect and accelerate until real and virtual assets become indistinguishable. High-speed networks of exchange produce excesses that can be neither contained nor controlled and, eventually, turn destructive. When enough is never enough, irrational exuberance overwhelms prudent investment policies and practices. Once again the Vegas Strip meets Wall Street and all bets are off.

6. Inefficient Market Hypothesis

....

Irrational Rationality

A few months before Hirst's confidence game and the concerns it provoked were in the news, leaders in China were worrying about how their version of Western capitalism was affecting people's daily lives. Contrary to widespread impressions, the Chinese people's feeling of well-being declined at the same time that their economic situation was dramatically improving. In a *New York Times* article "When Growth Outpaces Happiness," Richard A. Easterlin reported that the spread of state capitalism was creating more anxiety than satisfaction: "Hundreds of thousands of Chinese who worked at inefficient and unprofitable state companies were laid off. The loss of jobs meant the loss of the employer-provided safety net. Growing numbers of rural migrants took city jobs that provided no benefits. Among urban workers still employed, concerns about job security and the continuation of benefits mounted. Life satisfaction in urban areas declined markedly."[1]

With slight modification, this account might well describe attitudes among a growing number of people in the United States who are suffering under the sometimes conflicting demands of efficiency and austerity. The victory of free-market capitalism that has resulted in, among other things, the collapse of the Soviet Union and the liberalization of the Chinese economy, represents the culmination of the neoliberal economic revolution theorized by Milton Friedman and his followers and put into practice by Ronald Reagan and Margaret Thatcher. One of the cornerstones of these developments was the use of economic growth, calculated by the increase in the gross domestic product (GDP), to measure the economic well-being of countries and, by extension, individuals. The GDP is the market value of all products and services produced in one year by the residents of a country. In contrast to the gross national product (GNP), which determines production based on ownership, the GDP calculates production based on geographical location. The GNP includes all income earned by a country's citizens at home or abroad and subtracts income from non-residents living in the country.

Growth has not always been the standard by which economic success has been measured. In fact, the use of the GDP or GNP to evaluate the relative economic performance of different countries is largely a product of the Cold War. As more data became available, government officials, businessmen, and market watchers became addicted to "index economics" and would anxiously await monthly or quarterly reports on employment, trade, interest rates, inflation, industrial output, sales, exports, and imports. In the public as well as the private sectors, there was an unquestioned belief that economic growth is the highest good and the conviction that the best way for the economy to grow is for it to accelerate. E. J. Mishan's comment about England applies to America as well: "The belief persists that faster economic growth is the solution of last resort to our chronic economic infirmities. If only we can somehow get Britain 'moving' *fast* enough, inflation would cease to plague us and the balance of trade would return to equilibrium."[2] On both sides of the Atlantic as well as both sides of the political aisle in the United States, the commitment to economic growth continues to drive economic policy and financial markets.[3] In December 2012, Jared Bernstein, former chief economist and economic adviser to Vice President Joseph Biden, concluded an article entitled "Raise the Economy's Speed Limit" by arguing, "The first thing to do is keep applying the accelerator on pro-growth policies that strengthen near-term demand and labor quality, including paycheck supports (like the payroll tax break), training for unemployed workers and investment in bridges, tunnels and other infrastructure. Over the longer term, we might want to think of immigration reform as a way to counteract our decelerating work force."[4]

During much of the 1960s, the Soviet Union's economy seemed to be growing faster than the economies of Western capitalist countries. Robert and Edward Skidelsky point out that "the apostles of growth in the 1960s were mainly left-wing economists and politicians who had abandoned—or in the United States never embraced—public ownership as a mechanism, but retained their socialist aspirations for a more equal society." Two decades later everything was reversed—Thatcher, elected in 1979, and Reagan, elected in 1980, embraced a philosophy of growth as a fundamental tenet of their faith in the free market. According to this emerging ideology, "the way to faster growth lay not through planning, but freeing up markets from red tape, improving incentives through lighter taxes, reducing the power of trade unions and extending markets through privatization and deregulation." Reflecting principles that we have seen date back to the late medieval philosophy and the Protestant Reformation, this "economic system was geared to the maximization of individual satisfaction as expressed in markets. Individuals were no longer to be viewed as part of wholes; the wholes were simply the sum of individual parts. This reduction of economic life to a crude individualism can be dated from the 1970s."[5]

During the latter half of the twentieth century, an increasing number of politicians as well as economists used economic data expressed in the GDP to demonstrate the superiority of American-style free-market capitalism as compared both to European Socialism and to East European, Soviet, and Chinese communism. In the years following Reagan and Thatcher, President Clinton and Prime Minister Blair tried to find what they labeled a "third way" that staked out a position between Keynesian liberals and Friedman neoliberals. These efforts were marginally successful. But when Clinton cut social services and reformed welfare to help balance the budget, it was clear that neoliberal economic principles had spread even to what once had been the political Left. The arguments today between conservative Republican politicians and neoliberal economists, who want to eliminate government regulations, cut taxes, and reduce spending, and liberal Democratic politicians and liberal economists, who want greater regulation, higher taxes, and more extensive social welfare programs, are lingering traces of those Cold War debates.

While aggregate statistics about the GDP and GNP were collected before the war, it was not until the introduction of new technologies for recording, gathering, and analyzing information, many of which were developed by defense industries during the war, that it became possible to process these data fast enough to make them useful. The preoccupation with growth, greater accessibility of data, and more effective means of managing information led to a fundamental transformation of economic theory and financial practices. We have seen that the pioneers who laid the foundation for the modern understanding of markets were Scottish or British philosophers—Adam Smith, David Hume, and John Stuart Mill. By the middle of the twentieth century, economists had forsaken philosophy and wanted to transform their discipline into a science. The privileged science was physics, which, economists insisted, required rigorous analysis formulated in abstract mathematical equations. As computing power increased, the mathematics became more complex, until it was often unclear what economic theory had to do with Wall Street, to say nothing of Main Street. With the end of the Cold War, extremely high-speed computers, which previously had been used solely for defense purposes, were made available for civilian use. These machines enabled mathematicians and computer scientists to analyze financial markets quickly, and to develop new highly abstract and extremely complex financial instruments that could be used in programmed trading.

While it is both impossible and unnecessary to rehearse the history of economic and financial theory over the past fifty years, it is important here to understand the significance of three of its pillars: equilibrium theory, portfolio theory, and the efficient market hypothesis (EMH). The underlying assumption informing all of these theories is the belief—and I stress that it is a belief—in the rationality of markets. Developments over the past several decades have exposed serious flaws in this belief as well as each of these basic theories.

It is not too much to say that the principle of equilibrium is the hinge on which the scientific status of modern economics swings. According to general equilibrium theory, which dates back to the 1870s, supply, demand, and prices in different interacting markets in the economy result in an overall equilibrium. Proponents of this theory argue that the movement of markets can be modeled with complex mathematical formulas that abstract data from the real economy. Nobel laureate Edmund Phelps goes so far as to insist, "It is no accident that the formal introduction of the concept [of equilibrium] into economics is associated with those writers whose names are closely connected with the foundation of 'economic science.' It could be argued that its introduction marks the foundation of the discipline itself."[6] In spite of endless gyrations of financial markets, this theory remained largely unquestioned until the meltdowns of the 1990s. Adherence to the general-equilibrium theory combined with the increasing reliance on mathematics to lend markets an air of what would turn out to be specious rationality. With the growing insistence that the economy and financial markets can be modeled mathematically, many economists came to believe that if something cannot be quantified, it is not real.

For many years, academic economists' reliance on abstract mathematical formulas and models led to a split between theorists and practitioners like financial analysts and traders, who dismissed the usefulness of these abstractions in actual trading. This situation began to change in the 1950s and 1960s, when the new field of financial economics emerged. By the 1980s, the line dividing theory and practice had eroded considerably—analysts and traders were making investments on the basis of abstract mathematical formulas, and guided by models devised by so-called "quants." Both the models and the ability to use them in trading were made possible by the spread of network technology as well as the exponential growth in the speed and data-processing capacity of computers. As markets were wired and trading became algorithmic, financial transactions became infinitely more complex and markets became considerably more volatile. While general-equilibrium theory interpreted major market fluctuations as the result of external factors, in networked markets it was becoming clear that significant disruptions were a function of factors related to the internal structure and operation of high-speed trading networks. By the beginning of the twenty-first century, it was obvious to some observers but unfortunately not to many investors that markets operate far from equilibrium; instead they periodically drift toward the edge of chaos. I will consider the dynamics of disequilibrium in Chapter 8.

As financial markets expanded, accelerated, and became more volatile, the ability to manage risk effectively became much more important. Like industrial capitalism, which required new theories of scientific management and a new class of industrial engineers, financial capitalism required new theories of financial economics and a new class of financial engineers, who work in what is known as structured finance and tend to understand the economy as a game made up of a set of agreed-on rules. In this game, the challenge is to manipulate rules by creating new products designed to increase income, decrease taxes, and redistribute risk. One of the earliest and most important strategies for managing risk grew out of what is known as portfolio theory.

In 1952, Harry Markowitz, a twenty-five-year-old graduate student at the University of Chicago, published a seminal paper entitled "Portfolio Selection," which he eventually expanded first into his doctoral dissertation, and then the book *Portfolio Selection: Efficient Diversification of Investments* (1959). The notion of investment portfolios has become so popular that it is difficult to realize how revolutionary the idea was in the 1950s. Markowitz changed the way that investors large and small think about markets and, by so doing, set the course for much of financial economics for several decades. His most important innovation was to shift from calculating risk in terms of individual stocks to assessing the risk of a portfolio made up of different stocks. Instead of making investment decisions based solely on the fundamentals of a particular company or the past performance of its stock, as the legendary investor Warren Buffett tends to do, Markowitz seeks to determine the *relative* volatility and hence risk of different securities in the portfolio. This change in investment strategy anticipates the shift in determining the value of currencies that came with the end of the gold standard. In previously traditional investment strategies, the fundamentals and past performance of the stock function something like a real referent, which is analogous to gold, and the relative risk quotient of the securities in the portfolio fluctuates like the changing value of floating currencies. What Markowitz described as the efficiency of the portfolio is a function of the *relative differences* in the performances of its stock. It is possible to hedge risk, he argues, by buying and holding a diversified portfolio of securities. By purchasing different kinds of stocks, one increases the chance that losses will be offset by gains. Obviously this strategy also entails the possibility that gains will be offset by losses. The central question for investors is how much risk they are willing to bear and how much they are willing to pay to hedge risk. For Markowitz, the differences and diversity of a portfolio create stability, while similarities or the homogeneity of holdings breeds instability. A portfolio is considered "efficient" when high volatility and low volatility are in balance.

At the time Markowitz formulated his theory, the use of computers did not extend much beyond the military and universities. During the latter half of the twentieth century, the rapid spread of computers and networking technologies revolutionized financial markets. One of the most important financial innovations of the postwar period was the invention of hedge funds. Alfred Winslow Jones created the first postwar hedge fund in 1949. Whereas mutual funds are regulated and open to all investors, hedge funds are private, unregulated, and usually restricted to a limited number of institutional or very wealthy investors. Between the late 1960s and early 1980s, hedge funds grew significantly—today hedge funds are a $2.5 trillion industry. The practice of hedging, like portfolio investing, is based on the relativity of risk. In structured finance, the economy appears to be a quasi-equilibrium system made up of codependent variables. When hedging, investments are understood as offsetting pairs that are reciprocally or perhaps even dialectically related. An investor hedges by placing what he calculates are balanced bets and counter bets. Such wagers often involve a complex series of interrelated bets using the same or sometimes different financial instruments. Here too, what is important is not the value of individual assets but the relative movement of investments. The trick of the trade is to place bets balanced enough to be safe but risky enough to offer potential profits.

The final theoretical pillar of current financial markets is the efficient market hypothesis, which Eugene Fama, who is widely recognized as the father of modern finance, defined in his 1965 article "Random Walks in Stock Market Prices." We have already considered the importance of efficiency for the scientific management of industrial processes; here we encounter the importance of efficiency for the mathematical and scientific management of financial transactions. Fama's efficient market hypothesis depends on two interrelated variables: information and speed. The fundamental tenet of this theory is that market prices reflect all publicly available information and that prices change instantly to reflect new public information. The equal distribution of information results in efficient markets; unequal distribution of information, by contrast, makes markets inefficient. When everyone has the same information, a particular commodity, security, or bond ought to have one price; if, however, buyers and sellers do not have access to all relevant information, there will be a price disparity across different markets. Once again, time is money. An investor can make a profit by buying low on one market and selling high on another as long as the buyer doesn't know what the seller knows.

In the mid-1960s, Paul Samuelson became a convert to the EMH and spread the word through his popular teaching and influential writings. This new gospel was widely accepted until the financial upheavals of the late 1990s. According to EMH, prices immediately reflect all available information and anticipate future market movement by discounting the current prices of stocks. As a result of the increasing speed with which information is disseminated in wired markets, the market instantly "knows" more than any individual investor can process at a given time. The market, in other words, has something like a lightning-quick mind of its own that emerges from but is not reducible to the individuals who comprise it. Furthermore, since the market supposedly incorporates all available information at every moment, it approaches functional omniscience. When understood in this way, the mind of the market appears to be the functional equivalent of the mind of God, whose all-knowing invisible hand creates and maintains order in what otherwise would be a chaotic universe. Lowly human beings must follow the lead of God/the market; if they intervene, they will probably disrupt the system's orderly machinations.

Two other critical assumptions of the EMH prove questionable. First, the theory assumes that changes in the market are a function of external rather than internal causes, and consequently that stock prices are unpredictable. If stock valuations accurately reflect all available information at all times, price changes are unpredictable because they can only be caused by new and unexpected information. It is also important to stress that the equal distribution of information, like frictionless markets, is an ideal that is never realized in real-world trading. Not even the newest communication and network technologies make information available to everyone infinitely fast, and, therefore, some people inevitably receive it later than others. We will see in Chapter 8 that high-speed algorithmic trading makes money in the nanoseconds of difference in information accessibility.

Second, EMH assumes that investors are rational. In this context, rational conduct is defined as the effort to maximize expected returns for a given level of risk. Such rational agents or investors are regarded as homogeneous, that is, they are all supposed to have access to the same information, which they interpret in similar ways to make investments within the same time horizon. Economic agents, in other words, are like billiard balls or molecules that brush against and bump into each other but do not really interact. The information on which investors base their decisions is often generated and transmitted by the same financial institutions and news sources, but individual decisions remain independent of each other. This understanding of the actions of individual investors also implies that sequential moments of decision are isolated from each other. Just as agents acting at a given moment are independent of each other, so too the moments in a time series are discrete and independent. Markets, like dice, have neither memory nor history, and thus cannot develop either upward or downward momentum. From this point of view, investing in any financial market is little more than a crapshoot. In his highly influential book *Irrational Exuberance*, Robert Shiller draws the logical conclusion from this illogical theory. "If we accept the premise of efficient markets, not only is being smart no advantage, but it also follows immediately that being *not so smart* is not a *disadvantage* either. If not-so-smart people could lose money systematically in their trades, then this would suggest a profit opportunity for smart money; just do the opposite of what the not-so-smart money does. Yet according to the efficient market theory, there can be no such profit opportunity for smart money."[7] Obviously, this is not good news for financial analysts and bankers whose jobs depend on the promise of beating the market.

By the late 1990s, markets did not seem to be very rational. This was not only the result of questionable assumptions about how human beings make decisions (assumptions that were exposed by the growing field of behavioral economics), but was also a function of changes in the markets themselves caused by new federal regulations and technological innovations. Since trading networks initially were proprietary and in most cases limited to large institutional investors, smaller institutions and individuals did not have access to valuable information that had a significant influence on security prices. This led to market inefficiencies and potentially big profits for those institutions that could afford to pay for access to expensive information and trading networks. In many cases, these inefficiencies created significant price disparities on different markets. Armed with privileged information, investors could realize big profits with a relatively small number of bets. In an effort to create greater equality, the SEC required the opening up of proprietary news, information, and trading networks to all investors big or small, institutional or individual. These new regulations had the desired effect of making markets more transparent and, thus, more efficient.

But this increased efficiency had the unintended consequence of creating new inefficiencies. In any market, there are two ways to make money: you can make a lot of money on a few big bets, or a little money on lots of small bets. More equitable distribution of information had the predicted effect of decreasing price differentials across markets. This meant that it was much less likely that investors could reap big profits with a small number of bets, and, therefore, they had to vastly increase the number of bets they placed to make the same profit or to continue growing. The same networks that were distributing information more broadly were also accelerating the speed of trading.

Committed to the ideology of growth, the only way investors could keep up with competitors was to trade more and more securities faster and faster. This marked the birth of high-volume, high-speed trading, which I will consider in Chapter 8.

A final development that spread during the 1990s—the practice of borrowing money to speculate on financial markets—turned this volatile mix toxic. Throughout history, entrepreneurs, companies, and corporations have routinely borrowed to expand their operations. Until the latter half of the twentieth century, such borrowing was usually for the purpose of building new plants, stores, or facilities; purchasing needed equipment; maintaining inventory; and expanding the workforce. With irrational exuberance spreading faster than a computer virus, investors started borrowing to play the increasingly speculative financial markets. These investments were not limited to traditional stocks and bonds but extended to a burgeoning variety of exotic financial instruments, many of which were little understood and most of which were unregulated. With markets soaring, the rules of lending changed. According to traditional practice, a borrower provides collateral to secure the loan. For example, in the days before the securitization of mortgages and collateralized mortgage obligations (CMOs), when a person purchased a house, the bank, which was usually local, would hold the mortgage and would take possession of the house if the borrower defaulted on the loan. The amount of the loan would always be calculated in relation to the actual market value of the house. With the transformation of the banking industry brought about by the emergence of huge banking supermarkets and the corresponding disappearance of local savings-and-loan banks in the 1980s, this tried-and-true system quickly changed. In the 1990s, markets were running wild and individual and institutional investors eager for a bigger piece of the action started borrowing excessively to invest in increasingly volatile financial markets. Lenders, who knew or should have known better, were making too much money to restrain themselves voluntarily and did everything they could to keep the party going. Rather than imposing stricter lending requirements, banks actually lowered collateral requirements at the precise moment they should have been raised. This meant that individuals and institutions could borrow even more money with fewer assets required to secure their loans. As if this were not bad enough, an innovation designed to increase liquidity was introduced—lending institutions began allowing borrowers to use the very financial assets purchased with the loan as collateral. This system worked fine as long as the market was rising but proved disastrous when stock prices fell.

In the fall of 1997, this entire house of cards came tumbling down. A growing debt crisis in Russia and Asia led to the failure of the high-flying Long Term Capital Management fund (LTCM), which threatened to bring down the entire global economy. At the time, LTCM was leveraged 33:1. Because of the decreased margins created by the increased efficiency of markets, the firm had made far too many bets. Having followed the hedging strategy of distributing their bets, LTCM figured that if one stock went down, another would go up and could be sold to cover losses and pay off the loan. What its managers didn't anticipate was virtually all their bets going bad at the same time. With only one dollar in reserve for every thirty-three invested, they did not have sufficient liquidity to meet their debt obligations when the market collapsed. With decreasing price differentials on securities, bonds, and other financial securities, LTCM had started making huge bets. Furthermore, a considerable portion of the collateral its managers had used to secure the loans consisted of the very securities, bonds, and financial instruments they had purchased with them. Thus when the value of these securities dropped, the value of the collateral dropped, and lenders issued what is known as a margin call, which requires paying more money to bring the collateral up to the value it had at the time of the loan. But since LTCM was so highly leveraged, it did not have sufficient liquid assets to meet the margin call without selling the securities that its managers had purchased with the loan. Since the losses were so great, they had to sell lots of assets to pay the banks, and this drove the price of the securities even lower in a classic feedback loop. The more stocks and bonds LTCM sold, the lower their price went; the lower their prices went, the higher the margin call to cover the decline in the value of the collateral; and the higher the margin call, the more assets had to be sold. The very nature of the investments and the new trading network inevitably led to the extremely rapid acceleration of losses. In this case, as in most others, speed kills. The situation was all the more alarming because some of the major banks and financial institutions at home and abroad were heavily invested in the firm. The collapse of LTCM was as close as the world economy had ever come to complete collapse. As close, that is, until 2008.

Today this story sounds all too familiar—markets have become much more volatile and fragile and the world much more dangerous in the past fifteen years. In 1998, William McDonough, head of the New York Federal Reserve Bank, convened a group of fourteen banks and financial institutions and charged them to come up with a plan to bail out LTCM and save the global economy. The plan they came up with required each member of the group to contribute $100 to $300 million, which at the time seemed like an enormous amount of money but today seems almost insignificant. The total fund of $3.625 billion was sufficient to save the day. A decade later the tape would be rewound and played again, but this time the risk would be incalculably greater and the cost would be exponentially higher.

Inefficient Efficiencies

In 1992, just one year after the collapse of the Soviet Union, neoconservative political theorist Francis Fukuyama published an influential book, *The End of History*, which was derived from an article he had written in 1989. Summarizing his analysis he writes, "A remarkable consensus concerning the legitimacy of liberal democracy as a system of government had emerged throughout the world over the past few years, as it conquered rival ideologies like hereditary monarchy, fascism, and most recently communism. More than that, however, I argued that liberal democracy may constitute the 'end point of mankind's ideological evolution' and the 'final form of human government,' and as such 'constituted the end of history.' That is, while earlier forms of government were characterized by grave defects and irrationalities that led to their eventual collapse, liberal democracy was arguably free from such fundamental internal contradictions."[8] As Fukuyama's argument unfolds, it becomes clear that his understanding of liberal democracy is inseparable from capitalism. The past two decades have proven him and his neoconservative and neoliberal supporters wrong about most things but nothing more so than the purported rationality of capitalism. While capitalism has continued to expand and the number of democratic countries is increasing, recent history has exposed in this system inherent irrationalities, contradictions, and inefficiencies that have resulted in growing social inequality and impending natural disaster.

Paradoxically, these irrationalities grow out of the insistence on the rationality of markets, and these inefficiencies are a function of the increasing efficiency of markets. In place of the efficient market hypothesis, I would propose the inefficient market hypothesis (IMH). According to this theory, the pursuit of rationality and efficiency ends up making markets irrational and inefficient. Rather than the result of external factors, this reversal is the function of contradictions inherent in the ideology of growth that underlies the EMH. We have seen that the rationality of markets requires efficiency, which, in turn, depends on speed. As markets become more rational, they accelerate, and as they accelerate, they become more efficient. At a certain point, however, production becomes so fast and efficient that it is excessive. The only way to deal with the irrationality and inefficiency of overproduction is through overconsumption. This requires consumers to borrow and spend money they don't have for stuff they don't need. Financial capitalism transforms the all-consuming spectacle of consumer capitalism into the society of speculation's insistence that investors borrow and invest money they don't have in securities that are insecure.

During World War II, the nation's industrial capacity was deployed to support the war effort. This resulted in a dearth of consumer goods, which, in turn, led to pent-up demand. The end of the war ushered in what Vance Packard, in his classic study *The Waste Makers,* aptly labeled the "era of prodigality," which created pressure for sustained growth. During the decade immediately after the war, domestic demand kept pace with the renewed production of consumer goods, but by the late 1950s, demand had declined, and other outlets had to be developed.

With the engines of production running at full speed and consumers buying less, American businesses sought new markets for their goods in other countries. The ambitious plan to rebuild Europe was in large measure motivated by U.S. economic interests. But spatial expansion, I have noted, has unavoidable limits, and when they are reached, it is necessary to develop new strategies to keep the system running. In the postwar years, spatial expansion gave way to temporal acceleration— product cycles were introduced to entice consumers to buy more stuff faster. In 1958, for example, Detroit started introducing new models every year. As Packard points out, "American motorists by 1960 were trading in their 'old' car by the time it reached an average of two and a quarter years. The Ford Motor company in one of its advertisements said this showed how smart and shrewd the average motorcar owner was becoming. At that age, it pointed out, the car starts showing minor ailments and dents. Further, it stated, 'the car is two years old in style. Its fine edge is gone.'"[9] The strategy worked, at least for a while.

During the 1950s, Americans consumed more than twice as much as they did before the war, and by the 1960s, the United States was out-producing the Soviet Union in consumer durable goods by twenty to one. When Vice President Nixon met with Nikita Khrushchev at the opening of the American Exhibition in Moscow on July 24, 1959, it was clear that the war had shifted from the battleground to the market. While most people thought that Nixon had gotten the better of Khrushchev, the dark side of consumerism was beginning to raise its head. As early as the mid-1950s, marketing consultant Victor Lebow wrote in *The Journal of Retailing*, "our enormously productive economy . . . demands that we make consumption our way of life, that we convert the buying and use of goods into rituals, that we seek our spiritual satisfactions, our ego satisfactions in consumption. . . . We need things consumed, burned up, worn out, replaced and discarded at an ever increasing rate."[10] During the 1950s, consumer debt rose three times faster than income and when plastic credit cards were introduced in 1959, spending accelerated even faster. A *Business Week* report issued at the time summarized all relevant financial forces in five simple words: "Borrow. Spend. Buy. Waste. Want."[11] At this point, consumerism became a latter-day potlatch in which value is measured not only by excessive production but also by excessive consumption. Yet while it seemed that consumption had become irrationally exuberant, it turned out that the markets were just beginning to heat up.

Market capitalism has long been associated not only with rationality but also with the freedom of choice. By the latter half of the twentieth century, economic principles defined reason as much as reason characterized markets. Rationality came to be defined largely by what made economic sense, and what was not in a person's, a company's, or a country's economic self-interest was considered irrational by definition. Choice, defined by economic logic, came to be widely considered an unquestionable good—the more choices, the better. Within this regime, freedom of choice is little more than the freedom to buy and consume. According to this logic, economic progress can be measured by the increasing number of choices that consumers have. Though rarely acknowledged, increasing the number of choices is really less about improving human well-being than it is about expanding the market.

Think of it: 48,800 items in the average American supermarket,

500 or more stations on satellite TV, 125 beverage options in a single Coke machine, 65 different styles with 140 color and fabric options—a total of 9,100 options from a single dress company, a new Nook with 700,000 Google apps.[12] Does this endless proliferation of consumer products really give people more choices or just different variations of the same options? Is it really true that more choices are always better?

Modernization's strategy of planned obsolescence, entrepreneurs' insistence on incessant innovation, and modernism's dedication to making it new intersect in the world of contemporary fashion to expose the irrationality and inefficiency of today's markets. Modernism, we have seen, is defined by its thoroughgoing commitment to the new or, more precisely, to an endless process of renewal. Though rarely acknowledged, what artists promote as a stance of radical critique in the name of creative innovation turns out to reinforce the very economic forces many of them claim to resist. Since the new must always be renewed, something like planned obsolescence is intrinsic to modern art. While the avant-garde endorses as an aesthetic ideal that which often seems utterly impractical, for industry and finance it is actually both practical and necessary for economic growth. If the market is to flourish, the excessive is indispensable, the frivolous essential, and the useless useful. This is not to suggest that the lines joining the avant-garde and expanding markets are clear or direct. To the contrary, much innovative modern art struggles to subvert market forces. Yet as we have seen in our consideration of hedge funds and private equity funds for art, the market has extraordinary recuperative powers that enable it to incorporate opposition and turn resistance to its own ends. When artistic resistance is transformed into economic promotion, high art is popularized and commodified and commodities are further aestheticized.

Nowhere are these dynamics more clearly on display than in today's fast-fashion industry. If fashion is essentially modern, fast fashion is quintessentially postmodern. When the introduction of greater product differentiation and product cycles during fall and spring fashion seasons didn't meet the endless demand for greater profits and faster economic growth, there seemed to be only one solution—shift gears yet again and speed up the engines of production even more. In her revealing book *Over-Dressed: The Shockingly High Cost of Cheap Fashion,* Elizabeth L. Cline reports: "Fast fashion is a radical method of retailing that has broken from seasonal selling and puts out new inventory constantly throughout the year. Fast-fashion merchandise is typically priced much lower than its competitors'. The fast-fashion concept was pioneered by Spain's Zara, which delivers new lines twice a week in its stores. H&M and Forever 21 both get daily shipments of new styles."[13] Fast fashion is high-speed, high-volume trading in the world of commerce. Just as financial firms can make a little money on a few bets or a lot of money on a lot of bets, so can those in the fashion industry make a lot of money on a few items, in couture, or a little money on a lot of items, with fast fashion.

Taking a page out of the playbook of industrial scientific management, fast-fashion entrepreneurs integrate supply, design, production, and distribution as tightly as possible. One important innovation in fast fashion is to reverse the trend of outsourcing production to distant countries in order to cut the time required to get products into stores. As we will see in some detail in Chapter 7, new technologies now make it possible to gather, process, and transmit massive amounts of data about consumer preferences at high speed, thereby enabling the market to adjust to demand faster than ever before. A Harvard Business School whitepaper, "Zara's Secret for Fashion," reports that "this 'fast fashion' system depends on a constant exchange of information throughout every part of Zara's supply chain—from customers to store managers, from store managers to market specialists and designers, from designers to production staff, from buyers to subcontractors, from warehouse managers to distributors, and so on." In contrast to distributed networks that have become so "fashionable" in the past few decades, Zara's extraordinary success depends on a much more centralized network for managing both material and immaterial flows. The results have been impressive. "Zara's designers create approximately 40,000 new designs annually, from which 10,000 are selected for production. Some of them resemble the latest couture creations. But Zara often beats the high-fashion houses to the market and offers almost the same products made with less expensive fabric at much lower prices. Since most garments come in five to six colors and five to seven sizes, Zara's system has to deal with something in the realm of 300,000 new stock-keeping units on average, every year."[14]

If mass production had to produce mass consumption, fast fashion has to produce hyper-fast, hyper-mass consumption. The marketing strategy of the fast-fashion industry is to encourage the shortest of short-term decision making by encouraging impulse buying in two ways. First, items are priced high enough to maximize profit margins but low enough so people do not hesitate to make purchases because of price; second, merchants introduce and remove stuff so fast that customers worry that the item they are thinking of buying won't be available the next day. As fashion seasons give way to incessant "innovation," conspicuous consumption becomes constant consumption. The strategy of accelerating the change of styles to draw customers back to stores as often as possible has proved to be remarkably successful. The American clothing industry today is a $12 billion business and the average American family spends $1,700 on clothes. Cline observes, "Nowadays, an annual budget of $1700 can buy a staggering surfeit of clothing, including 485 'Fab Scoopneck' tops from Forever 21 or 340 pairs of ladies' sandals from Family Dollar or 163 pairs of seersucker Capri pants from Goody's or 56 pairs of Mossimo 'Skinny Utility' cargo pants from Target or 47 pairs of glitter platform wedges from Charlotte Russe or 11 men's Dockers suits from JCPenney or 6 Lauren by Ralph Lauren sequin evening gowns."[15] In much of Europe, where fast fashion started, the situation is even crazier. In an article entitled "Britain's Bulging Closet: Growth of 'Fast Fashion' Means Women Are

Buying HALF Their Body Weight in Clothes Each Year," Paul Sims reports that the average woman in England has twenty-two garments hanging in her closet that she has never worn and will spend on average $201,000 on clothing during her lifetime.[16]

In an effort to meet growing demand from people whose high-speed lives don't even leave them enough time to shop, some companies are combining fast fashion and mass customization. According to Adeline Koh, a company named Stitch Fix combines algorithms "with human oversight to create a personalized consumer experience. When you sign up for Stitch Fix, you fill out a very extensive style profile along with notes about your own personal preferences. All this algorithmically generates some suggestions tailored for you. The results then go to your personal stylist, who takes these suggestions and any of your own detailed notes (e.g. you hate frills; you want something in stripes), skims through your online profiles for a sense of your style (such as your Pinterest boards), and finally makes a selection to send to you. Stitch Fix then sends you five items (clothes and accessories), in a 'fix' (or shipment)."[17] Prices are not fixed but are customized to fit within each consumer's budget. The company's website boasts, "Our unique process tracks each customer's preferences over time, making Stitch Fix the only shopping experience that can learn as much about women as their favorite shopping partners." Style profiles provide valuable information that can be used in future advertising and promotions. For many people, fashion is as addictive as the technology that delivers it. To insure increasing product churn, Stitch Fix fixes can be scheduled monthly or as often as customers would like.

The trend of product cycle acceleration is not limited to fashion; it can be found in all sectors of the economy. In Japan, for example, the preoccupation with the new has led to inefficiencies that are creating problems for the country's one-time leader in consumer electronics— Sony. In an article entitled "Fad-Loving Japan May Derail a Sony Smart- phone," Hiroko Tabuchi writes, "For years, Japan's three largest mobile network companies have pressed phone makers . . . to update their handsets every three or four months. Phones with digital TV broadcast receivers were once all the rage; a phone without it was never going to sell. Then it was thumbprint scans; you'd be hard pressed to find those on many phones today. The same is true of swiveling screens, and to a lesser extent, electronic wallets." Only four months after Sony introduced its highly touted Xperia Z smartphone, Japan's largest mobile carrier, NTT DoCoMo, stopped selling it. Tabuchi explains, "Sony's Xperia Z got caught in this marketing buzz saw. Phones, like fashion, have become seasonal and the seasons are getting shorter and shorter. DoCoMo started selling the Xperia Z in Japan on Feb. 9 as part of the carrier's spring 2013 collection, replacing the Xperia AX of the winter collection. A month later, on March 15, DoCoMo announced its summer collection of 11 new phones, with the Experia Z replaced by the Experia A, which went on sale a month earlier." At this point, the accelerating speed of turnover, which for awhile had increased profits, becomes counterproductive and even destructive. Yuichi Kojure, professor of information technology at Aomori Public University, admits, "Mobile phone makers are exhausted. . . . I think more people here [in Japan] are starting to realize that the way its mobile phone industry works is unsustainable."[18]

Errol Morris's timely film *Fast, Cheap and Out of Control* might well have been about today's fast fashion, fast phones, and high-speed, high-volume financial networks. While the absurdity of the situation would seem to be undeniable, people who continue to believe that they are in control still insist that the only way to respond to economic slowdown is to push the pedal to the metal. But the constant acceleration of today's economy and financial capitalism is reaching the limit where system failure becomes inevitable and a major crash is unavoidable. This limit is marked by three interrelated crises: choice, waste, and debt. In anticipation of issues to be considered in more depth later, I will consider each briefly here.

Choice. In books like *Capitalism and Freedom* (1962) and *Free to Choose* (1980), Milton Friedman expresses one of neoliberalism's foundational doctrines, one that illuminates the crisis of choice. "What the market does is to reduce greatly the range of issues that must be decided through political means, and thereby to minimize the extent to which government need participate directly in the game. The characteristic feature of action through political channels is that it tends to require or enforce substantial conformity. The great advantage of the market, on the other hand, is that it permits wide diversity."[19] Diversity, in turn, is supposed to create a greater range of choices. But is this really true? Does the market actually permit or create a wide diversity of choices? And is it really true that the more choices we have, the better off we are? Genuine innovation is rare; most of what is marketed as the new is, in fact, a repackaging of the old, which results in the eternal return of the same. Same thing, different color, same product, different package. 1.0, 2.0, 3.0, 4.0, 5.0. . . . More often than not, what are touted as more choices actually are a limited menu of options designed to meet the needs of business rather than the needs of people. What is surprising is that so many people still fall for the con. More choices are not necessarily better and often can make life more stressful. While too few choices can be discouraging or even depressing, too many choices are overwhelming. The increasing number of possibilities sometimes becomes paralyzing, and can actually lead to more anxiety and less freedom. The ideology of choice extends beyond products and investments to all aspects of life—abortion, guns, schools, health care, retirement, on and on and on—until choice overload creates decision fatigue. So many choices, so little time. This condition is not limited to adults—there is trickle-down anxiety from parents to children.

Waste. The fast-fashion and fast-phone industries serve as metaphors for all kinds of waste that plague the world today, ranging from human to atomic, economic, financial, and environmental. The problem of waste surely is not new. Like everything else, however, the production and accumulation of waste has accelerated dramatically during the past five decades. The Environmental Protection Agency (EPA) reports that every year Americans throw away 12.7 million tons of textiles; this amounts to an astonishing sixty-eight pounds per person. Only 1.6 million tons of this waste are recycled or reused.[20] The harmful effects of excessive production are not limited to material waste. Cline correctly stresses that the textile industry consumes excessive amounts of fossil fuels, energy, and water: "The process of making textiles has never been green. Avtex Fibers, one of the world's largest rayon factories based in Front Royal, Virginia, was shut down in 1989 for poisoning the surrounding water and soil and is still listed as an EPA Superfund site. The technology and regulations to make textile manufacturing less environmentally harmful have improved dramatically in the United States, but the textile industry has largely moved overseas in recent decades to countries that are ill-equipped or simply too poor to reduce the impact of the fiber-making process." In China, where 10 percent of the world's textiles are produced, air and water pollution are at record high levels.[21]

The situation with electronic waste, or eWaste, is even more dangerous. Each year the United States produces 5 to 7 million tons of eWaste, and this is increasing at a rate of 3 to 5 percent a year. Most of this waste is highly toxic, containing hazardous materials that include lead, beryllium, cadmium, barium, PVC, mercury, PCBs, and bromide flame retardants (PBB and PBDE). In recent years, the United States has enacted some regulations to control or prohibit the disposal of eWaste in this country. But this has merely shifted, not solved the problem by encouraging the export of eWaste to foreign countries, especially those in Asia, while at the same time opposing international regulations to address this global problem. Only about 20 percent of eWaste is recycled. The rest is sent to countries like India, Pakistan, Vietnam, and especially China, where there are virtually no controls on waste disposal. In cities like Shanton and Guiyu, dubbed China's Electronic Waste Village, hundreds of thousands of workers labor for just $1.50 a day and are exposed to dangerous chemicals while they break down computers, mobile phones, tablets, and other devices in order to salvage minute traces of rare metals. The absence of adequate supervision and regulation has led to severe environmental problems. In Shanton, for example, the soil has two hundred times and the water two thousand times the accepted levels of lead. In addition, the burning of waste materials creates dangerous air pollution, which has resulted in widespread health problems. Once again, immaterial and material flows are inseparable— monitors from American computers whose screens are filled with lead end up in roadside ditches in what was until recently rural China. Waste and pollution, like money circulating in today's financial markets, know no boundaries and never sleep. When everything is connected, other countries' problems are our problems and vice versa.[22]

Debt. What greases the wheels and heats the wires of today's markets is debt—personal debt, consumer debt, credit card debt, student debt, corporate debt, and government debt at every level—local, state, and federal. The graphs tell it all.

While the trends are obvious, the debt problem is even worse than these graphs suggest because it is compounded by the positive feedback systems operative in today's complex financial markets. Accelerating compound interest on all kinds of debt makes it increasingly difficult to meet payments on time. Furthermore, as the economy slows or stalls, revenues decline, making it even harder to service debt. While economists and politicians argue about whether cutting taxes and austerity (Friedman's neoliberal approach) or raising taxes and spending (Keynes's liberal approach) is the better short-term strategy for addressing the debt problem, there is no doubt that in the long run, the current trajectory is unsustainable. With all the acrimony swirling in Washington, it is easy to overlook how much supposedly opposing parties actually agree about problematic assumptions. On the Left and the Right, there remains an unwavering commitment to the principle of

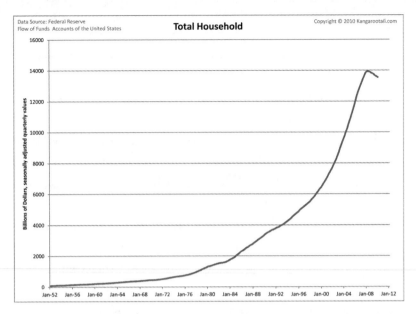

Total outstanding household debt, 1952–2012. Pages 168–71: reprinted with permission by Carsten Mundt, Ph.D., from "Debt by Outstanding Sector—Quarterly Charts 1952 to Now," available at http://www.kangarootail.com/uncategorized/debt-outstanding-by-sector-quarterly-charts-1952-now. Data from Federal Reserve, *Flow of Funds Accounts of the United States.* Copyright © 2010 Kangarootail.com.

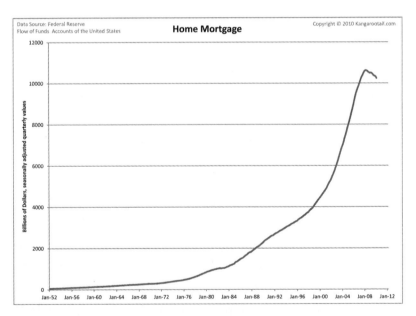

Total outstanding home mortgage debt, 1952–2012.

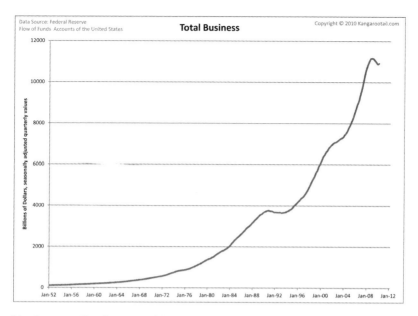

Total outstanding business debt, 1952–2012.

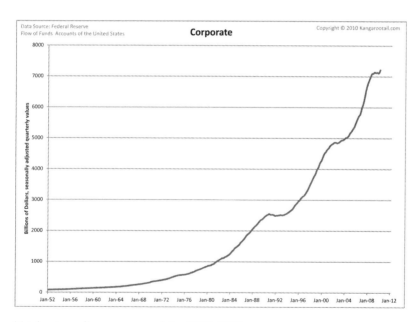

Total outstanding corporate debt, 1952–2012.

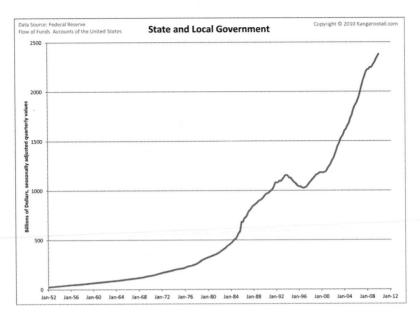

Total outstanding state and local government debt, 1952–2012.

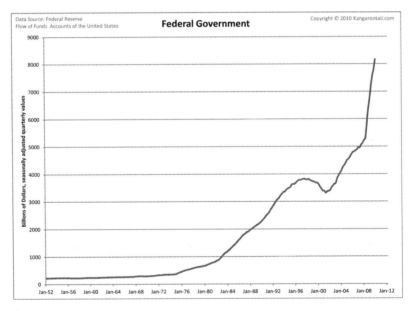

Total outstanding federal government debt, 1952–2012.

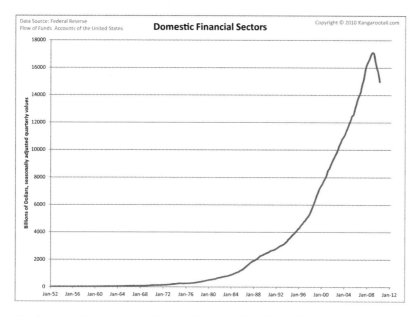

Total outstanding domestic financial-sector debt, 1952–2012.

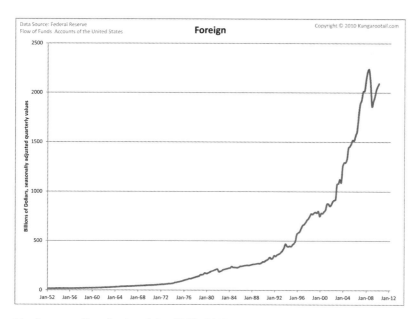

Total outstanding foreign debt, 1952–2012.

economic growth as a measure of national and personal well-being. Furthermore, there continues to be an assumption that the best way for the economy to grow is to increase the efficiency and speed of production and investment and to encourage people to spend more money faster. If individuals and companies do not borrow and spend money they don't have, and investors do not borrow and invest in securities and financial instruments that are more virtual than real, liquidity dries up and material as well as immaterial flows freeze.

Artful finance. Irrational rationality. Inefficient efficiencies. These problems have not befallen the economy and financial markets from the outside but are intrinsic to the very operation and logic of what capitalism has become today. On November 18, 1956, just three short months before his Kitchen Cabinet with Nixon, Khrushchev famously declared, "We will bury you!" Long before the Berlin Wall fell, it was clear that this prediction was fatally flawed. But the confident assertions of neoliberal economists and neoconservative politicians about the final victory of global capitalism after the collapse of the Soviet Union are premature. It is not communism or socialism that will bury us but ever-increasing speed, which continues to create more material and immaterial waste than we can process—waste that threatens to bury us all.

7. Dividing by Connecting

······································

Lost Horizon

When *Time* magazine published its Death of God cover on Good Friday in 1966, the issues raised were as much social and cultural as religious and theological. The phrase "death of God" effectively captured the tenor of the tumultuous decade of the 1960s. With the war in Vietnam raging; cities burning; and sex, drugs, and rock and roll the gospel of the day, one world seemed to be passing away but it was not yet clear what was emerging to take its place. While many people believed that America had lost its way, others were convinced that the Age of Aquarius marked the dawn of spiritual revival and moral renewal. In the years since the 1960s, the conflicts that plagued the era have deepened and continue to contribute to the gridlock currently paralyzing the country. Once again, the origin of many of these problems can be traced to the Protestant Reformation.

When Thomas Altizer declared the death of God in his infamous book *The Gospel of Christian Atheism* (1963), he was invoking an image that dates back to the Reformation. We have seen that modernism begins with Luther's turn away from the outward rituals and hierarchy of the Catholic Church and toward his own private personality, where he believed the only certain truth could be found. More than two centuries later, Kierkegaard's famous declaration that "truth is subjectivity" summarized this trajectory in a way that rendered explicit the momentous implications of this individualization and privatization of truth and certainty. The unlikely bridge between nineteenth-century Europe and twentieth-century America is the writing of Friedrich Nietzsche. The twentieth century effectively begins with the publication of Freud's *Interpretation of Dreams* and Nietzsche's death in 1900. Freud always said that he refused to read Nietzsche because he feared he would be too influenced by him. These fears were well founded because Nietzsche, more than anyone else, anticipated the confusions, uncertainties, and anxieties of the twentieth century. His metaphor for this seismic cultural shift is the death of God, and it is noteworthy that the site of Nietzsche's most memorable declaration of the death of God is the marketplace.

> The madman jumped into their midst and pierced them with his eyes. "Whither is God?" he cried; "I will tell you. *We have killed him*—you and I. All of us are his murderers. But how did we do this? How could we drink up the sea? Who gave us the sponge to wipe away the horizon? What were we doing when we unchained this earth from its sun? Whither are we moving now? Whither are we moving? Away from all suns? Are we plunging continually? Backward, sideward, forward, in all directions? Is there still any up or down? Are we not straying as though through an infinite nothing? Do we not feel the breath of empty space? Has it not become colder? Is not night continually closing in on us? Do we not need to light lanterns in the morning? Do we hear nothing yet of the noise of the gravediggers who are burying God? Do we smell nothing as yet of the divine decompositions? Gods, too, decompose. God remains dead. And we have killed him.[1]

By the mid-1960s, social, political, and cultural turmoil had created a profound sense of disorientation for a growing number of people. Having lost every stable center as well as foundations that once seemed secure, it was no longer clear what was right and what was wrong, what was up and what was down. Night indeed seemed to be closing in.

The images Nietzsche uses are calculated to provoke: death, graves, and decomposition not only for humans but even for God. There is another image, however, that is always overlooked but is equally telling: "How could we drink up the sea? Who gave us the sponge to wipe away the horizon?" The inward turn to the subject that begins with Luther and Descartes ends with the disappearance of the objective world in subjective experience. This erasure of horizons seals everyone in bubbles that are difficult to escape. Since the images of God, self, and world are always interrelated, it is necessary to amend Nietzsche's proclamation of the death of God. The transcendent God has died and been reborn as the all-powerful human subject, who creates the world in his or her own image. Martin Heidegger recognized Nietzsche's displacement of the traditional creator God with the modern creative subject as the culmination of the entire Western theological and philosophical tradition. In his influential essay "The Question Concerning Technology," he writes that through modern science and technology, man "exalts himself to the posture of lord of the earth. In this way the impression comes to prevail that everything man encounters exists only insofar as it is his own construct. This illusion gives rise to one final delusion: It seems as though man everywhere and always encounters only himself."[2]

Nietzsche calls the bubbles or silos within which individuals are confined "perspectives." He was convinced that there is no underlying or overarching meaning or purpose to life; rather, the world is nothing more than the ceaseless flux of insubstantial appearances that can be interpreted in an infinite number of ways. In one of his most notorious aphorisms, Nietzsche writes, "Against positivism, which halts at phenomena—'There are only *facts*'—I would say: No, facts is precisely what there are not, only interpretations. We cannot establish any fact 'in itself': perhaps it is folly to want to do such a thing."[3] For Nietzsche, there is no such thing as absolute truth or objective facts because truth as well as facts are always interpreted from the perspective of a particular individual. "'Interpretation,' the introduction of meaning—not 'explanation,'" he insists. "There are no facts, everything is in flux, incomprehensible, elusive; what is relatively most enduring is—our opinions." If there are no facts but only interpretations, and if all interpretations are determined by contrasting and often conflicting perspectives, then truth is relative. Nietzsche's conclusion echoes a moment in Fyodor Dostoyevsky's *The Brothers Karamazov*.

> The deeper one looks, the more our valuations disappear—meaninglessness approaches! We have *created* the world that possesses values! Knowing this, we know, too, that the reverence for truth is already the consequence of an illusion—and that one should value more than truth the force that forms, simplifies, shapes, invents.
>
> "Everything is false! Everything is permitted!"[4]

By the late twentieth and early twenty-first centuries, Nietzsche's perspectives, which he interpreted as conflicting expressions of "the will to power," had become bubbles and silos created and reinforced by proliferating high-speed, 24/7 information and media networks. Contrary to expectation, increasing connectivity has led to deeper divisions and more hostile oppositions. It would be a mistake, however, to attribute growing local, national, and global conflict solely to emerging technologies. During the past half-century, religious and cultural disagreements have promoted social and political divisions, which eventually led to a largely unnoticed internal migration that has further fragmented the country. To appreciate the magnitude of the problems this fragmentation has created, it is necessary to understand how and why these divisions have emerged. Once again, the mutually reinforcing interplay of flows that are both material (people) and immaterial (data and media) have proven transformative.

Bubble Machines

In the spring of 1969, university campuses in the United States and many other countries erupted. While diagnoses of the specific ills plaguing society differed, young people were united in labeling the cause of the problems they sought to remedy "The System." Though it was rarely clear precisely what this term specified, it captured a widespread sense that invasive social and political structures had become repressive. According to many young people in the 1960s, the burning question became how to cultivate experiences and activities that could elude, resist, or even overturn the system. Some followed Freud and Timothy Leary and argued that it was necessary first to change consciousness before it would be possible to change the world. Turning further inward, they, like countless Eastern and Western mystics before them, sought from drugs a transformation of awareness that they believed would lead to a New Age. Others, following Marx and Herbert Marcuse, insisted that it was necessary to change the world in order to change individual awareness, values, and practices. Turning outward, they sought to transform society through radical political action, which would usher in the utopia in which the modern artistic avant-garde had always believed. While followers of mainline religion saw this youth rebellion as a rejection of everything in which they believed, the counter culture was actually a spiritual movement that paralleled important developments that were beginning to take place on the fringes of Catholic and Protestant Christianity.

The New Religious Right emerged as a counter-counter culture that was made possible by forging unlikely alliances. In the early years of the twentieth century, Protestant fundamentalism burst on the scene as a strident anti-Catholic reaction to the influx of Italian, Eastern European, and especially Irish immigrants in many East Coast cities. Tensions between Protestants and Catholics persisted until the late 1960s, when church leaders and their followers decided that social issues trumped theological disagreements. A major factor contributing to this unexpected development was the increasing diversity of the United States. Protestants and Catholics found common cause in their opposition to new immigrants, who seemed to be socially, economically, and politically more different from them than the two religious camps were from each other. Both groups also believed that growing secularism and creeping humanism posed the threat of a godless society, which for true believers would mark the end of Western civilization. From its inception, the New Religious Right has been vehemently anti-communist and has radically opposed anything its followers think even hints at socialism.

It is important to stress just how much the role of religion in American life changed during the latter half of the twentieth century. In 1960, John Kennedy had to travel to Houston to reassure fundamentalists and evangelicals, who were nervous about the prospect of a Catholic in the White House, that he believed "in an America where the separation of church and state is absolute—where no Catholic prelate would tell the President (should he be Catholic) how to act, and no Protestant minister would tell his parishioners for whom to vote—where no church or church school is granted any public funds or public preference—and where no man is denied public office merely because his religion differs from the President who might appoint him or the people who might elect him."[5] By 2004, this situation had changed completely: Cardinal Joseph Ratzinger, with the support of Pope John Paul II, intervened in the American presidential campaign *against* the Roman Catholic John Kerry and in support of the evangelical Protestant George W. Bush. Ratzinger wrote a letter to American bishops instructing them to deny communion to any Catholic candidate who refused to criminalize abortion. Underscoring his point, the future pope wrote: "The case of a Catholic politician consistently campaigning and voting for permissive abortion and euthanasia laws" was "guilty of formal cooperation with evil and so unworthy to present himself for Holy Communion." The difference between the 1960 and 2004 presidential elections shows both how much and how little things have changed since then.

After the end of World War II, the emergence of a national liberal political agenda, consumer culture, and the Cold War combined to create conditions favorable to a widespread return of fundamentalism and evangelicalism. Three factors in the political, social, and cultural developments of the 1960s were decisive in changing the aversion to politics that had long characterized conservative Christianity: (1) the expansion of government power and growth of social welfare programs, (2) what was perceived as an increasingly active federal judiciary, and (3) the revolution in values brought by the counter culture. During the postwar period, there was an unprecedented increase in federal spending for national defense, public education, and entitlement programs. What began with Roosevelt's New Deal culminated in Johnson's Great Society. By the 1960s, social welfare programs and civil rights initiatives were coming together in a broad range of policy initiatives that religious and political conservatives found very troubling. With the rapid expansion of the federal government, there was an inevitable growth in regulations governing many aspects of life.

In the polarized climate created by the Cold War, many conservatives argued that these political and economic initiatives were leading the country down the road to socialism, which eventually would lead to communism. Such fears seemed to be confirmed by the actions of the federal judiciary, especially during the era of the Warren Court (1953–69). In the 1950s, the growing Soviet threat had led to the resurgence of anti-communism and, correspondingly, a marked rise in nationalism and patriotism. With Joseph McCarthy fanning the flames of a second Red Scare, Congress passed legislation to insert "under God" into the pledge of allegiance; a year later a bill to add the inscription "In God We Trust" on all currency and coins was approved. Less than a decade later, in 1963, the country seemed to reverse direction when the Supreme Court banned school prayer. Writing for the majority in two critical cases, Justice Hugo Black stated that it was "no part of the business of government to compose official prayers." The following year, the Court ruled that Bible reading in schools is unconstitutional. As one of the most outspoken critics of these decisions, Billy Graham declared that the ruling was "a most dangerous trend" and signaled "another step toward secularism in the United States."[6] For many conservatives, these decisions represented a further move to the Left that had begun with the *Brown v. Board of Education of Topeka* ruling in 1954. As one Alabama legislator put it, the justices had "put Negroes in the schools and now they've driven God out."[7]

Just as the counter culture was not monolithic but instead consisted of contrasting personalistic and political poles, so too the counter-counter culture was not uniform but initially was split between Evangelicals and Pentecostals, on the one hand, who were preoccupied with personal transformation brought about through an individual relationship to Jesus Christ, and on the other, Fundamentalists, who believed in scriptural inerrancy and sought to impose their literalism on not only the Supreme Court but also what they took to be the Constitution. Jimmy Carter, not Ronald Reagan, was the first born-again president, and there is considerable evidence to support the claim that Carter took religion much more seriously than Reagan ever did. During his campaign, Carter enjoyed widespread support among many religious conservatives as a result of his decision to make restoration of the integrity of the family a cornerstone of his campaign. After the election, however, Evangelicals began to wonder whether Carter was their kind of conservative. While they were disillusioned by his failure to cut taxes and curtail welfare, the issue that led to Carter's split with the New Religious Right was his support for the Equal Rights Amendment. Concerned about the impact of this bill on the family, a group of conservative religious leaders, which included Oral Roberts, Jerry Falwell, Jim Bakker, and, most important, Timothy LaHaye, met with Carter to discuss his position. When he insisted on the importance of ensuring equal rights for women, these religious leaders decided to withdraw their support. That decision as much as anything else led to the election of Ronald Reagan as the fortieth president of the United States. The New Religious Right joined forces with neoconservative politicians to forge a program that was largely defined by what it opposed. These new true believers were antimodernists, antisecularists, anticommunists, antisocialists, antihumanists, antiliberals, antirelativists, antifeminists, antielitists, antiscience, and antigay. Unfortunately, this agenda still sounds all-too-familiar today.

While there were many reasons for these developments, the major contributing factors were racial politics and economic policies that had been designed to provide a social safety net and ensure a more equitable distribution of wealth. Religious ideology often masked personal and political prejudice as well as economic self-interest. With segregation breaking down and big government expanding, once-solid Democratic Dixie turned red. But something else was going on that eventually would intersect with these developments in unexpected ways. Some talented kids dropping acid in the suburbs of San Francisco were hanging out in garages, meeting at the Home Brew Computer Club, and creating the personal computer, which they believed would liberate individuals from systems they deemed repressive.

One or Many?

Throughout the history of Western philosophy, the most persistent issue has been the problem of the one and the many. Is reality fundamentally one or many? This question is theological as well as philosophical—Is there only one God (monotheism), or are there many gods (polytheism)? We have discovered that images of God, self, and world are inseparable; it is, therefore, important to note that the question of the one and the many also raises psychological, social, and political issues. Is the self unified or plural? Is society integrated or segregated? Are communities inclusive or exclusive? The perennial issue of the relation between the whole and parts is a variation of the problem of the one and the many. Since the 1960s, the sense of the whole has been steadily eclipsed by the progressive fragmentation of both self and society. New technologies like the telegraph, radio, television, and, more recently, the Internet and World Wide Web, hold out hope of restoring or creating this sense of wholeness by providing the means of communication that will enable people to overcome their differences. The reality invariably turns out to be very different—technologies intended to unite people usually end up dividing them. Instead of a global village animated by the nervous system of electronic technology, we have been left with a fragmented world in which real walls are built to keep out illegal immigrants, and virtual walls are created to protect government secrets and virtual financial assets circulating around the world at the speed of light. In a pattern we will see repeated elsewhere, increasing connectivity through high-speed transportation, information, communications, and financial networks not only draws people closer together, but also creates deep social, political, and economic divisions.

In his extremely illuminating book *The Big Sort: Why the Clustering of Like-Minded America Is Tearing Us Apart,* Bill Bishop argues that during the past several decades, there has been an "ideological Balkanization of America," which has been the result of a massive internal migration. This shift is reflected not only in the division between red and blue states, but more important, in the redistribution of the population at local and county levels. The numbers are surprising—4 to 5 percent of the people in the United States move to a different county every year; during the 1990s, more than one hundred million people changed counties. Bishop's data are significant because they show not only the number of people who have moved, but also the pattern of their movement. People are moving from more diverse to more homogeneous communities and as a result, the country is becoming less integrated and more segregated. "The picture the United States had of itself in the 1950s, 1960s, and 1970s," Bishop writes, "was of a nation that was increasingly becoming one—religiously, politically, and economically. From the 1950s through the mid-1970s, communities did grow more politically integrated."[8] But in the early 1970s, this trajectory suddenly reversed: the country started becoming more divided and communities became increasingly segmented.

There were many reasons that this tectonic shift was not widely recognized at the time. The cultural conflicts of the 1960s set in motion a political, economic, and religious movement to the right whose far-reaching implications would not become clear for several decades. Earlier internal migrations in the United States were largely the result of economic rather than cultural factors. People who otherwise might not have wanted to move were forced to leave familiar communities for other parts of the country that they often found strange or even hostile. While economic hardship contributed significantly to internal migration after 1970 and continues to be a major factor in immigration from foreign countries today, Bishop insists that the population flows from 1970 to 2000 were motivated by different factors. People "were reordering their lives around their values, their tastes, and their beliefs. They were clustering in communities of like-mindedness, and not just geographically. Churches grew more politically homogeneous during this time, and so did civic clubs, volunteer organizations, and, dramatically, political parties. People weren't simply moving. The whole society was changing."[9] This very important point deserves emphasis. People were moving not simply because of economic hardship, though in many cases this has continued to play a role. Instead they were relocating by free choice, influenced as much or perhaps even more by matters of faith, culture, education, and lifestyle as by economic duress. As a result of these changes, more and more like-minded people were living in enclaves of homogeneous communities. Examining data gathered in Texas between 2004 and 2006, Alan Abramowitz and Bruce Oppenheimer report, "Americans are increasingly living in communities and neighborhoods whose residents share their values and they are increasingly voting for candidates who reflect those values."[10] In a growing number of communities, real and virtual fences along with real and virtual security guards are being enlisted to protect these enclaves from intrusions by strangers deemed undesirable or even dangerous.

These changes pose a puzzling question: Do deliberate political policies and practices lead to geographical migration, or does the process of self-sorting reform the political landscape? In ways that will become clear later, high-speed information and communications networks contribute to this process. On the one hand, some analysts argue that faster computers make it possible to collect, store, and process more data that can be used to develop blueprints for sophisticated gerrymandering, which makes elections less competitive. This creates a self-reinforcing loop that is further strengthened when fast, cheap, and ubiquitous media networks promote candidates with limited political agendas. On the other hand, some analysts maintain that internal migration at the grassroots level is reflected in the redistribution of political power between the two parties. In other words, population movement drives politics and hence policy, rather than the reverse. The truth lies somewhere in between. The flow of real people influences the flow of ideas and information, and the flow of ideas and information influences the flow of real people. While this situation is not new, the speed at which it is occurring is unprecedented.

This process of self-sorting has led to deepening political, social, and economic divisions. To appreciate the significance of these changes, it is important to underscore how recent they are. During the 1950s, only one-third of voters could identify the differences between the two political parties, and even in the wake of Senator Joseph McCarthy's Red Scare, only half the people in the country knew the policy differences between conservatives and liberals. "The American ideal," Bishop argues, "was to get along. The national goal was moderation and consensus. Given the trauma of the Great Depression and the horrors of World War II, these were reasonable objectives." But there can be a downside to consensus. Though it seems incongruous today, during the postwar period some commentators feared that political parties were losing their distinct identities and argued that bipartisanship and moderation could go too far. In 1950, the American Political Science Association actually issued the results of a four-year study that concluded by "calling for the return of ideologically distinct and powerful political parties."[11]

Another important difference between the 1950s and 1960s that contributed to these developments was the change in people's attitudes toward government. In the late 1950s, eight in ten Americans supported most government policies, programs, and actions, but by 1976, the approval level had dropped to only 33 percent.[12] The economic, political, social, and cultural upheavals of the 1960s were the primary factors contributing to this change in attitudes. It is rarely noted, however, that this mistrust of government was shared by people on both ends of the political spectrum. As is often the case, extremes meet—the views of some members of the counter culture (Left) and some members of the counter-counter culture (Right) overlapped more than they realized.

We have seen that there were two poles of the counter culture in the 1960s—a politically active pole that sought to change the world in order to change individual lives, and a more spiritually oriented pole that sought to change individual consciousness to change the world. While Evangelicals and Pentecostals cultivated personal renewal through religious rituals and a personal relationship with Jesus Christ, hippies searched for authenticity through personal experiences brought about through sex, drugs, and rock and roll. During the 1960s, youthful protesters from both camps called for dismantling a political system that they found individually and socially repressive. For the political activists, the solution was not less government but bigger government modeled on socialist or even communist systems. Hippies, by contrast, were preoccupied with individual experience and remained suspicious of all government interference. To the extent that they had any politics, they tended to be libertarian. Though opposite in countless ways, religious, political, and cultural radicals on the Right as well as the Left joined in the call to get government off the backs of people.[13] Once again, the underlying issue was the relationship between the individual and the larger social whole. Conservative Christians and drug-crazed hippies and yippies placed the highest value on individuality and were relentlessly critical of any system, structure, or institution that might infringe on an individual's rights. This strange alliance between the counter culture and the counter-counter culture created the conditions for the technological and economic revolutions that began in the 1970s.

Splicing and Dicing Big Data

Though I lived through this period, I did not understand much of what was going on around me until several decades later. Having been introduced to the worlds of art and architecture through my discussions with artists, architects, and museum directors during the late 1980s and 1990s, I became aware of how much technology was transforming creative endeavors in many areas as well as the infrastructure of society and the economy. In an effort to gain a better understanding of this new world, in the spring of 1988 I visited the MIT Media Lab, which had begun as a branch of the architecture school. The director, Nicholas Negroponte, and his colleagues were most cordial and very generous with their time. The lab was divided into teams, each of which was working on different projects. The three groups I remember best were robotics, prosthetics, and the personalized newspaper. At the time, the idea of publishing an individualized newspaper for every person seemed to be a complete fantasy. It was, however, clear that Negroponte and his colleagues were not only serious about this project, but also had no doubt such publications would soon be available to anyone who wanted them. Seven years later, Negroponte described his vision for the future of news media and the world their new format would represent in his best-selling book *Being Digital.* "Imagine a future in which your interface agent can read every newswire and newspaper and catch every TV and radio broadcast on the planet, and then construct a personalized summary. This kind of newspaper is printed in an edition of one." He called this innovation *The Daily Me.*[14]

The longer I thought about Negroponte's project, the more I began to see that it is actually the logical conclusion of the print revolution that started with Gutenberg's printing press and Luther's Bible five centuries earlier. While the printing press led to the standardization of publications and transformed the way people write, it also privatized communication. Oral culture was of necessity more communal than print culture; with print and the advent of silent reading, people could wrap themselves in their own cocoons. Commenting on the solitude and isolation of the reading experience, some early critics of print sounded like today's parents worried about their kids sitting alone in front of computer screens or mobile devices playing video games and texting with friends they rarely, if ever, see.

By 1995, the pieces were in place to begin to make Negroponte's dream a reality. *Being Digital* appeared at what former Intel CEO Andy Grove has labeled an "inflection point" between old and new ways of communicating and, equally important, advertising. We have seen that for mass production to be profitable, it was necessary to create mass consumption. This required developing new industries ranging from mass transportation and mass communication to mass advertising. Throughout World War I the primary medium for advertising was print and to a lesser degree radio, but after World War II, mass advertising shifted to television. Although the first regular television station was established in 1940 (WNBT in New York City) and CBS and NBC started commercial transmission in 1941, network telecasts did not begin until 1949. What made television so attractive to businesses was its capacity to expand advertising beyond anything that previously had been possible. Nationwide advertising vastly extended mass markets and led to growing product standardization. While regional and personal differences did not completely disappear, the increasing uniformity of products contributed to greater social homogenization throughout the 1950s. Colors might differ but models remained pretty much the same. Gray flannel suits and Levittown had become emblematic of a sameness that a growing number of people found stifling—so much so that philandering "mad men" on Madison Avenue and "desperate housewives" in the suburbs sought relief behind closed doors by crossing lines they still imposed on their teenage children.

By the end of the decade, technologies were beginning to emerge that would change the way the world does business and people live their lives. As late as the 1990s, most major advertisers still thought TV was the most effective medium for promoting brands and selling products. A few prescient entrepreneurs, however, quickly realized that the Internet and World Wide Web marked the end of the era of mass communications and everything that went with it. One of the reasons it took people so long to recognize the commercial potential of the Internet was that it had been invented for military purposes. In the early 1960s, the U.S. government became concerned about the possibility of the disruption or even the destruction of the nation's communications system. The Department of Defense undertook an intensive research program that resulted in a robust communications system comprised of multiple computers connected in a network made up of smaller, more localized networks. The structure of this system was cellular. What came to be known as the Internet, then, was from the beginning quite literally an inter-net, that is, a network of connected and communicating networks. The decentralized and distributed structure of the Internet was intended to provide security that was not possible with a centralized system. It is important to note that the contrast between hierarchical, centralized networks operating through a mainframe and decentralized, distributed networks operating through personal computers and eventually mobile devices mirrors the difference between the structure of communism or socialism (totality over individuals; whole over part) and capitalism (individuals over socio-political totality; parts over whole). While there was some recognition of the commercial potential of this new technology, for security reasons, the early use of the Internet was largely restricted to military use and in some cases to research at major universities, much of which was classified.

These restrictions were eventually lifted, but other hurdles remained. In the early days of the Internet all communication was text-based. When I taught a tele-seminar with Helsinki in 1992, no student at Williams College or the University of Helsinki had used the Internet and all of our online exchanges were typed; just three years later, there were over twenty-five million Internet users. This rapid growth created both unprecedented opportunities and unexpected challenges. With more users and a greater amount of information circulating around the world faster and faster, it was increasingly difficult to navigate the Net and to find the information for which one was searching quickly and easily.

This situation suddenly changed with the introduction of the graphic interface—first Mosaic (1993) and then Netscape (1995). The success of Netscape was the result of collaboration between two unlikely partners, Marc Andreessen, a twenty-one-year-old graduate student at the University of Illinois, Urbana-Champaign, and Jim Clark, founder of Silicon Graphics and Healtheon and a major Silicon Valley investor. By developing an intuitive graphical interface, Netscape made the Web both accessible and potentially ubiquitous. While at the University of Illinois, Andreessen had worked at the National Center for Supercomputing Applications and had been a member of the team that created Mosaic, which used simple graphic software. "When Mosaic appeared," John Cassidy reports, "less than one percent of Internet traffic was on the World Wide Web. Two years later, the Web was the most popular thing on the Internet, accounting for about one quarter of all traffic. Mosaic was responsible for the transformation."[15] In 1994, Clark and Andreesen founded Mosaic Communications, which they later renamed Netscape as part of the settlement of a legal case that the University of

Illinois had brought against the company. Clark provided initial funding of $3 million and within a year, the legendary Wall Street analyst Mary Meeker took the company public. Netscape's stock soared to $170 a share, giving the company a valuation of $6.5 billion in less than six months. This IPO started the dot-com boom, which, of course, eventually went bust. Shortly thereafter, Meeker and Chris DePuy published *The Internet Report,* which quickly became the bible for dot-com entrepreneurs and investors. Morgan Stanley distributed over 300,000 copies of the report before HarperCollins issued a paperback edition. The lengthy study predicted that the explosive growth of information and network technologies would create a period of unprecedented financial opportunity.

What almost no one noticed at the time was that a seemingly insignificant technical decision in the design of Netscape would transform business and by extension change the world. This innovation was the cookie. In his book *The Daily You: How the New Advertising Industry Is Defining Your Identity and Your Worth,* Joseph Turow goes so far as to suggest that ultimately the cookie "would do more to shape advertising—and social attention—on the Web than any other invention apart from the browser itself." A cookie consists of data sent from a website that is stored on a user's computer in order to collect and transmit data about a person's online activity. Over time, cookies record a history of use that provides valuable information about a person's interests, preferences, activities, personal friends, and professional associates. The cookie was developed in 1994 by Lou Montulli to solve a marketing problem for Netscape. The code was initially intended to serve as something like a shopping cart that "enables a website to keep track of the different items that a customer sets aside for purchase. Without a way to identify the customer, every click to put an item in the cart would appear to the online store as if it were originating from a different person."[16] Once installed, the cookie could track the activity of users at any time, including all purchases and every website visited. Montulli and his colleagues made a fateful decision about the deployment of cookie technology—they allowed cookies to operate without asking users' permission to install them. In 1995, Microsoft followed Netscape by incorporating cookie capability in the first version of Internet Explorer. Michael Wallent, who was the director of Microsoft's browser project, admitted that the prospect of profits trumped concerns about transparency and privacy. "I don't think anyone ever thought that cookies were anything that could be excluded in the browser and have that browser become a success in the marketplace."[17] Today the fifty leading Internet sites install an average of sixty-four cookies each on the computers of every user who visits them.[18]

The deregulation of the telecommunications industry during the 1980s prepared the way for early commercial networks like Compu-Serve (1979), Prodigy (1982), and AOL (1985), which was founded by one of my former students at Williams, Steve Case. The National Science Foundation did not turn over control of the network structure on which the Internet depends to commercial interests until 1994. The timing for Netscape could not have been better. During the 1990s, it was not clear how the Internet and World Wide Web could be monetized. Since the Internet had begun with government support and initially had been used by universities for scholarly purposes, there was a tradition of not charging for material distributed online. This policy was reinforced by the political persuasions of many early innovators and users whose motto was "information wants to be free." By "free" they meant free to circulate without either restrictions or cost. To make money in the highly competitive financial and consumer markets of the 1990s, however, information could neither circulate freely nor cost nothing.

Early strategies for monetizing the Internet and World Wide Web involved advertising. Companies, advertising agencies, and dot-com entrepreneurs took magazines and newspapers as their model for marketing campaigns. The accepted method of assessing the value of companies for potential investors was to calculate potential advertising revenue based on the number of "hits," or site visits. The problem with this method of assessing advertising effectiveness was speed—even with cookie technology it was at that time impossible to collect, process, and manage data quickly enough to adjust production, marketing, and distribution in a timely manner. The bottom line was that there was absolutely no way to determine the real or potential value of any of these new online companies. Implicitly acknowledging this fact, venture capital firms adopted their own version of hedging by betting on ten companies: although the managers knew nine would fail, the hope was that one would hit it so big that it would more than make up for any losses.

By 2010, everything had changed and once again the reason was a significant increase in computational and processing speed. In 2009, Facebook founder Mark Zuckerberg responded to Twitter's rapid growth by reassuring his one billion active monthly users that the company would "increase the pace of the stream" and "continue making the flow of information even faster."[19] The extraordinary changes in media and technology during the past few years are the result of the intersection of four technological innovations: super high-speed, low-cost computing; super high-speed algorithmic data-processing capabilities; the cloud for storage of massive amounts of information; and what is widely labeled "big data."

These changes have brought about a fundamental transformation in the way people do business. New media, information, and communications technologies have led to a shift from mass consumption to mass customization. We have seen that markets can expand spatially, by opening stores and offices in new cities and countries; differentially, by introducing more options for consumers; and temporally, by accelerating the product cycle. When increasing speed and efficiency lead to excess production, businesses often use all three of these strategies to increase their profits. During the first half of the twentieth century, mass production, mass consumption, and mass media formed feedback loops in which each drove the others. During the latter half of the twentieth century and first decade of the twenty-first century, the emergence of super-high-speed computers that can gather, store, and process information as well as personal computers, portable tablets, and mobile phones created the possibility of tracking and targeting customers and consumers with products designed for their individual interests and tastes.

Big data has become big business. Omar Tawakol, who founded Blue-Kai, one of the biggest of the big data companies, in 2008, has rightly declared, "Oil was to the industrial revolution as data is to our information economy."[20] In recent years, the speed of computers has continued to increase at the same time that relatively low-cost machines have been connected in distributed networks that can store data and access it quickly. With the advent of cloud computing, businesses effectively outsourced their information-technology operations and started to share resources to achieve economies of scale. Companies provided what is known as "converged infrastructure" and shared services that work something like a utility similar to the electricity grid. Rent, don't own is the motto for cloud computing. While individual commercial networks remain proprietary, increased connectivity among networks makes it possible to process more data at a higher speed.

It is difficult to calculate the scope of the recent data explosion. In a special issue of the *Harvard Business Review* devoted to big data, Andrew McAfee and Erik Brynjolfsson report that "as of 2012 about 2.5 exabytes of data are created each day, and that number is doubling every month. More data cross the internet every second than were stored in the entire internet just 20 years ago. This gives companies an opportunity to work with many petabytes of data in a single data set—and not just from the internet. For instance, it is estimated that Wal-Mart collects more than 2.5 petabytes of data every hour from its customer transactions. A petabyte is one quadrillion [that is, 1,000,000,000,000,000] bytes, or the equivalent to about 20 million filing cabinets' worth of text. An exabyte is 1,000 times that amount or one million gigabytes." The incomprehensible amount of data that is being collected and the astonishing speed at which it is being processed and distributed are transforming business as well as life. McAfee and Brynjolfsson continue, "For many applications, the speed of data creation is even more important than the volume. Real-time or nearly real-time information makes it possible for a company to be much more agile than its competitors. For instance, our colleague Alex 'Sandy' Pentland and his group at the MIT Media Lab used location data from mobile phones to infer how many people were in Macy's parking lots on Black Friday—the start of the Christmas shopping season in the United States. This made it possible to estimate the retailer's sales on that critical day even before Macy's itself had recorded those sales. Rapid insights like that can provide an obvious competitive advantage to Wall Street analysts and Main Street managers."[21] McAfee and Brynjolfsson argue that these innovations are creating an unprecedented management revolution. What few commentators realize is that these developments are actually an extension and acceleration of the management revolution brought about by the invention and networking of the telegraph, telephone, and stock ticker, as well as the copying, calculating, organizing, and filing systems that accompanied the Industrial Revolution.

One of the first people to recognize the implications of big data for marketing was Jeff Bezos, the founder and CEO of Amazon. In the early years of commercialization of the Internet and World Wide Web, most people thought that money would be made by selling ads on websites or selling what could be transmitted over networks: music, video, financial assets, and eventually, even educational materials. Bezos did not deny that there were profits to be made that way, but he was more interested in selling real stuff online. He also knew that in virtual space, unlike real space, there are no limits to expansion—hence the name Amazon. Most people were skeptical when Bezos founded his company in 1994, but he remained boundlessly optimistic. His high-powered pitches always included impressive charts and graphs predicting a rosy future for Amazon and an entirely new model for retailing. Bezos's calculations presented what he referred to as "pro-forma profits," which, he explained, "is what our profit will be when we start making a profit." Though it took a few years, Bezos eventually had the last laugh and former skeptics were left scrambling to catch up, which in networked economies is nearly always a losing position. Books were just the beginning; it is now clear that the company's ambition is to sell everything and become the largest retailer on earth.

Amazon's success was due not only to the size and speed of its operation but also to Bezos's early recognition of the value of data. From the first days of the company, Amazon's leadership developed software to collect and manage data about consumers' preferences and habits, which they used to promote its products. Others were slow to grasp the implication of Amazon's strategy. Information is valuable not only to sell commodities; it can also be commodified and sold for big profits. Amazon seeks to have it both ways—it uses the data it gathers to market its own products and, with its big bet on the cloud computing business, it sells its data to other companies to market their own products.

The more companies know about their customers, the better they can be tracked and targeted. By employing increasingly sophisticated surveillance technologies, advertisers are devising new ways not only to respond to consumer demand but also, more perniciously, to shape their desires. In a 2010 *Wall Street Journal* interview with Holman Jenkins entitled "Google and the Search for the Future," Google CEO Eric Schmidt offered a glimpse of the world he believes is just around the corner. "I actually think most people don't want Google to answer their questions. They want Google to tell them what they should be doing next." Schmidt predicts that increasingly powerful handheld devices will make it possible to produce serendipity electronically. Google telling us what to search; Google telling us what to think; Google telling us what questions to ask; Google telling us what to want; Google telling us what to do; Google telling us what to buy; Google programming serendipity. The problem is that programmed serendipity is not serendipity at all.

If data is the oil of the information age, then the search engine is to the information revolution what the steam engine was to the Industrial Revolution. Information and data do you no good if you can't access them quickly. Though the competition has become fierce, the big winner in the search engine wars for now is still Google. Google has become such a pervasive and invasive presence in the lives of everyone that it is difficult to recall how new the company is and how fast it has grown. Founded in 1996 by two Stanford graduate students, Larry Page and Sergey Brin, the company went public in 2004. Google's technology is so transformative because of its size and speed—its competitors cannot match the amount of data Google collects and the speed at which it processes and distributes them. "To understand why marketers would get so excited about search engine advertising," Turow explains, "consider that for decades they had been fixated on what they call the 'purchase funnel' or 'consumer decision journey'—the multistage trip that people take when they make a purchase, from awareness of product choices to action on those choices. Google's innovations meant that, for the first time, advertisers could reach out to huge numbers of *individuals* as they took consumer decisions journeys online. Marketers hoped to connect to those individuals conducting Google searches with products that mirror the interests expressed by the search terms, using two approaches: search-engine optimization (SEO) and paid search."[22]

The extent of Google's domination of the search market is stunning —80 percent of all searches and 98 percent of mobile searches are done on Google. Just four years after Google's IPO, the company controlled 78 percent of the global search business and was making $22 billion annually. In 2010, Schmidt disclosed that in two days Google creates as much data—approximately 5 exabytes—as the world produced from the beginning of humanity to 2003.[23] Since time is money in the search business, Google has developed Spanner, the largest database in the world, to synchronize the entire network by using GPS and atomic clocks to ensure global consistency. Andrew Fikes describes Spanner as "a new-age database . . . that stretches across the globe while behaving as if it's all in one place. . . . It's the first worldwide database worthy of the name—a database designed to seamlessly operate across hundreds of data centers and millions of machines and trillions of rows of information. Spanner is a creation so large, some have trouble wrapping their heads around it. But the end result is easily explained: With Spanner, Google can offer a web service to a worldwide audience, but still ensure that something happening on the service in one part of the world doesn't contradict what's happening in another."[24] Once omnipresence and omniscience become technological realities, can omnipotence be far behind?

Even such rapid exponential growth is not enough for Google; engineers are now working 24/7/365 to increase the efficiency and speed of search. Data companies are in a high-speed race for what is known as "semantic search" capability. Trained as computer scientists, Page and Brin have always seen Google as an artificial-intelligence company; their genius has been to develop a search engine that uses a combination of page ranking and targeted terms or categories. One of the difficulties with this method, however, is that the meaning of terms is often lost when they are taken out of context. Though computers are capable of storing and processing massive amounts of information, they are actually dumb because they cannot understand the meaning or significance of the information they store. This limitation creates inefficiencies in searches. Everyone has had the experience of typing in a specific word or term and instantly receiving dozens of irrelevant references. Semantic search would overcome this difficulty by taking the context of the term into consideration and thereby determining a greater specificity of meaning, which would greatly increase the efficiency of searches.

In January 2013, Google announced the appointment of Ray Kurzweil —author, inventor, entrepreneur, futurist, prophet of the approaching "singularity," and co-founder of Silicon Valley's fashionable Singularity University—as its new director of engineering. The goal of Kurzweil's research at Google is to develop computers that can understand the language of the texts they process. It was appropriate that Kurzweil gave his first interview about his new position at Singularity University's NASA campus. According to its website, Singularity University was created by Kurzweil, Larry Page, and several other Silicon Valley tycoons "to educate, inspire and empower leaders to apply exponential technologies to address humanity's grand challenges." While its founders regard Singularity University as a radically new kind of educational institution, it actually stands in a long tradition that dates back to the beginning of the modern era. Singularity University is where New Age utopianism meets high-tech for the twenty-first century. For Kurzweil, creating computers that can read and think is part of meeting humanity's greatest challenge, which is death. To many high-powered software engineers and virtual reality virtuosos, the body is little more than meat, and death is nothing more than one more engineering problem. Though the technology Kurzweil and his buddies deploy is new, the dream is as ancient as humanity—immortality. These latter-day devotees actually believe that in less than fifty years, technology will enable people to live for several hundred years and in the not-too-distant future, it will be possible to live forever. This dream, however, is as much an illusion now as it was in the time of Plato. Since the immaterial and the material are inseparably intertwined, it is impossible to escape bodily mortality.

For those who cling to the future of this illusion, an important step toward this goal would be the creation of an artificial brain that can understand the meaning of concepts. Schmidt explains the importance of semantic search by using what he describes as "the hotdog problem." "Is it a 'hot dog' or a 'hotdog.' And, if you knew something about whether the person had dogs, or whether the person was a vegetarian, you'd have a very different potential answer to that question." With the ability to understand meaning contextually and to track the activity of people both online and offline, semantic search would enable Google to anticipate questions and provide answers before a person even asks them. Kurzweil's plan is to create what he calls a "cybernetic friend"—a search engine so powerful that "it knows users better than they know themselves." Ever the futurist, he confidently predicts, "I envision in some years that the majority of search queries will be answered without your actually asking."[25] Reclusive Russian multimillionaire and former online media tycoon Dmitry Itskov takes this idea even further. He has launched 2045 Initiative, which is dedicated to the "mass production of lifelike, low-cost avatars that can be uploaded with the contents of a human brain, complete with all particulars of consciousness and personality."[26] At this point, the human-machine loop begins to close and we enter what technophiles label "the posthuman era."

Google's domination of the search business should not obscure the recent emergence of other powerful companies whose names most people have never heard. Consider, for example, Acxiom, which was founded in 1969 and is based in Little Rock, Arkansas, where the company has more than 23,000 computers on five acres. Every week more than one trillion transactions take place on Acxiom's network. During the fiscal year ending in 2012, Acxiom posted a profit of $77.26 million on sales of $1.13 billion.[27] According to Eli Pariser, the company has data on about 96 percent of American households and half a billion people worldwide. Acxiom makes money by providing this data to its clients, most of whom use it for marketing purposes. It is, of course, possible to use data for other purposes, which might be either beneficial or harmful.

Scandals in Washington have raised awareness and increased concerns about the theft, misuse, and sale of data by individuals, criminals, corporations, and most disturbing, governments. In response to growing resistance to big data, Acxiom recently launched a public-relations campaign to reassure people that personal information would not be misused. A website, AbouttheData.com, now allows consumers to view personal data that the company stores in its marketing databases. Natasha Singer reports that the data on this site include "biographical facts, like education level, marital status and number of children in a household; homeownership status, including mortgage amount and property size; vehicle details, like the make, model and year; and economic data, like whether a household member is an active investor with a portfolio greater than $150,000. Also available will be the customer's recent purchase categories, like plus-size clothing or sports products; and household interests like golf, dogs, text-messaging, cholesterol-related products or charities."[28] It remains to be seen whether Acxiom's new policy will provide more transparency or is just another way for the company to collect more data. The initial signs are not encouraging. When Singer went to AbouttheData.com, she was unable to access her own marketing profile. Upon investigation, she discovered that after she had published an article about having trouble accessing her Acxiom files, the company had excluded her from its marketing databases.

While new companies continue to proliferate and in some cases grow at an unprecedented rate, the big keep getting bigger. Until recently, Apple accounted for 4.3 percent of the S&P index and 1.1 percent of the global equity market. Amazon continues to dominate online retail as well as electronic books. Less often noticed but probably more important for the future, Amazon is making a huge bet on cloud computing, which is predicted to result in big profits from big data. While Facebook has not come up with a proven financial model, its strategy involves monetizing the personal data of its billion users. One of the reasons Amazon is willing to sell the Kindle at such a low price is that the value of the device derives less from selling books than from gathering data about consumers' choices. While it is still too early to know what Bezos's plans are for the *Washington Post,* there can be little doubt that this publication will provide additional data that he can turn to financial advantage in other business ventures. Sales, data, and information are mutually reinforcing. The more products sold, the more data are collected, and the more data at companies' disposal, the more products they can sell, which in turn provides yet more data to increase sales even more. While Facebook has grown at an astonishing rate, it is still very much a work in progress. Without a proven model for revenue, executives are betting that they can turn the social graph, which is the basis of their platform, to their economic advantage. The social graph provides in effect a global mapping of everybody on the network and how they are connected. This information is potentially valuable to companies that are trying to identify patterns of people who share interests and have similar consumer preferences. It remains unclear, however, whether Facebook users will consent to allowing the company to use their personal information in this way. If growing concerns about privacy make people reluctant to allow Facebook to use or sell their personal data to marketers, the over-eager investors who prematurely jumped at the chance to buy the stock when the company went public will turn out to be big losers.

Google, of course, remains the leader in the big data business and its lead is growing every day. Even though Microsoft has poured billions of dollars into developing its search engine, Bing, Google still controls two-thirds of the search traffic in the United States and 90 percent in Europe. All of the company's strategies for growth are designed to expand its capacity to collect, store, and process data: consider Gmail, Calendar, Texting, Instant Messaging, Google News, Finance, Shopping, Wallet, Play, Photo Editing, and YouTube. Appearances to the contrary notwithstanding, nothing is free—the price users pay for Google services is providing the company with valuable data. The future of Google depends on profits from data more than from advertising—Google monetizes what people give them for nothing. Google's partnership with the popular Android operating system, as well as its global mapping projects Google Earth and Google Street View, soon will make it possible to target potential consumers anytime and anywhere in the world. Marc Andreessen and Facebook COO Sheryl Sandberg claim that these technologies create the possibility of "situational awareness," which enables companies to know not only where a person is but also what he or she is doing. For marketers, it makes a difference whether someone is shopping, having lunch with a friend, watching television, or sleeping. But when companies are armed with these data, Kurzweil's so-called cyber-friend will not necessarily serve the user's best interests. Siva Vaidhayanathan correctly warns of the dangers this technology harbors: "We are not Google's customers: we are its product. We—our fancies, fetishes, predilections, and preferences—are what Google sells to advertisers. When we use Google to find out things on the Web, Google uses our Web searches to find out things about us. Therefore, we need to understand Google and how it influences what we know and believe."[29]

The aim of these giant companies is to hook consumers on their own company's platform and to use their size and speed to crush the competition. In the past decade, huge information and data monopolies have emerged that control most of the traffic on the Internet. There is a profound irony in this development. We have seen that in the early days of the information revolution, personal computer enthusiasts promised a new age in which decentralized and distributed networks would put information in the hands of the people. This, in turn, would promote greater competition by giving individuals access to technologies that previously only major businesses and corporations could afford. Greater efficiencies were supposed to result from disintermediation, which would cut out middlemen and put sellers and buyers into direct contact with each other, thereby reducing the cost and time of transactions. What is happening is the exact reverse. Instead of decentralization, distribution, and disintermediation, information monopolies are creating new centralized structures for gathering, distributing, and selling information. Expanded platforms and a growing menu of data management services are creating new intermediaries between producers and consumers as well as users and clients. Like the industrial monopolies of the early twentieth century, the information monopolies of the early twenty-first century raise troubling economic, financial, social, and political questions. Making today's information monopolies even more dangerous are their invasive capacities, which create a serious threat to personal privacy and national security.

In this tangled network of networks, it is no longer clear where to draw the line between data and money. When currency is current, money is effectively information or data, and data, information, and customized advertising are money. This situation raises pressing questions: Who really owns my data? Where is my data? How is it gathered? What is known about me? Who has access to personal data I thought were my own? What happens to my data after I die? As data monopolies have expanded, concerns about privacy have grown. On March 12, 2013, a *New York Times* article by David Streitfeld entitled "Google Concedes that Drive-by Prying Violated Privacy" reported that Google "acknowledged to state officials that it had violated people's privacy during its Street View mapping project when it casually scooped up passwords, email and other personal information from unsuspecting computer users." According to the report, for years Google had been secretly collecting personal information from millions of unencrypted wireless networks throughout the world.

Today's growing problems of secrecy and lack of transparency can be traced back to Netscape's decision to insert cookies in software without informing users. As technology has become more sophisticated, the ability to monitor what people are doing online has grown very quickly. Though consumer groups have raised security concerns for years, lobbying efforts on behalf of major companies so far have successfully persuaded government agencies that the imposition of regulations would be bad for business. As I have suggested, there are other reasons that municipal, state, and federal governments have been reluctant to impose regulations. In many cases, government agencies use the same technologies as companies to gather information and conduct surveillance in the name of national security and, therefore, are reluctant to encourage legislation that would limit their own activities. Furthermore, the very companies that should be regulated often ingratiate themselves to government officials and agencies by providing additional information to them. In the media-crazed post-9/11 world, it is impossible to be sure whether threats are real or government and business officials are using scare tactics to frighten people into accepting surveillance tactics that are problematic at best and unconstitutional at worst. In an article cleverly entitled "Invasion of the Data Snatchers," *New York Times* columnist Bill Keller observes, "When our privacy is invaded in the name of national security, we—and our elected representatives, afraid to be thought of as soft—generally go along quietly. Our complacency is reinforced by a popular culture that has forsaken Orwell's nightmares for a benign view of authority. In many of my own guilty-pleasure television favorites, 'The Wire,' the British thriller series 'MI-5,' the Danish original 'The Killing,' and the addictive 'Homeland'—surveillance is what the good guys do, and it saves the day."[30] But does it?

With technology developing faster than our ability to control it, a new condition has emerged that can best be described as "asymmetrical transparency." Here we discover another unexpected trace of the death of God. The relentless gaze of data snatchers has replaced the omnipresent surveillance that once was the privilege of God. In a world where knowledge is power, big data is creating the most powerful companies, corporations, and governments in the history of the human race. Information monopolies as well as countless smaller businesses know far too much about individuals, and individuals know far too little about companies. People have no idea what many of these companies are, who is running them, or how they operate; moreover, it is virtually impossible to find out what information they have and what they are doing with it. To make matters even worse, it is difficult, if not impossible, to opt out of these data-collecting systems. The information intentionally or unintentionally provided by the use of credit cards, loans, mortgages, automatic toll-payment transponders, mobile phones, tablets, online commerce and finance, Social Security, healthcare, and even the Internal Revenue Service makes it impossible to escape the reach of information monopolies whose machinations remain deliberately opaque. No matter what business is involved, the less transparency, the greater the chance for abuses of all kinds. The effect of asymmetrical transparency is actually dehumanizing. When churches, companies, and corporations keep secrets, it is usually to protect themselves or to exploit others.

Secrecy is different for individuals. People willingly and unwillingly keep secrets for many reasons. In today's world of talk radio, reality TV, tweeting, Facebook, and YouTube, secrecy has become as obsolete as last week's fashion. Nothing, it seems, is too personal or too horrible to confess or expose. There is, however, something dehumanizing, even obscene, about total transparency. Sometimes to see everything is to know nothing. Not all secrets are malevolent; some even make us who we are. Human beings are not machines whose every code can be decrypted. They are instead irreducibly mysterious to others as well as themselves. To steal secrets is to rob a person of what makes her who she is.

The practice of targeting consumers on the basis of secret and not-so-secret preferences is not new. Mass customization is a technological upgrade of niche marketing, which was introduced after World War II. Bishop points out that in 1956, Wendell Smith, an advertising executive, "introduced the idea of 'market segmentation.' Smith described the old mass-marketing strategy as 'bending . . . demand to the will of supply.' In this model, Smith wrote, manufacturers looked upon the national market as a large cake and worked to take a full layer. Smith suggested that firms slice in a different direction. Manufacturers should consider tailoring their products to the specific needs of a small number of consumers."[31] Within five years, niche marketing was driving the advertising industry, and three decades later high-speed computers and networking technology led to what marketing gurus Don Peppers and Martha Rogers confidently predicted would be the "one-to-one" future, which will be "a tribal society at the speed of light." While providing unprecedented marketing opportunities, they warn that this one-to-one future will also inevitably lead to what they call the "fractionalization" of society.[32]

With data flying through networks at the speed of light and ubiquitous handheld devices, it is possible to target consumers and clients on the fly and even to individualize prices at the site of sale. Several supermarket chains are experimenting with eye-tracking devices that can detect where a customer's gaze pauses when scanning shelves. This information is transmitted on high-speed computers to data warehouses, where it is processed and used to determine which ads for special prices for the product should be sent to the consumer's mobile device. All of this takes place in real time. At this point, the retinal scan and optical-recognition system of Steven Spielberg and Tom Cruise's *Minority Report* is no longer science fiction. But who would have guessed that ad men and supermarket chains would make it a reality?

For online advertisers, the most important commodity is the consumer's attention and, when attention is at stake, timing is everything. Turow reports that according to one advertising industry observer, "the holy grail of targeting" is "capturing the individual consumer" through "real time bidding" for ads while individuals are using a particular site. As computational speed has continued to ramp up, new players have emerged that are developing software applications that facilitate real-time online auctions for website ads. One of the most successful of these companies was DoubleClick, founded in 1995 and bought by Google for $3.1 billion in 2007. DoubleClick's initial business model was to provide display ads for websites like MySpace, America Online, and the *Wall Street Journal*. Google's purchase was a preemptive strike against Microsoft's effort to get into the display ad business, but what really interested the search giant about DoubleClick was the company's recent introduction of a Nasdaq-like exchange for online ads. This system brings together Web publishers and advertisers on a site where they can participate in real-time ad auctions. The adaptation of algorithms for high-volume trading on high-speed financial networks is transforming the way in which online advertising is bought and sold. High-speed algorithmic auctions further fragment the market by customizing ads for individual users while they are visiting a particular site. Here's how it works. Let's say you are planning a trip to Iceland and log on to a travel site to book a flight. The ads that first show up reflect your recent history of site visits and purchases. Assuming you do not travel to Iceland regularly, you are probably not a very valuable prospect for Reykjavík hotels. But once Google's DoubleClick lets its clients know that you are going to Iceland, your value to hotels there goes up and the immediate value to advertisers pushing other products goes down. Software running on extremely high-speed computers conducts an auction for advertising space on the website and ads for Reykjavík hotels pop up on the travel site you are visiting. All of this is driven by algorithms and takes place in a matter of milliseconds.

With the advent of mass customization, individualized pricing, and real-time ad auctions, the advertising and marketing strategies used to promote mass consumption are fast becoming a distant memory. By radicalizing the strategy of product differentiation and real-time ad auctions, mass customization takes the strategy of accelerating product cycles to another level. In industrial and consumer capitalism, information technologies and big data are deployed to sell and buy actual consumer products. In today's accelerated consumer capitalism, high-speed computing, big data, and algorithmic trading are being used to sell more products faster than ever before. But even this speed of commerce pales in comparison to what happens when the currency of exchange is light rather than stuff. Before considering high-speed, high-volume trading on today's financial markets, it is necessary to consider some of the troubling social and political implications of the trajectory I have been charting.

Fragmenting Fragments

The modernity that began with Luther's privatization, deregulation, and decentralization of the subject, which resulted from the inward turn to the individual, appears to be reaching closure with the personal, religious, social, political, and economic fragmentation brought about by today's high-speed networks. While industrial grids and post-industrial networks are structurally very different, both are characterized by the contrasting and sometimes contradictory rhythms of connection and separation, and splicing and dicing. Just as print standardizes production and individualizes consumption (that is, reading), so too networks of networks create global connections that divide as much as connect. Some walls fall and other walls rise, sealing individuals and communities in silos and cutting them off from genuine connection and conversation. The more sophisticated the technology and the faster the connectivity, the more these fragments are fragmented until the horizon disappears and each person becomes sealed in a bubble where it is difficult if not impossible to hear anything but the echo of one's own voice or the voices of those who are just like oneself. The result of this fragmentation is the loss of common knowledge and shared values that are the basis of every community.

We have seen that mass communication began with the invention of the printing press and the mass circulation of Luther's Bible, sermons, and tracts. Attentive observers quickly realized that print both standardizes and individualizes. Kierkegaard, who was one of Luther's most faithful followers, was the first critic of what he regarded as the dehumanizing effect of mass media. His focus was the newspaper industry in nineteenth-century Europe. Ever the champion of the individual, Kierkegaard was convinced that modern mass media repressed individual thinking and acting by transforming people into unknowing vehicles for the opinions and interests of others he labeled "the crowd." In his brief 1845 book *The Present Age,* which was the first influential work of media criticism, he writes, "And eventually human speech will become just like the public: pure abstraction—there will no longer be someone who speaks, but an objective reflection will gradually deposit a kind of atmosphere, an abstract noise that will render human speech superfluous, just as machines make workers superfluous. In Germany there are even handbooks for lovers; so it probably will end with lovers being able to sit and speak anonymously to each other. There are handbooks on everything, and generally speaking education soon will consist of knowing letter-perfect a larger or smaller compendium of observations from such handbooks, and one will excel in proportion to his skill in pulling out the particular one, just as the typesetter picks out letters."[33]

The correlative dangers of depersonalization and homogenization that Kierkegaard identified so early become even more evident with the spread of mass media throughout the twentieth century. With the introduction of national radio, television, newspapers, and magazines, the dissemination of information expanded but the channels of communication were controlled by a few major corporations. By mid-century, the information people received tended to be as uniform as the half-hour format of nightly news programs around which housewives scheduled family dinners. Television and radio did not immediately eclipse newspapers and magazines. While many local and regional newspapers continued to flourish, national newspapers like the *New York Times* and magazines like *Time* and *Life* were widely read and came to be accepted publications of record. As these media became more pervasive, the power of new media conglomerates to shape opinion and thereby influence political, social, and economic developments increased considerably. Though these early information monopolies created a conformity that often stifled creativity and criticism, there were certain counterbalancing advantages to mass media. People from widely different backgrounds with radically divergent views had ready access to a shared body of news and information. They might not agree in their assessment of the news but at least they were all reading the same newspapers and listening to the same TV networks.

All of this has changed with the shift from mass production, mass consumption, and mass media to mass customization. Negroponte and his colleagues at the Media Lab designed the *Daily Me* to liberate people from the conformity that had been imposed on them by mass media over which they had no control. Individualized newspapers, they believed, would do for print media what the remote control and later the VCR did for television by putting power literally in the hands of the people. Each individual would be able to create his or her own newsfeed that would reflect personal interests and would be accessible anywhere at any time. But excessive individualization, privatization, and decentralization creates another whole set of problems. As PCs gave way to mobile phones and tablets, as networks expanded, and as big data became virtually ubiquitous, the media-scape was again transformed. Producers began unbundling programs and let consumers slice and dice the news any way they wanted. While this new mode of distributing news and information seems to put much more power in the hands of the consumers, the new information monopolies have continued to exert their own extraordinary power, which is all the greater because it is invisible. That is, the power has shifted from television networks to high-speed computer networks, where code, algorithms, and platforms program the news. Apple TV is designed to replace television networks with Internet television, which not only will provide profitable programming opportunities but also will increase the data available for customer tracking and microtargeting. While companies like Microsoft and Yahoo have very successful news platforms, Google News, which was introduced in July 2010, leads the field. Pariser reports that "Google's CEO [Eric Schmidt] doesn't beat around the bush when he describes where this is all headed: 'Most people will have personalized news-reading experiences on mobile-type devices that will largely replace their traditional reading of newspapers,' he tells an interviewer. 'And that kind of news consumption will be very personal, very targeted. It will remember what you know. It will suggest things that you might want to know. It will have advertising. Right? And it will be as convenient and fun as reading a traditional newspaper or magazine.'"[34] Fast computers and big data enable news sources to update personalized newsfeeds on the fly in real time 24/7. Not only is your personal "newspaper" different from everybody else's, but it is also changing faster than you can possibly read it.

These developments in media and advertising are additional examples of the profound paradox of connection/division that lies at the heart of the wired world: the more connected we are, the more separated we become. The self-sorting in real time and space is both reflected and promoted by the self-sorting taking place through high-speed media, information, and communications networks. Rather than breaking down the silos that isolate individuals and communities and creating webs that draw them together, these networks have led to the emergence of new silos that make communication and debate all but impossible. Just as mass communication can lead to standardization and uniformity and so repress individual creativity and criticism, mass customization can also lead to fragmentation and privatization and so repress the shared knowledge and values that make consensus and cooperation possible.

The problems created by mass customization are exacerbated by political operatives' use of advertising methods designed to fuel consumption to run political campaigns. I have already considered the political implications of the internal migration that has occurred since the 1970s. The combination of this red versus blue self-sorting and gerrymandering has made many states and congressional districts uncompetitive. Where people live, however, doesn't matter if they don't vote. Once again, Republicans were the first to realize the importance of technological innovation for influencing voter turnout. George W. Bush's victory over John Kerry in 2004 was in no small measure the result of the Republican's effective use of high-speed computers, big data, and microtargeting. In the age of big data, political campaigns and advertising campaigns both depend on what software entrepreneur Stephen Wolfram labels "personal analytics."

In his revealing analysis of the use of information technologies in recent political campaigns, *The Victory Lab: The Secret Science of Winning Campaigns,* Sasha Issenberg writes, "To social scientists and campaign operatives, breaking the electorate into clusters represented a holy grail; to outsiders, it was an alternately dazzling and dystopic symbol of modernity as democracy entered the computer era." The 2004 campaign compiled 182 pieces of information, which, Bishop explains, was "the kind of consumer data that has been used for a generation to target consumers for candy bars to computer gizmos. Then the sharp-penciled boys at Bush headquarters cross-referenced this data with political polls. With the resulting calculations, Republican organizers could tell (with a reported 85 to 90 percent accuracy) whether a person—any person—was a Republican or a Democrat."[35] They used these data to turn out the vote among Republicans rather than to try to convince independents and Democrats to cross party lines.

Democrats never saw their defeat coming. They depended on traditional methods of polling and advertising and completely overlooked the political opportunities brought about by the high-speed data revolution. But they learned their lesson quickly and by 2008 and especially 2012 were beating the Republicans at their own game. Writing less than a week after the 2012 presidential election, Zeynep Tufekci reported how the Democrats did it. According to Obama's campaign manager, Jim Messina, the "campaign made an 'unparalleled' $100 million investment in technology, demanded 'data on everything,' 'measured everything' and ran 66,000 computer simulations every day." Issenberg explains the significance of the Obama campaign's investment and innovation: "Sandwiched between the heroic presidential candidate who positioned himself as uniquely able to loosen a nation's intellectually sclerotic politics, and the unrivaled hordes of volunteer activists and supporters who believe in him, sat one of the vastest data mining and processing operations that had ever been built in the United States for any purpose. Obama's computers were collecting a staggering volume of information on 100 million Americans and sifting through it to discern patterns and relationships. Along the way, staffers stumbled onto insights about not only political methods but also marketing and race relations, scrubbing clean a landscape that had been defined by nineteenth-century political borders and twentieth-century media institutions and redrawing it according to twenty-first-century analytics that treated every individual voter as a distinct and meaningful unit."[36] It is important to note the irony at the heart of the Obama campaign. The candidate was marketing himself as the person who could overcome political, social, economic, and racial divisions by employing data obtained through the advertising tactics of super-segmentation and the microtargeting of individuals according to these same divisions. The strategy worked, and data dicing appears to have made the difference. Obama's lead in the critical states of Ohio, Virginia, Colorado, and Florida was only 400,000 votes, which was approximately 1 percent of all eligible voters. In the new age of big data and mass customization, smart campaigns might be the way to win elections, but these victories could turn out to be empty. Dicing more than splicing reinforces ideological predilections that make governing virtually impossible.

The paradoxes of connectivity are also vividly evident in online education. Like print, online courses both regularize and individualize, standardize and privatize. With the recent explosion of massive open online courses, or MOOCs, tens of thousands of students take the same course from the same teacher. These courses follow the traditional broadcast model of one-to-many communication and do not take advantage of the possibilities for many-to-many communication created by networking technologies. Individual students set their own pace, but the approach of the course and the material taught are the same for all students. While making courses available to as many people as possible at little or no cost serves a very important social and economic purpose, there are also disadvantages to the uniformity of this approach.

While MOOCs standardize the content and delivery of education, new technologies also make it possible to customize courses just like people can customize news feeds and playlists on their iPods and iPhones. In 1999, New York investment banker Herbert Allen and I founded Global Education Network, whose mission was to provide high-quality online education in the liberal arts to all people in all places at all times at a very low cost. Though the company failed, we learned many important lessons. In developing new ways to deliver education online, we anticipated the trend of mass customization by unbundling our courses and letting students—or more accurately, consumers—put together their own courses. While our goals were educational, this tactic was, in all candor, a marketing decision. We discovered that many people were not interested in taking an entire course but wanted to pick and choose the classes to fit their individual interests and needs. By modularizing courses, unbundling them, and allowing consumers to mix-and-match individual class sessions from different courses, we enabled them to create their own personalized educational experience. In this way, we created an educational network that was more flexible and adaptable to consumer interests and needs as well as the demands of the marketplace. But as a lifelong teacher, I relearned an important lesson—students do not always know best. In education, as in advertising and politics, there are disadvantages to mass customization. When every student is free to compile his or her personal educational experience, students no longer are introduced to the common body of knowledge that has shaped society and culture and that forms the basis for the shared values on which communities, societies, and even nations depend.

The mass customization of education represents the logical conclusion of developments that began in the 1960s. Throughout the latter half of that decade, the growing diversity of the student body and faculty as well as their interests created pressure for diversifying the curriculum. New students and eventually new faculty members demanded new courses that would deal with cultures, societies, traditions, and writers who had been overlooked for far too many years. Giving in to faculty and student pressure, most schools not only made courses in Western civilization optional but also dropped almost all requirements, thereby giving much more freedom to students to design their own programs. In the 1980s, these academic issues were politicized in Allan Bloom's *The Closing of the American Mind: How Higher Education Has Failed Democracy and Impoverished the Souls of Today's Students,* which struck a nerve and set off a national debate about what was labeled "the core curriculum." For Bloom and his neoconservative supporters, a vital democratic society depends on what they consider to be core values that were developed exclusively within the Western tradition.

Not all colleges and universities have given in to student and faculty pressure to do away with required courses in "Western classics." Columbia University, where I now teach, for example, has not only kept its core curriculum, but recently has doubled down on its commitment by making it the cornerstone of a major new fundraising initiative for the arts and sciences. Columbia students are now required to take nine courses, which amounts to more than a quarter of their entire education, in the core. While there have been efforts to diversify the core by including other traditions that reflect a more globalized world, a core by any other name is still a core. In today's pluralistic, globalized world, it no longer is clear what constitutes a core but it is clear that we need shared knowledge and common values if we are going to be able to address the problems dividing us.

The core curriculum and customized courses represent two extremes that parallel the poles of mass communications and mass customization. Too much uniformity is as problematic as too little commonality. On the one hand, standardization represses creativity and discourages individual expression; on the other hand, customization and privatization atomize society and isolate individuals in ways that inhibit the shared knowledge and values necessary for a civil society and discourage the cross-fertilization of ideas that creates a vital educational ecosystem. Here the abiding problem of the one and the many returns as a critical educational issue. We are neither one nor many. For the nation, as for the world, the ideal of *e pluribus unum* lies somewhere in between.

Google Glass

Nietzsche had notoriously bad eyesight, which was made worse by insufferable migraine headaches. His weak vision made it difficult for him to read and write and often required him to wear dark glasses when he was in the sunlight. Perhaps this is why he was so sensitive to the disappearance of the horizon. As his madman makes clear, the loss of the horizon that accompanies the death of God has profound implications—though these implications did not become fully explicit until Heidegger's magisterial four-volume study, which interprets Nietzsche's philosophy as the culmination of the inward turn of consciousness that began with Luther's privatization of faith and Descartes's search for certainty. Arguing that everywhere modern man turns he encounters only himself, Heidegger anticipated the postmodern world in which the processes of privatization and customization have sealed individuals and homogeneous groups in separate cells that become echo chambers.

Google engineers are now developing the technology that will make Nietzsche and Heidegger's vision a reality. In May 2012, the company announced Project Glass, which combines the idea of head-mounted displays for augmented reality with the functionality of the smartphone.

These wearable devices that look like eyeglasses represent the next phase in omnipresent computing, in which users are able to access the Internet anywhere at any time without using their hands. Google Glass uses the Android operating system, which is able to display text messages, maps, video chats, and photographs in real time through voice commands. While initial demonstrations have shown how Google Glass would work for skydiving and mountain biking, the real target market once again is advertising. As Jeffrey Rosen correctly argues, "Advertising has always been an arms race, with ads chasing people and people finding ways—TiVo, for example—to avoid ads. But once ads move onto our smart phones and, possibly, onto wearable devices like Google Glasses that aspire to project ads directly to our retinas, avoiding the ads that are following us everywhere will become much harder than simply deleting our cookies: smart phones have persistent identification numbers that can't be easily reset."[37]

Google is not alone in extending the human-machine interface in ways that make it difficult to know where one ends and the other begins. Affectiva, which was spun out of MIT's Media Lab, is developing artificial intelligence in a new field known as affective computing. The company's website explains, "Affectiva understands the importance of emotions—in every aspect of our lives. It shapes our experiences, our interactions and our decisions. In an increasingly technology-driven world, emotion is either absent or oversimplified. Our mission is to digitize emotion, so it can enrich our technology, for work, play and life." The primary application for this new technology is, of course, advertising. More sophisticated biosensors make it possible to study facial expression to assess the effectiveness of "digital branding in terms of engagement, attention, emotional connection and influence." In one six-week study, the company focused on how display advertising impacts consumers in a digital world that is inundated with marketing messages. The result: "The new approach to display advertising . . . delivered an entirely new state of impact at every level of the purchase funnel vs. standard ad units."[38] In addition to the eyes and face, the voice is being mined for data that can be sold to companies seeking more subtle methods of targeting consumers. The Beyond Verbal communications company has patented technology that claims to extract a person's full set of emotions and character traits, using people's raw voice in real time as they speak. The company boasts, "This ability to extract, decode and measure human moods, attitudes and decision-making profiles introduces a whole new dimension of emotional understanding which we call Emotions Analytics™, transforming the way we interact with machines and with each other."[39] As these and other examples suggest, the technologies we have developed are turning back on us and transforming us by reprogramming our bodies and minds. It is no longer clear whether we can control what we have created.

8. Extreme Finance

Beating the House

Oliver Stone has an uncanny sense of timing. Released just two months after the 1987 stock market crash, the film *Wall Street,* which he directed, captured the new age of markets just at the moment they seemed to be imploding. By 2010, when the film's sequel, *Wall Street: Money Never Sleeps,* was released, the more recent collapse of financial markets had made that 1987 crisis seem like a minor blip. In this sequel the main character, Gordon Gekko, played by Michael Douglas, has done his eight years of prison for insider trading and is promoting his book *Is Greed Good?* while looking for the newest new thing. His future son-in-law, Jacob Moore, played by Shia LaBeouf, is a propriety trader and the protégé of Louis Zabel (Frank Langella), who is trying to raise money for an alternative energy company working on fusion technology. When the stock plummets and investment rival Bretton James (Josh Brolin) blocks the bailout as payback for Zabel's refusal to support him years earlier, Jacob's mentor commits suicide by jumping in front of a subway train. With Zabel out of the way, James moves in and offers young Jake a job. To test his mettle he challenges the kid to a motorcycle race. A helicopter picks up Jake from the top of a Manhattan skyscraper and takes him to Connecticut, where he meets James at what he calls his "second office."

The scene that unfolds repeats exactly the initial encounter between Gekko and his protégé Bud Fox (Charlie Sheen) in the original *Wall Street* film. This time, however, it's not fine art and the Japanese but high-speed motorcycles and the Chinese that frame the action. James greets Jake:

> "Might be dangerous. Think you can keep up?"
> "World's crashing; we'll see."

As they mount their bikes, it's all about testosterone and speed. Decked out in Ducati's finest leather jacket, pants, and boots, and riding a high-end Ducati Desmosedici RR and a MotoCzysz C1, James and Jake push each other to the limit.

When the kid beats the boss, James vainly attempts to save face by saying, "Not bad, Jake, though I think I might have given you the faster bike." He then proceeds to explain that he has always believed that one time in his life every man should be a mentor and have a protégé. He tells Jake that he has a great future and offers to be his mentor. But when he informs him that he has diverted the Chinese money from Zabel's fusion project to an oil deal, Jake objects and James, echoing Gordon Gekko's pitch to young Bud Fox, replies,

> "Are you an idealist or a capitalist?"
> "I'm a realist. You're not my mentor; Lou Zabel was. Whether you admit it or not, you destroyed Zabel and forced him to suicide so you may talk about moral hazard but you are the moral hazard."
> "Is that a threat?"
> "Absolutely."[1]

Biking, skateboarding, free skiing, snowboarding, surfing, running, skydiving, hang gliding, bungee jumping, cliff diving, rock climbing, car racing, high-speed, high-volume trading. The faster the speed, the higher the high. For big-time players in today's extreme finance, speed, wherever it can be found, is addictive.

On October 20, 2001, just one month after 9/11, I journeyed to Las Vegas to join Tom Krens, director of the Guggenheim Museum, and his colleagues for the opening of one of the most unlikely museums that can be imagined—Guggenheim, Las Vegas. While Vegas tycoon Steve Wynn had introduced high art to Vegas at his Bellagio casino resort, Tom's play upped the ante. For many years, the Guggenheim had a museum on the Grand Canal in Venice and the museum was now opening a counterpart along the fake canal in the hotel, casino, and resort complex called Venetian Las Vegas. Tom's partner in this venture was Sheldon Adelson, CEO of the Las Vegas Sands Corporation, who would go on to finance a super PAC that supported the most conservative politicians in the 2012 presidential elections. Explaining the history of the Guggenheim-Vegas Venetian alliance, Krens recalled Robert Venturi and Denise Scott Brown's famous 1968 Yale seminar that led to their influential book, *Learning from Las Vegas*.

> I remember being captured almost thirty years ago by Robert Venturi's argument—presented in his compact but landmark book, *Learning From Las Vegas*—about the *derivative* authenticity of Las Vegas "vernacular" architecture. Although I could have scarcely imagined working with Las Vegas as a site even one year ago— since my very first visit to the city took place only at the beginning of this year—the fascination of the place is undeniable. When Sheldon Adelson and Rob Goldstein first approached us about bringing "The Art of the Motorcycle Exhibition" to Las Vegas, it still did not seem likely that the Guggenheim could be there until we began talking about architecture. Sheldon's and Rob's willingness to consider a permanent new building—and an ambitious

architectural statement—and their agreement that Rem Koolhaas would be the architect, created the possibility for the Guggenheim to engage the image of Las Vegas head on and come up with a creative solution that would add substantially to the character of Las Vegas on the one hand, as it maintained the dignity of a traditional cultural institution on the other. From a purely museological standpoint, it is our plan to build a space of an absolutely unique character and capacity.[2]

Krens, who had long been a devoted rider of BMW motorcycles, brought low and high culture together on Fifth Avenue in 1998 by mounting the highly controversial show *The Art of the Motorcycle,* sponsored by BMW. The exhibition included a fascinating collection of motorcycles from different periods with highly stylized designs. Always sensitive to the importance of multiple media, the curators included a film series entitled *The Motor Cycle on Screen* with Dennis Hopper, whom *Easy Rider* had made a 1960s counter-culture icon, doing the voice-over. To promote the show, Krens began what became one of his signature initiatives, the Guggenheim Motorcycle Gang, which included Hopper as well as Jeremy Irons, Laurence Fishburne, Lauren Hutton, Bob Geldof, and Lyle Lovett. Hopper was at the Guggenheim-Vegas opening in all his glory.

The 63,700-square-foot museum, designed by award-winning architect Rem Koolhaas, consisted of two main sections. The first was space that resembled a traditional white-box museum gallery, but the walls were made of luscious rusted corten steel, reminiscent of the work of Richard Serra (for whose sculptures Frank Gehry had designed the largest gallery in the Guggenheim, Bilbao). On the walls of the gallery hung paintings from yet another Guggenheim partner—the Hermitage Museum in Saint Petersburg. To make the evening even more bizarre, representatives from the venerable Hermitage were in Vegas hanging out with Dennis Hopper as well as people from the Guggenheim and

Left to right: Mark C. Taylor, Jean Nouvel, Victoria Duffy, and Dennis Hopper at the Guggenheim–Las Vegas opening, October 2001

the Venetian. The second part of the museum was a large exhibition space designed explicitly for *The Art of the Motorcycle,* which featured the installation designed by Gehry. With wealthy investors seeking to diversify their portfolios, the art market was soaring. There was a lot of buzz and hopes were high. But the Guggenheim, Las Vegas turned out to be a bad bet and on May 11, 2008, it closed. Commenting on the closing in the *Las Vegas Sun,* local art collector Patrick Duffy explained, "You don't get a return on investment if you overpromise and underdeliver."[3] But that was only part of the problem. What was not known at the time was that Adelson was hedging his bets by turning his attention to China, where he was planning a huge resort and hotel in Macau. This bet has paid off big time. Today Macau dwarfs Las Vegas; on the west side of the Macau Strip stands the Venetian, which Tom Daniell describes as "a pastiche of a pastiche: a bigger version of the 'original' in Las Vegas, it's the world's largest casino, and one of the largest buildings of any kind, anywhere."[4] A perfect sign of the times; Macau is pastiche of a pastiche, copy of a fake, sign of a sign, figure of a figure—all image, no substance. Virtual reality for the virtual global economy.

We have already discovered that Las Vegas and Wall Street have a strangely symbiotic relationship. For investors, as for gamblers, the name of the game is how to beat the house. What is less often recognized is that Vegas also has a close relationship to both information theory, which has shaped financial markets for more than half a century, and wearable computers, which were the precursors of head-mounted displays like Google Glass. As James Weatherall explains in his informative book *The Physics of Wall Street,* Claude Shannon, who is credited with founding information theory, the digital computer, and digital circuit design theory in the late 1940s and early 1950s, had a life-long fascination with gambling and used to spend weekends in Vegas with MIT mathematician Edward Thorp. Shannon, Thorp, and John Kelly, their colleague from Bell Labs, successfully applied the principles of game theory and information theory to blackjack. In 1961 Thorp had studied mathematics and quantum physics at New Mexico State University, but for a long time his real interest had been playing roulette. When he was appointed to an instructorship at MIT, he met Shannon and the two began seriously investigating what gambling could teach them about financial markets and what information theory could teach them about gambling. In 1961, Thorp gave a talk at the American Mathematical Society entitled "A Winning Strategy for Blackjack," which received wide coverage in the national media. His strategy depended on card counting, and the primary insight he drew from his success is that information counts in games that seem to be of chance. He suspected this was also true for financial markets.

One of the distinctive things about games of chance like roulette and craps is that, unlike card counters and poker players, the wheel and dice have no memory and, therefore, the games are random. No matter how many times you have rolled snake eyes, the odds the next time don't change. In an effort to develop an algorithm that would predict the odds, this most unlikely pair combined Thorp's understanding of roulette wheels in terms of game theory and Shannon's information theory. While their math seemed to work for assessing the odds, the problem they faced was how to make the necessary calculations and communicate the results fast enough to be able to place the bets in time. The novel solution Thorp and Shannon devised was a wearable computer. Weatherall explains that their scheme involved two people—one who "would be wearing the computer, which would be a small device about the size of a cigarette pack. The input device would be a series of switches hidden in one of the wearer's shoes. The idea was that the person watching the wheel would tap his foot when the wheel started spinning, and then again when the ball made one full rotation. This would initialize and synchronize it to the wheel. Meanwhile, a second person would be sitting at the table, with an earpiece connected to the computer. Once the computer had a chance to take the initial speeds of the ball and rotor into account, it would send a signal to the person at the table indicating how to bet."[5] While Thorp and Shannon were not able to determine the precise number the ball would land on, they were surprisingly successful at predicting the general area where the ball would land. This proved to be sufficient to greatly improve their odds of winning. Thorp kept the wearable computer and their experiment in Reno secret until he published his best-selling book *Beat the Dealer* in 1966.

Thorp was intrigued by gambling but always knew the big money to be made was on Wall Street, and he regarded his visits to Reno as research for developing investment strategies. Gambling and investing are similar in many ways, but Thorp realized that there is one important difference that he could turn to his advantage.[6] When playing roulette you can only bet on which number the ball will land on but you cannot bet where the ball will not land; when investing, you can simultaneously bet for and against a stock by using a tactic known as shorting. Shorting is a complex variation of an option that involves selling securities or other financial instruments that are not owned, with the intention of repurchasing them if the price goes down. In order to sell shares of a stock you don't own, it is necessary to borrow them from someone who does own them but doesn't want to sell at that time. These shares can be sold with the understanding that at some time they will be repurchased and returned to the lender. If the price goes down between the time the stock is borrowed and the time it must be repaid, the investor makes money because he repurchases them at a lower price than he purchased them; if it goes up, of course, he loses money. This is a sweet deal for the lender because he keeps the stock, while at the same time receiving a premium for renting it to another investor.

According to Weatherall, the practice is at least three hundred years old—there is evidence that it was banned in England in the seventeenth century. While shorting is common today, it was still considered risky as recently as the early 1960s.[7] Thorp's genius was to see that shorting could be used for hedging bets in financial markets. He developed a strategy known as "delta hedging," which for almost five decades has resulted in returns averaging 20 percent. In 1967 he wrote a follow-up best-seller entitled *Beat the Market,* and in 1974, Thorp founded Convertible Hedge Associates, which effectively marks the beginning of the hedge fund era.

Hedge funds, combined with other innovations that were emerging in financial economics in the 1960s and 1970s, fundamentally changed financial markets by carrying the interrelated processes of dematerialization and virtualization of financial assets that had been going on for a long time to a whole new level. We have already seen how portfolio theory shifts the determination of the value of securities and other financial instruments like currencies and derivatives from their connection to something real like a company with tangible assets to their worth relative to other securities and financial instruments. In portfolio theory, investors try to hedge risk by purchasing securities that counter-balance each other, that is, when one goes up, another is likely to go down; in shorting, investors bet that a stock will go both up and down. As Michael Lewis has brilliantly explained in *The Big Short,* during the financial crisis of 2008, fund managers at major investment firms like Goldman Sachs were advising their clients to purchase stocks that they, the managers, were shorting at the same time. That is to say, they were urging clients to purchase securities that they, without telling those clients, were betting against. By playing the market both ways, investment firms made money even when their advice was bad. To make matters worse, during the previous several decades, individual and institutional investors had increasingly been playing with borrowed money. Consumer capitalism's mandate, "borrow and spend," became financial capitalism's mandate, "borrow and invest." By the first part of the twenty-first century, many investment firms were leveraged at an unsustainable level of 50:1. In little more than a decade, the dire consequences of the failed hedge fund Long-Term Capital Management had been forgotten. With hedge funds proliferating faster than the SEC could control them, the approaching collapse of global financial markets should have been clear to anyone willing to consider the situation honestly. For the full impact of these new financial instruments and trading strategies to be felt, however, other changes had to occur. Most important, Thorp and Shannon's feedback loop, created by gathering and communicating information with the wearable computer, had to morph into high-speed networked computers processing big data in real time.

Changing the Guard by Changing the Rules

On December 20, 2012, the *Wall Street Journal* carried an article that shook much of the financial world: "NYSE to Sell Itself in $8.2 Billion

Deal: Planned Takeover Highlights Rise of Electronic Trading." Jenny Strasburg and Anupreeta Das reported,

> The New York Stock Exchange, the cornerstone of American capitalism for 200 years, agreed to be sold as part of an $8.2 billion takeover by International Exchange, Inc.
>
> If regulators and shareholders approve, the combined company would own 14 stock and futures exchanges and five clearing operations that serve as middlemen between buyers and sellers of futures and other contracts, doing more things in more places than any rival.
>
> The takeover would also seal the triumph of electronic trading over "open outcry" floor trading that long dominated financial markets, as well as push the exchanges to embrace new and lucrative kinds of trading.
>
> ICE, based in Atlanta and started 12 years ago as an electricity-trading market, said it would hold on to the NYSE Euronext name and the New York company's trading floor at the corner of Wall and Broad streets in Lower Manhattan. But it is too late to stop the erosion of the Big Board's clout. So far this year [2012], the iconic floor has handled just 20% of all trading volume and NYSE-listed stocks, down more than 40% in 2007, according to analysts at Sandler O'Neil + Partners, LP.
>
> "The trading floor is going to become like the Roman Forum," said Wall Street historian Charles Geisst, a Manhattan College finance professor. "It'll be a nice place to visit, but nothing much going on there."[8]

We might well say of the New York Stock Exchange what Andy Warhol said of department stores—it has become a museum.

The sale of the NYSE and the disappearance of the trading floor into the ether of worldwide webs brings together all of the trajectories we have been tracing: speed, dematerialization, virtualization, connectivity, privatization, individualization, customization, fragmentation, market omniscience, omnipresence, omnipotence, fragility, volatility, excess, and collapse. These developments are the result of four interrelated changes in financial markets during the past several decades: technological innovations that make possible high-speed, high-volume trading, which I will consider in the next section; changes in regulations governing markets; the privatization of markets; and the increasing fragmentation of markets.

For more than two hundred years, the NYSE had what amounted to a monopoly on stock trading in the United States and had disproportionate influence on global markets. Like many other established institutions, it was dedicated to tradition and was slow to change. Until quite recently, buying and selling on the NYSE resembled bartering in local shops before the introduction of display windows. The function of any market is, of course, to bring together buyers and sellers. When an individual, institution, or corporation wants to buy or sell a security, the trade usually goes through a financial intermediary. On the NYSE, the trade was traditionally executed on the actual floor of the exchange by a specialist, who represented the member firm responsible for trading a specific security. One specialist was designated for a given stock but dealers could be specialists in several stocks. Each specialist had a designated place on the exchange floor where his particular stocks were traded. When individual or institutional investors wanted to sell or buy a security, they would notify their broker, who, in turn, called his representative on the floor. This representative would then physically go to the place designated for the particular security and the specialist would "make the market" in the security by conducting an actual auction among all buyers and sellers at that particular moment. The specialist would receive a small percentage of the sale price in exchange for this service. While this fee-for-service was not inconsequential, the real advantage that specialists and market makers had in this system was access to information—they were the only ones who knew the actual bid-ask spread and the depth of the market at any given time. Since here, as in all transactions, money is made in the gap created by the spread, this information was very valuable.

By the late twentieth century, technology had made this system obsolete. We have seen that during the 1980s, electronic communications networks (ECNs) spread rapidly. The rise of NASDAQ during the 1990s foreshadowed the descent and eventual disappearance of the traditional NYSE in the early twenty-first century. Like so many other financial institutions and policies, the roots of NASDAQ go back to the Depression era. In the wake of the turmoil of the 1920s and 1930s, the National Association of Securities Dealers (NASD) was created to bring order and stability to over-the-counter (OTC) markets, which were unregulated at the time. In the absence of any method for collecting and distributing stock quotes, brokers resorted to phones and telegrams among themselves to determine prices and execute trades. This practice created many opportunities for fraud. One of the primary ways that the NASD initially sought to bring order to chaotic OTC markets was by gathering and publishing price information for both investors and traders.

In 1971, NASD became NASDAQ (National Association of Securities Dealers Automated Quotation System), and on February 8 of that year it started trading as the world's first electronic stock market. Initially it was little more than a computer bulletin board system that did not actually connect buyers and sellers, but as relevant technologies evolved, the exchange quickly adapted. Though the technology for universal on-line trading was in place by the 1980s, political wrangling and conflicting interests delayed its introduction until the early 1990s, when NASDAQ became a fully operational electronic trading network. Due to its origins as a means of gathering and distributing information about over-the-counter stocks, which were not listed on the NYSE and other major exchanges in the 1990s, NASDAQ became the exchange of choice for new technology stocks, most of which did not have Big Board status.

In networks and markets as in buildings, architecture makes a difference. In contrast to the stately building, reminiscent of the original mints in Roman temples, which was the home of the NYSE, NASDAQ never had any real trading floor. From the beginning, the exchange was nothing more than a computer network whose hub, located in Trumbull, Connecticut, links hundreds of thousands of computers as well as individual investors trading on the Internet. Rather than real people on a real trading floor, in NASDAQ's virtual exchange, market makers were never physically present and their transactions were mediated electronically at a distance. As computers improved and networks expanded, this function was completely automated and real traders were eliminated. Another important difference was that unlike the NYSE, NASDAQ market makers—real or virtual—did not have a monopoly on the stocks they handled and usually broadcast their best bid and ask prices over the network rather than keeping it to themselves. Competition among market makers led to greater access to price information, which made markets more efficient but, as we will see, also more volatile. In retrospect, it is clear that accelerating speed doomed the NYSE to unplanned obsolescence. With financial markets wired globally and computer speed following Moore's law by doubling approximately every eighteen months, the only way for markets to survive was to get human beings out of the loop and let the machines take over.

Throughout the last decade of the twentieth century and opening decades of the new millennium, technology and financial innovation have been changing faster than most investors and all government regulatory agencies can comprehend. Under the inept leadership of Arthur Levitt, who served as chairman of the Securities and Exchange Commission during the critical period from 1998 to 2001, regulations were enacted that were intended to increase transparency and make markets both more efficient and equitable. Unintended consequences of these actions, however, completely transformed markets in ways that made the explosion of high-volume, high-speed trading inevitable.

A series of new regulations that began in the 1990s proved decisive for the transformation of financial markets in the past two decades. We have seen in the discussion of the efficient market hypothesis that a more equitable distribution of information makes markets more efficient by decreasing the difference between the price for buying and selling securities as well as commodities. In 1997, the SEC issued an order display rule that "required specialists and market makers to publish 'the best price at which [they] were willing to trade.'" With the proliferation throughout the 1980s and 1990s of proprietary electronic communications networks, which collectively were labeled alternative trading systems (ATS), the new regulation had to be strengthened less than a year later. In 1998, the SEC issued Reg ATS, a regulation that required all ECNs "to display their orders to the public."[9]

Greater transparency increased market efficiency but also created unanticipated problems that were compounded by another seemingly inconsequential decision the SEC made. On April 9, 2001, the SEC ordered all U.S. stock markets to switch from listing prices in fractions to a decimal system. The practice of fractional denomination of securities dated back four hundred years to the time when Spanish traders had used "a currency of Spanish doubloons to facilitate trade. These doubloons were divided into two, four or even eight pieces so that traders could count them on their fingers. Since these traders excluded the use of thumbs, their system was a base eight rather than a base ten, i.e., digital."[10] This meant that the smallest price fraction for buying or selling a stock was 1/8 of a dollar or 12.5 cents, which was the minimum spread for investors as well as specialists and market makers. The size of this spread created the opportunity for significant profits and losses. The NYSE eventually recognized the problems with this system and adopted a 1/16th standard that still left the minimum spread 6.25 cents, which was not insignificant. With the introduction of decimal pricing, however, the bid/ask spreads on stocks dropped precipitously. The decrease in this spread led to a decrease in profits, which, in turn, encouraged an increase in the volume of trading. As I explained in the consideration of the efficient market hypothesis and fast fashion, there are two ways to make money: a lot of money on a few bets, or a little money on a lot of bets. When the bid/ask spread dropped from 12.5 or 6.25 cents to fractions of a cent, the only way to make the same amount of money was to increase the number of trades. The result was an explosion in the volume of trading. Sal Arnuk and Joseph Saluzzi report that "in June 2007, just before Reg NMS [a series of initiatives designed to increase competition among both different markets and individual investors] was implemented, average daily volume across all exchanges was 5.6 billion shares per day. Two years later, in June 2009, it had increased more than 70% to 9.6 billion."[11] Since that time, trading volume has continued to grow at an even faster rate.

These regulations had another unintended consequence that has proven to be very important. When NASDAQ was created in the early 1970s, markets were quite fragmented and it was difficult for traders to find reliable comparative price information. Stocks that the NYSE controlled could be traded on regional or over-the-counter exchanges, but the Big Board ticker tape did not report these prices and transactions. In 1975, Congress authorized the SEC to devise a system that would facilitate a national market. More than a quarter-century later, Reg NMS, which was expected to create a more integrated market in the spirit of the SEC's long-term goal, instead led to the excessive proliferation and fragmentation of financial markets. This process was facilitated and accelerated by the privatization of financial markets.

Until recently, stock exchanges were member-owned nonprofit businesses that functioned something like a utility. With the explosion of ECNs in the 1990s, established exchanges could no longer compete effectively. In an effort to keep up with the competition, NASDAQ became a for-profit business in 2000, and six years later NYSE went private. This development transformed the structure and the operation of stock exchanges from quasi-utilities providing services for investors and businesses seeking capital to for-profit enterprises that had to answer to their own investors. Since income is generated by trades, the only way they could increase profits was to increase the number of trades on exchange networks. When SEC regulations decreased spreads and, correspondingly, increased the volume of trades, security markets in search of profits began to privilege high-volume traders at the expense of small institutional and individual investors. The shift from nonprofit to for-profit also created incentives for the creation of new exchanges. During the first decade of the twenty-first century, the stock market was no longer primarily controlled by the NYSE and NASDAQ; instead it became "one big conflicted, for-profit web of more than 50 trading destinations." The advantages to investors of lower transaction costs and commissions were offset by significant disadvantages of computerized trading. Wall Street veterans Arnuk and Saluzzi argue persuasively that "our markets today are not about executing your trade and investment ideas in a way that is beneficial to you. It is about how dozens of HFT [high-frequency trading] computers touch and manipulate your order so they can make money from your ideas—without you even knowing."[12]

The pattern here is exactly what we discovered in our analysis of information monopolies like Google, Microsoft, Amazon, and Facebook. Market whales started swallowing smaller fish until ten of the thirteen exchanges in the United States were at that time owned by the Big Four:

NYSE, NYSE Amex, and NYSE Arca
NASDAQ, NASDAQ PSX, and NASDAQ BX
BATS and BATS Y
EDGX and EDGA (Direct Edge)

The interrelated problems of market fragmentation and consolidation are compounded by a recently devised strategy to elude transparency known as "dark pools." Official markets are open to everyone, but dark pools are private markets that are hidden from investors and only available for large trades by big financial institutions. Since these trades are unregulated and anonymous, they allow investors to buy or sell large blocks of securities without tipping their hand and thereby influencing the market in a way that would have negative consequences for the transaction. High-volume trading in private pools does not have the same impact that it has on public exchanges like the NYSE and NASDAQ, where quick access to this information would probably depress the stock. With the proliferation of exchanges and dark pools, it becomes possible to hide the size of the trade by breaking it up into smaller units and using different trading venues. In his provocative book *Dark Pools: High-Speed Traders, A.I. Bandits, and the Threat to the Global Financial System,* Scott Patterson reports that "by 2012, the amount of stock trading that took place in dark pools . . . was a whopping *40 percent* of all trading volume—and it was growing every month."[13] Since both "official" markets and dark pools are privately owned, trading has become so fragmented that it is difficult to know what is really going on. The expansion of dark pools reduces the transparency that SEC regulations were devised to create. The inability of regulatory authorities to address the problems introduced by such innovations underscores the growing problems created by the accelerating speed of financial markets.

The evolution of financial markets during the past two decades repeats patterns and paradoxes that we have discovered elsewhere: instead of creating greater integration, growing connectivity leads to more fragmentation; the pursuit of greater transparency, efficiency, and equality leads to more secrecy, inefficiency, and inequality; and decentralized and distributed networks create consolidation in which the big get bigger and smaller businesses, firms, and individuals are increasingly disadvantaged. The combination of the automation, size, and speed of networked exchanges deepens the problem of asymmetrical transparency that lies at the heart of today's marketing strategies for consumer products. The capability to collect, process, and distribute data from every transaction provides financial exchanges with resources that enable them to grow exponentially. The more trades they execute, the more money they make and the more information they collect, and the richer their data, the more profitable their trades are. In a world where information is power and power is money, the rich are getting richer faster than ever before.

Toxic Speed

Today's globally wired financial markets represent postmodernism on steroids. Patterson catches the drift when he writes, "With electronic trading, a placeless, faceless, postmodern cyber-market in which computers communicated at warp speeds, that physical sense of the market's flow had vanished. The market gained new eyes—*electronic eyes.* Computer programmers designed hunter-seeker algorithms that could *detect,* like radar, which way the market was going."[14] Just as postmodern art and architecture stage a play of signs of signs that are grounded in nothing beyond themselves, so financial assets circulating in global networks at the speed of light are grounded in nothing real. We have traced the progressive dematerialization of tokens of exchange from metal to inscription to paper to image to information. There has been a correlative change in the way value is determined. Rather than being established by its relation to a real commodity, product, or asset like inventory, a factory, or *real* estate, the value of the monetary sign in financial capitalism is determined by its relationships to other financial signs like currencies, options, futures, derivatives, swaps, collateralized mortgage obligations (CMOs), Bitcoins, or countless other so-called financial innovations.

With extreme finance's high-speed, high-volume trading, the decoupling of the virtual from the real reaches what is for the moment its most advanced form. Financial markets have become almost completely detached from the real economy. With unemployment remaining stubbornly high, the government obsessed with cutting spending, and businesses too wary about the future to expand, the stock market records record highs day after day. In November 2012 Bain & Company issued an informative report entitled "A World Awash in Money," in which analysts write, "We discovered that the relationship between the financial economy and the underlying real economy has reached a decisive turning point. The rate of growth of world output of goods and services has seen an extended slowdown over recent decades, while the volume of global financial assets has expanded at a rapid pace. By 2010, global capital had swollen to some $600 trillion, tripling over the past two decades. Today, total financial assets are nearly 10 times the value of the global output of all goods and services." The report concludes that "for the balance of the decade, markets will generally continue to grapple with an environment of capital superabundance. Even with moderating financial growth in developed markets, the fundamental forces that inflated the global balance sheet since the 1980s—financial innovation, high-speed computing and reliance on leverage—are still in place. . . . More than any other factor on the horizon, the self-generating momentum for capital to expand—and the sheer size the financial sector has attained—will influence the shape and tempo of global economic growth going forward."[15] The accompanying graphic makes the point unmistakable.

The implications of this situation are staggering. The tipping of the scales from the real to the financial economy can be traced to the neoliberal reforms that began in the 1980s, which I considered earlier. For the foreseeable future, as it has for the past two decades, the huge volume of global financial assets will continue to rest on a relatively small global GDP, which is projected to total $90 trillion by 2020 (versus $63 trillion today). According to the Bain & Company report, this means that total capital will remain ten times larger than the total global output of goods and services and three times bigger than the base of nonfinancial assets that constitute the world GDP.

Based on these calculations, the global volume of money will grow

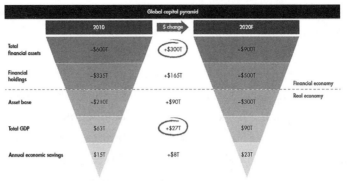

Global capital pyramid. A $27 trillion growth in global GDP will support a $300 trillion increase in total financial assets by 2020. Data sources are International Monetary Fund; OECD; and Bain Macro Trends Group analysis, 2012. Image used with permission from Bain & Company; see the original image at http://www.bain.com/publications/articles/a-world-awash-in-money.aspx.

by 50 percent to $900 trillion by 2020. This estimate, however, lowballs growth in the financial sector. The investment analyst Michael Lewitt, author of *The Death of Capital,* points out that the situation is even worse than Bain predicts because the report does not account for two additional variables: first, the role of the Federal Reserve in printing money, and second that the vast majority of newly created money is in the form of debt and not equity. "The fact that debt is growing as a percentage of total global money," Lewitt explains, "has profoundly negative implications for future economic growth and stability. Unlike equity, debt has to be serviced. As global debt grows, so does the volume of capital required to pay interest and repay principal. To the extent that debt is used for purposes that fuel economic growth, the capital used to service this debt can itself be considered contributing (albeit indirectly) to growth. But to the extent that debt is used for non-productive purposes, the capital used to service it is also unproductive. It is fair to say that much of the debt that has been created over the last decade has been devoted to unproductive and speculative uses rather than productive uses."[16]

There is an additional factor that complicates this already tenuous situation—speed. We have repeatedly discovered that the way markets continue to expand after reaching their spatial limits is through acceleration. In this regard, financial assets are no different from consumer goods like cars, clothes, and iPhones—the faster the churn, the more the profit. "High frequency trading," Lewitt explains, "has transformed the very art of investing into a race for speed. And custodians no longer hold anything in their accounts but an endless chain of promises as they lend and relend their customers' securities to other counterparties. At the end of the day, investors are left with the reality that not only is the world awash in money, but that most of this money is owed to somebody else. Like the listener in Wallace Stevens' great poem, they behold money as 'Nothing that is not there and the nothing that is.'"[17] This nothing, however, has real consequences.

It is difficult, perhaps even impossible, to comprehend the speed of today's financial markets. In the early 2000s, it was possible to trade in milliseconds or thousandths of a second, which is two hundred times the average speed of human thought. By the end of the decade, this time had been reduced to microseconds, or one-millionths of a second, and now trades are executed in nanoseconds, or one-billionths of a second. In 2011, NASDAQ released its NanoSpeed Market Data Mesh system, which enables its clients to receive data in six hundred nanoseconds, that is, six hundred billionths (600/1,000,000,000) of a second. This incomprehensible acceleration has four important consequences. First, as the speed of trading increases, the time a security is held decreases. In the world of high-speed, high-frequency trading, everything is about the shortest of short-term investments. Calculations are not made in terms of years, weeks, days, or even hours, minutes, or seconds, but in nanoseconds. In this world, a second can be a long-term investment. Such high-speed and high-volume trading make it possible to make or lose money on price differentials of as little as one-tenth, one-twentieth, or even one-hundredth of a cent. Commitment to radically short-term investing is reinforced by traders' practice of beginning and ending every day with a clean slate; that is, all positions are settled before the trading day ends.

Second, as I have suggested, the movement of stock prices in high-speed markets has virtually nothing to do with economic conditions in the real world. Rather than a reflection of actual economic conditions, financial markets have become a speculative play of mirrors in which reality is virtual. Technological and financial innovations have combined with regulatory reform to create two economies that are rapidly moving apart. The best way to understand their growing difference is in terms of speed: the real economy and the financial economy move at different speeds. In our consideration of industrial and consumer capitalism, we have seen that people and companies make money by selling labor or stuff, much of which is material—such as commodities, products, real estate, and so on. Investors try to make money by investing in business and innovations that increase productive capacity. In financial capitalism, by contrast, people try to make money by investing in immaterial speculative assets that proliferate at the speed of light. In this new world, time is money in a completely new sense. As Lewitt observes, "We have created a system that is wholly dependent on the ability of money to keep circulating through the global financial system." The faster virtual assets circulate, the more money investors can make or lose. When circulation stops because liquidity freezes up, as it did during the 2008 financial crisis, the entire global financial system suddenly screeches to a halt. While many commentators have expressed concern about the increasing acceleration of financial markets, few, if any, have recognized the importance of speed in the growing inequitable distribution of wealth. Since the real economy and the financial economy scale differently, the wealth gap is actually a speed gap. In the real economy, you can only produce so much stuff, labor so many hours, or serve so many patients or clients in one hour. In the financial economy, there seems to be virtually no limit to the number of trades you can execute in one second. In August 2011, Nanex, "a high-tech firm that tracks speed trading, processed a staggering one *trillion* [that is, 1,000,000,000,000] bytes of data in all U.S. stocks, options, futures and indexes on a single day. That was quadruple the peak spikes of information the market had seen just two years earlier."[18] With the fast getting faster, the slower will never catch up no matter how long they work or how fast they run.

At this point another unexpected reversal takes place. Speed increases so much that rather than annihilating space by making one's location irrelevant, as many analysts had long predicted, it reinforces the importance of place. After several decades of so-called real-time trading on placeless global networks, real estate has become really important—once again it's all about location, location, location. With trades being executed in nanoseconds, the time it takes to transmit buy or sell orders from brokers to exchanges becomes critical. If the computers of financial firms are not located close to the servers of the exchange on which they trade, they are at a disadvantage. Chicago firms, for example, cannot trade successfully on New York exchanges. This development has led to a trend called "colocation" in which exchanges build big data centers right next to their own server farms. Large firms trading on these markets rent space in the facilities to cut down on transmission time. In August 2010 the erstwhile venerable New York Stock Exchange, now known as NYSE Euronext, opened a massive new data center and trading hub in Mahwah, New Jersey, that is longer than three football fields. The complex includes a 100,000-square-foot colocation with 20,000-square-foot pods that all rented immediately. Reporting on the new facility, Rich Miller writes, "The need to execute a trade in a microsecond ahead of rivals has created an arms race in ultra-low latency colocation, and is reshaping the playing field in the trading industry. NYSE Euronext expects its New Jersey data center, and a similar facility in Basildon, England, to house ecosystems of hedge funds and trading firms eager to conduct trades in microseconds."[19] In a nod to the era that has passed away, on the grounds of the new facility there are six buttonwood trees to serve as a reminder of the buttonwood tree on Wall Street under which twenty-four brokers signed the Buttonwood Agreement on May 17, 1792, establishing the New York Stock & Exchange Board.

Third, the expansion of high-speed networks and trading, combined with the frequent creation of new financial instruments designed to take advantage of these technologies and novel trading strategies, creates new possibilities for market manipulation. The most pernicious form of this tactic is momentum manipulation. In high-speed markets, "nothing" takes many forms. Much high-speed trading involves orders that are sent out but are intentionally never executed; their purpose is instead to be a diversionary tactic to trick other large investors. To appreciate the implications of this strategy, it is necessary to understand what is known as front running. Front running is an illegal practice that involves a firm using its knowledge of pending trades for its customers to the advantage of the firm itself. When trades are large, as they tend to be on high-speed exchanges, purchases can move the price of a stock significantly. Knowledge of imminent trades is, therefore, valuable information that can be exploited. If a trader uses this information to place his own order before placing the order of his client, he can make a significant profit. Arnuk and Saluzzi recount their first encounter with this trading strategy and their effort to figure out what was going on.

> We first began to notice it when we would bid for a stock in order
> to accumulate a large position for our clients, and, upon entry of
> every bid that we made, automated front running was triggered.
> An offer gets lifted in front of us. Then another. The rapid-fire

order sequence continued, where bids were entered ahead of us, canceled, and then entered again only higher, and then canceled again. Often this sequence involved hundreds or even thousands of entered orders and cancellations, whereby only a few hundred shares ultimately get executed by the HFT [i.e., High Frequency Trading] firms. Market participants frequently hear that the reason HFT firms entered and canceled 95% of their orders without a trade is because HFTs are just "managing risk" in their marketing activities. In reality, HFT firms are trying to create momentum. They are trying to mislead institutional algorithmic orders that follow along these price changes, which are created with the intention to manipulate a stock higher after the HFT firm has already bought the stock at a cheaper price.[20]

These comments point to the final consequence of high-speed trading that must be considered in this context. Speed has become superhuman and, therefore, it is impossible both to comprehend the high-speed of markets and, more important, to manage them. While programmed trading has been going on for several decades, today's algorithmic trading has completely changed financial markets and, by extension, is transforming the world. Markets are no longer driven by testosterone-pumped speed junkies who ride fast motorcycles, but increasingly are driven by geeks and quants with doctorates primarily in physics and astrophysics. James Simons, founder of Renaissance Technologies, which with over $15 billion under management is one of the largest and most successful hedge funds, will not even interview anybody who does not have a doctorate in physics or astrophysics. The impact of big data on financial markets is greater than on consumer markets, because timing is even more important for high-speed trading than it is for customer targeting. If information is to be useful in financial transactions, massive amounts of data must be processed and communicated virtually instantaneously. Quants create algorithms, which are rules or procedures sometimes known as bots, designed to cruise different financial and news networks as well as data banks for information that will create a transactional advantage. These data and information are fed to other algorithms that actually execute the trades. To appreciate the significance of these changes, it is important to recall that more than 70 percent of all trades on U.S. markets are algorithmic. Once an algorithm has been created and selected, traders lose control over the entire process.

But the situation is even more complicated because it is now possible to program algorithms to adapt to the rapidly changing investment environment on the fly. Algorithms, in other words, have been programmed to evolve. At this point, artificial intelligence bleeds into what computer scientists describe as artificial life. The evolutionary dynamics of trading algorithms are governed by rules that are similar to biological organisms. Indeed, it is possible to interpret evolution itself as an algorithmic process. The algorithm that governs evolution is the rule of the survival of the fittest—those algorithms that adapt, survive, and even propagate through the interrelated processes of self-programming and self-organization flourish, and the algorithms that are too slow or unproductive die. At this point, something very strange begins to happen —financial markets begin to resemble biological organisms that develop according to their own adaptive programming rules.

If high-speed financial markets emerge from but cannot be completely reduced to the actions of individual agents, then where does their evolution stop? I began this book by citing Michael Crichton's novel *Prey,* which tells the story of self-replicating and self-organizing microbots that escape into the wild. In the introduction to his novel Crichton writes, "Sometime in the twenty-first century, our self-deluded recklessness will collide with our growing technological power. One area where this will occur is in the meeting point of nanotechnology, biotechnology, and computer technology. What all three have in common is the ability to release self-replicating entities into the environment."[21] In the tale Crichton tells, individual microbots resemble ants that are dumb but whose interactions lead to the emergence of something like a mind of the colony. To use another analogy, the human mind arises from the firing and interaction of millions of dumb neurons. As ants are to the mind of the colony, neurons are to the mind of human beings. This line of reasoning can be extended to financial markets. Through the decisions and interactions of individual agents whose perspective is necessarily limited, something like the mind of the market emerges. This collective mind is more than the mere sum of the individuals who make it up. Though the mind of the market cannot exist without the intelligence of investors, the market knows things that individuals cannot know, and acts on individual investors through feedback loops that are both limiting and mutually reinforcing.

Didier Sornette, a professor of geophysics whose work is important for reasons that will become clear in Chapter 10, writes, "If or when greater-than-human intelligence will drive progress, this progress will be much more rapid and will probably involve the creation of still more intelligent entities, on a still-shorter time scale. In the evolutionary past, animals adapted to problems and made inventions, the world acting as its own simulator in the case of natural selection of time scales in millions of years. Superhuman intelligences can lead to a drastic acceleration of natural evolution by executing simulations at a much higher speed."[22] As evolution migrates from carbon to silicon, the rate of change will accelerate and eventually lead to systemic failure. Since we have already passed the point at which the speed of financial networks far exceeds the speed of the human mind, natural processes, and the real economy, periodic meltdowns become inevitable even if their precise timing cannot be predicted. Science fiction has become everyday reality. The problem is that too many people do not understand how the complex networks that are transforming the world and human life function in social, cultural, natural, and financial systems.

Fat Tails, Short Circuits, Flash Crashes

It is important to recall that economics did not exist as an independent discipline and field of research until the 1870s. Prior to that time, what today passes for economics was part of natural philosophy. Adam Smith, after all, was a professor of moral philosophy at the University of Glasgow. Not many professors of economics or finance could claim that title today. The tradition of natural philosophy dates back to a time before disciplinary specialization began and the lines separating fields and subfields characteristic of today's academic world had not been clearly drawn. During the latter half of the nineteenth century, the academy became specialized by discipline in ways that mirrored and extended the differentiation of labor that Smith had identified as the heart of the market economy. This has led to educational institutions and disciplines that follow the industrial model of segmentation and competition, with each discipline establishing its own niche. Though not always explicitly acknowledged, the emergence of economics as an autonomous discipline presupposed the differentiation of the economy from other social, political, psychological, and even religious processes. Increasing specialization has led to a fragmentation of knowledge that makes it difficult to understand the interrelations of various systems and subsystems operating in complex networks.

The decisive break that began the differentiation of economics from other areas of inquiry resulted from the effort to establish the subject as a science by appropriating methods used in physics. In 1900, Thorstein Veblen coined the phrase "neoclassical economics" to characterize this shift. The most important consequence of this privileging of physics for explaining economics was the use of quantitative mathematical formulas and models. When they are stuck in isolated silos and infatuated with mathematical abstractions, economists tend to ignore the extent to which their field rests on ideas and metaphors borrowed from other thinkers and disciplines. Consider, for example, how economic theory and practice have been influenced, both implicitly and explicitly, by the ideas, images, and analyses that are explored in this book, including Ockham's individualism, Luther's privatization, the decentralization and deregulation of religion, Calvin's invisible hand, Descartes's mechanism, Newton's equilibrium, Darwin's evolution, Mandeville's beehive, Bentham's utilitarianism, Taylor's efficient scientific management, Mandelbrot's fractals, and Shannon's information theory.

The mathematization of economics that began in the 1870s reached a turning point in the 1950s and 1960s with the emergence of financial economics and increasingly high-speed computers, which made it possible to use abstract mathematical models to analyze markets and generate trading programs. As the earlier discussion of portfolio theory and the efficient market hypothesis suggests, these mathematical models made fundamental assumptions that are as much philosophical or even ideological as scientific. To appreciate how high-speed computers and networking technologies are transforming financial markets, it is important to understand the foundational principles of neoclassical economics:

1. Each individual is an autonomous agent who acts independently of all others.
2. The whole is nothing more than the sum of its parts, and therefore the market is an aggregate of the actions of individual agents.
3. All actors are rational agents who always act in their own self-interest. Since they all act the same way, such individuals tend to be homogeneous.
4. When information is equally distributed and available in a timely manner, markets are efficient and converge on one price.
5. Markets are governed by the principle of equilibrium and therefore tend to be cyclical.
6. The movement toward equilibrium presupposes a negative

feedback system that reduces imbalances when they become excessive.

7. In this closed system, significant changes are the result of external (exogenous) rather than internal (endogenous) disruptions.

8. The operation of markets is similar to games of chance like dice and roulette. This means that markets do not have a memory and, thus, the past does not influence present decisions. Just as the chance of heads or tails is always fifty-fifty regardless of previous results, so the likelihood of a stock going up or down is independent of past performance. From this point of view, markets are random walks. Random events, however, are not arbitrary and, therefore, are not completely uncertain; rather, they are probabilistic.

9. Since markets are probabilistic, financial economists can devise ways to manage risk by calculating probability and thereby reducing uncertainty.

10. Change in markets follows a normal (or Gaussian) distribution, which conforms to a bell curve.

11. Since effects are always proportionate to causes, small events never have catastrophic effects.

12. Extreme events, outliers, or fat tails are rare enough to be irrelevant for investors.

In the wake of the 1987 market crash, it became apparent to a growing number of people that all of these assumptions are false. As volatility increased with the acceleration of financial markets, most reasonable observers acknowledged that traditional models were outdated and fundamental changes in market theory and investment practices were needed.

During the late 1980s, an alternative interpretation of financial markets began to emerge among researchers investigating complex systems in a variety of contexts. This new line of analysis differed from traditional approaches in both method and substance. Instead of viewing the economy as an independent sphere that is the private domain of specialists, complexity theorists regard the economy as an intricate network that intersects and interacts with other networks. This network of networks forms a web whose structure is fractal. That is, every part of the network, from the individuals or parts that make it up to the whole, have the same structure and follow similar rules. Far from isolated individuals, agents are something like relational nodes in a web that continues to expand and change as a result of their activities even as the overall structure of the web establishes the parameters of constraint for all actions. Since individuals and systems are neither separate nor autonomous but are irreducibly connected, they can only be understood by bringing to bear insights drawn from multiple fields and disciplines. In his book *The Self-Organizing Economy, New York Times* columnist and Nobel laureate Paul Krugman explains the value of this approach: "Some of the ideas that come out of the interdisciplinary study of complex systems—the attempt to find common principles that apply across a wide variety of scientific fields, from neuroscience to condensed matter physics—are, in fact, useful in economics as well."[23]

Regardless of the context or medium—be it natural, biological, social, political, cultural, or economic—complex systems have the same structure. Furthermore, they are not static but evolve over time through a process of co-adaptation among the individuals and subnetworks that comprise them. Since this process leads to the emergence of new, more effective configurations, a more accurate way to describe these systems is as *emergent* complex adaptive networks. The structure and operation of these networks call into question all of the assumptions of neoclassical theory. After considering the general features of emergent complex adaptive systems regardless of their medium, I will examine how they work in today's financial markets.

1. Emergent complex adaptive networks (ECANs) are comprised of many different parts that are not autonomous but

are connected in multiple ways. These connections or relations determine the specific identity and characteristics of the members and components of the network.

2. ECANs display spontaneous self-organization, which complicates the relationship between interiority and exteriority in such a way that the line that is supposed to separate them becomes porous. In other words, ECANs are open rather than closed. Like the individuals that comprise them, the networks that make up complex webs are codependent and coevolve through mutual interactions.

3. In ECANs, the whole is more than the sum of the parts. Whole and part are co-emergent, that is, neither can be itself apart from the other, and each becomes itself in and through the other. This means that there are no individuals apart from communities and no communities without individuals.

4. The whole emerges from but is not reducible to its parts. Accordingly, no form of reductive analysis can understand the operation of the whole. Since ECANs are holistic structures, they cannot be understood solely by an analysis of their separate parts.

5. Individual agents, elements, or components of ECANs always act within parameters of constraint that are determined by their place in the overall network. Complete autonomy and radical freedom of choice are illusions.

6. Since webs comprised of interrelated networks evolve over time, each configuration is also conditioned by the history of the network. ECANs, therefore, have a memory.

7. Diverse components can interact both serially and in parallel to generate sequential as well as simultaneous effects and events. This means that there is no simple and direct relationship between a single cause and a single effect. Interactions can be both linear and nonlinear.

8. The complexity of the relationships among the members of a network creates positive feedback loops that move away from equilibrium. While negative feedback systems create checks and balances that tend toward equilibrium, positive feedback creates increasing acceleration that moves toward disorder, which can approach the edge of chaos.

9. As positive feedback accelerates, ECANs approach a condition of self-organized criticality or the tipping point, where a minor event can have a catastrophic systemic effect.

10. Catastrophic effects are not caused by external (exogenous) factors, but are a function of the multiplicity of relations combined with positive feedback loops, whose effects can be disproportionate to their causes. This is the well-known butterfly effect. Far from accidental, "accidents" that break symmetries and upset equilibria are periodic occurrences.

11. Since disruptions are systemic and therefore unavoidable, development is not continuous; periods of stability are punctuated by periods of instability that are always destructive but sometimes can be productive if adaptation occurs in a timely manner.

This understanding of emerging complex adaptive networks provides a better framework for interpreting today's financial networks than either neoclassical or neoliberal economic theories. Markets—especially today's wired global networks—are network phenomena. Within these networks individual agents and systems—be they human or nonhuman—are intrinsically interrelated. That is to say, individuals do not first exist in isolation from each other and then come together to form groups; to the contrary, individuals become what they are through their participation in a whole that is more than the sum of its parts. This whole might be an ecological system, a religious community, a political party, or a financial market. The relation between the individual and the network, or the part and the whole, is two-way and, therefore, the system is nonlinear. Instead of separate and isolated, as conceived by neoclassical and neoliberal economic theory and much of recent financial economics, agents are interconnected members of networks in which all action is interaction. The interrelation of investors creates the market, which in turn creates possibilities for investors to play their games. In today's financial markets, agents can be either human or algorithmic.

In a book suggestively titled *The Economy as an Evolving Complex System,* complexity theorists John Holland, professor of psychology, electrical engineering, and computer science, and Brian Arthur, an economist who developed the modern theory of increasing returns (discussed later), make a very important point with their co-authors Blake LeBaron and Richard Palmer. "Asset markets," they write, "have a recursive nature in that the agents' expectations are formed on the basis of their anticipations of other agents' expectations, which precludes expectations being formed by deductive means. Instead, traders continually hypothesize —and continually explore—expectational models, buy or sell on the basis of those that perform best, and confirm or discard these according to their performance. Thus, individual beliefs or expectations become endogenous to the market, and constantly compete with an ecology of others' beliefs or expectations. The ecology of beliefs coevolves over time."[24] The use of ecological and biological metaphors for understanding economic process points to important similarities among information, economic, and natural systems that I will consider in Chapter 10. At this point, it is necessary to consider how artificial agents work in ECANs.

One of the most important features of these complex networks is that they are distributed and not subject to any centralized control mechanism. In an effort to understand how distributed networks operate, and to create simulations of markets, investigators have conducted a variety of experiments using "cellular automata," or computer codes that function like algorithms. The interactions of these codes are formally similar to the interactions of cells in other organisms, structures, and organizations. Each cell has a set of instructions that tells it how to respond to the behavior of surrounding cells. In the absence of any overall program or design, cells evolve according to simple rules that respond to altering circumstances created by changes in surrounding cells. As the cells interact, complex forms and patterns begin to emerge. To understand how evolving algorithms work, consider a flock of birds. There is no pilot directing the flock; rather, each bird communicates with the other birds immediately around it and adjusts its movements in a coordinated way. Though no bird knows the overall pattern or precise direction of the flock, the flock "knows" where it is going. In other words, a "mind of the flock" emerges from and guides the movements of the birds, which remain ignorant of it.

In a similar way, the market, which emerges from the activity of individual investors or increasingly different algorithms, loops back to nudge them toward endpoints of which they are not always aware. There is, then, a mind of the market in more than a metaphorical sense. Since markets function like ECANs, they have both a short-term and a long-term memory: thus, the past establishes the parameters of future investment decisions without completely determining outcomes in advance. Markets are characterized by the interplay of freedom and constraint that is found in all domains of human life. Far from consistent and continuous, the interaction of agents and the interrelation of past and future in the present lead to unavoidable disruptions. The historical development of markets is best characterized by what biologist Stephen Jay Gould described in another context as "punctuated equilibrium." Like living organisms, economic systems coevolve through a long process in which periods of relative stability are punctuated by catastrophic events, which, I have stressed, can be both creative and destructive. The gradual accumulation of small changes eventually leads to a qualitative shift.

According to complexity theorists, these moments of discontinuity are when emergence occurs. Since new patterns of order develop from within and are not imposed from without, ECANs are self-organizing. In retrospect, it is clear that Hayek had a much more sophisticated understanding of the relationship between parts and wholes in complex systems than most of his epigones, whose obsession with individualism made them blind to network dynamics.

> Adaptation to the unknown is the key in all evolution, and the totality of events to which the modern market order constantly adapts itself is indeed unknown to anybody. The information that individual organizations can use to adapt to the unknown is necessarily partial and is conveyed by signals (e.g., prices) through long chains of individuals, each person passing on in modified form a combination of streams of abstract market signals. Nonetheless, the whole structure of activities tends to adapt, through these partial and fragmentary signals, to conditions foreseen by and known to no individual, even if this adaptation is never perfect. That is why the structure survives, and why those who use it survive and [sometimes] prosper.
>
> There can be no deliberately planned substitutes for such a self-ordering process of adaptation to the unknown. Neither his reason nor his innate "natural goodness" leads man this way, only the bitter necessity of submitting to rules he does not like in order to maintain himself against competing groups that had already begun to expand because they had stumbled upon such rules earlier.[25]

Like his followers, Hayek remains unaware of the theological history of his interpretation of markets. He has, in effect, developed an economy of salvation that is a story of the fortunate fall in which the market always brings good out of evil by turning individuals' sin (self-interest) into the good of all. This vision is thoroughly Christian and, more specifically, profoundly Protestant. As we have seen, in contrast to medieval Catholic theology in which the individual can be redeemed only through participation in the larger totality of the church universal, Luther privatizes, decentralizes, and deregulates religion. Calvin systematizes Luther's theological innovation by developing a doctrine of creation in which the omniscient, omnipresent, and omnipotent God's invisible hand providentially guides the world. In a world fraught with conflict and torn by self-serving competition, believers are saved from despair by their faith that God works in mysterious ways to bring good out of evil. In this model, the order that gives meaning to life is imposed from without by the transcendent (that is, exogenous) God.

During the years between Luther and Calvin, on the one hand, and Smith, Hayek, and Friedman, on the other, this theological vision did not disappear but was secularized in ways that made it invisible to people who know little or nothing about history, philosophy, and theology. The most important revision in the translation of theology into economics was the change in the source of order and, by extension, ground of meaning. The notion of self-organization represents a reinterpretation of Calvin's providential God and Smith's invisible hand in terms of emerging complex adaptive networks. Smith effectively transforms the external governor into an internal principle of self-regulation to form an account of the order and meaning of markets. From this point of view, the market is a self-organizing, self-regulating system in which the interactivity of networked individuals gives rise to the emergence of organizational patterns, which, in turn, guide agents toward ends that are not always what they had intended. By the late twentieth century, this network had become both virtual and global. Furthermore, human beings had been taken out of the loop—that is, disintermediated—and the networks were taking on a life of their own and evolving in ways that mere mortals could not comprehend. For today's true believers, the market always knows best. But does it really? Is the faith in markets justified or is it a dangerous illusion? While today's constantly expanding markets are virtually omnipresent and seemingly omnipotent, they definitely are not omniscient.

On May 6, 2010, at 2:45 in the afternoon, the Dow Jones Industrial Average plunged about 1,000 points or 9 percent, then recovered most of the losses in a matter of minutes. It was the second largest point swing—1,010.14 points—and the biggest intra-day decline and recovery —998.5 points—in the history of the Dow.[26] In a ten-minute period, the stock market lost and then regained approximately $700 billion in a total swing that amounted to $1.4 trillion. While excessive market volatility has become common in the past two decades, this event was extreme and rattled investors, regulators, and government officials. The plunge immediately rippled through the market, creating a bizarre and unexplainable instability. During the disruption, the stock of major companies like Procter & Gamble and Accenture were trading for as little as a penny and as much as $100,000 in intervals of less than a second. This event, which has come to be known as "The Flash Crash," exposes the instability and vulnerability of emerging complex adaptive trading networks.

In the wake of the crash, industry and government investigators identified multiple causes of the problems. The common denominator in all of these analyses is the increasing speed of financial networks and transactions. The best analysis of the Flash Crash is a little-known documentary by Dutch filmmaker Marije Meerman entitled *Money and Speed: Inside the Black Box*. This film, which has only been released in this country as an iPad app, presents a detailed analysis of the crash nanosecond-by-nanosecond. The film describes the beginning of the crash: "On May 6, 2010 at 1400 hours, 42 minutes, 44 seconds and 75 milliseconds an E-mini future that traded on the Chicago market begins to show erratic price swings. The fluctuations affecting this E-mini are an important indicator of market moods, soon spread to other shares within the U.S., ultimately leading to the fastest and most dramatic fall of Dow Jones ever."[27] But the crash was brief, so brief that my son Aaron's question after the 1987 crash—"Where did the money go?"— becomes ever more urgent.

In the short time since the Flash Crash, there have been similar incidents. In March 2012 a single trade of Apple caused the stock to drop 9 percent in a matter of seconds; later that year 148 stocks listed on the NYSE, many of which were the most popular on the exchange, displayed "irregular trading patterns." Investigators eventually identified a "rogue algorithm" of one of the most powerful brokerage firms in the country, Knight Capital Group, as the cause of the problem. At the height of the crisis, Knight was losing $10 million a minute and by the end of the trading day, the stock was down 25 percent. On May 18, 2012, Facebook's IPO, which was one of the biggest ever in technology and the biggest in Internet history, faltered because of a NASDAQ computer malfunction during the first hours of trading, which led to tens of millions of dollars in trades being wrongly priced. Perhaps most telling of all, in May 2012 Bats Global Markets prematurely released a trading platform for high-speed, high-volume traders that malfunctioned because of programming errors. All stocks with symbols between A and BFZZZ, including its own, stopped trading, causing an instantaneous precipitous drop. Analysts attributed the debacle to the pressure to keep up in an ever-accelerating competitive market. It is clear, however, that another contributing factor was the continuing fragmentation of markets. In the wake of the string of disasters in 2012, Nathaniel Popper of the *New York Times* reported that "regulators are still grappling with whether the rise of high-speed firms has become a net benefit or loss for investors. . . . Many market experts have argued that the technical glitches that have recently hit the markets have been the result of a broader trend of the market splintering into dozens of automated trading services and a lack of human oversight."[28]

In an effort to reassure the public and to obscure the magnitude of the problems, defenders of the way that financial markets have evolved over the past two decades attribute these failures to "rogue algorithms" or "rogue traders," like former Goldman Sachs board member Rajat Gupta, who was sentenced to two years in prison for insider trading. Others blame large banks and brokerage houses for inadequate oversight and insufficient risk management. When JPMorgan Chase's golden boy, Jamie Dimon, recently came under fire when his risk management team lost $6 billion dollars, he blamed the "mistake" on "a London Whale" (that is, a super-high-volume trader) and hung his own golden girl, Ina Drew, out to dry by blaming her and her risk-management group for inadequate oversight. But this is not the 1980s and the problems with today's markets are not the result of the failure of either individuals or institutions. The problems are structural and, therefore, systemic.

Because of this increasing volatility, both domestic and foreign investors are becoming wary of U.S. financial markets. Between May and October of 2011, investors withdrew $90 billion from domestic equity funds. Alarmed by these developments, former SEC chairman Arthur Levitt published an article in the *New York Times* on August 2, 2012, entitled "Errant Trades Reveal a Risk Few Expected" in which he urged the SEC to hold hearings as quickly as possible to address these problems. Levitt's comment is bitterly cynical because, as we have seen, he was responsible for enacting the rules and regulations that transformed financial markets in ways that made both the increasing speed and the volatility that accompanies it inevitable. To make matters even worse, after leaving his post as chair of the SEC, Levitt reportedly became a consultant for some of the very same high-speed, high-volume trading firms that he first enabled and then disingenuously criticized. He was not the only influential figure to change his tune. The morning after the Flash Crash, Duncan Niederauer, CEO of the NYSE, who had been a cheerleader for high-speed trading, said in an interview on the floor of the exchange, "Everybody has to compete on technology, and what we're all going to ask ourselves is how fast is too fast, when is enough enough?" And then, pausing, "It's not sustainable."[29]

But the sense of urgency has not been reflected in the measures taken to address the problem. Since today's global markets are all connected, concern has been growing as well in countries other than the United States. In 2012, the German government approved "legislation that would, among other things, force high-speed trading firms to register with the government and limit their ability to rapidly place and cancel orders, one of the central strategies used by the firms to take advantage of small changes in the price of stocks. A few hours later, a European Union committee agreed on similar but broader rules that would apply to the entire Continent if they win approval from the union's governing bodies."[30] With growing volatility and bubble after bubble, other countries are beginning to share Europe's concern.

In the United States, reforms are, predictably, moving much more slowly. Trying to justify his own mistakes, Levitt doubled down on speed in a *Wall Street Journal* article entitled "Don't Set Speed Limits on Trading: Why Penalize Efficiency? It Creates Deep and Liquid Markets." Touting the advantages of the faulty system he created, he writes, "Due to the rise of high-frequency trading, investors both large and small enjoy a deeper pool of potential buyers and sellers, and a wider variety of ways to execute their trades. There are today more than 30 execution venues—ranging from established global exchanges to a plethora of specialized markets—catering to the particular trading needs of institutions and individuals. Choice abounds, and investors now enjoy faster, more reliable execution technology and lower execution fees than ever before." The flaws in Levitt's argument are too numerous to list. In the face of mounting evidence to the contrary, he concludes, "We should not set a speed limit to slow everyone down to the pace set by those unwilling or unable to compete at the highest levels of market activity. Investors large and small have always been served well by those looking to build the deepest possible pool of potential buyers and sellers, make trades at a better price, and all as quickly as possible. More liquidity, better pricing and faster speeds are the building blocks of healthy and transparent markets, and we must always affirm those goals."[31] Better pricing? Healthy and transparent markets? Advantages to more, and more choices? Fragmentation into thirty trading venues? Reliable execution technology? More liquidity in markets that suddenly freeze up? Levitt and those who agree with him are living in a parallel universe that has nothing to do with the real economy or the real world.

The aversion to regulation is, of course, widespread in the United States and has led to stopgap measures that amount to little more than Band-Aids. The most common step is the imposition of circuit breakers to halt trading briefly and give markets a chance to adjust to whatever sharp movement has occurred. But the circuit breakers proposed by the SEC don't work because they are too slow or, alternatively, trading networks are too fast. The most common practice is to halt markets if the prices move more than 10 percent in five minutes. But in a world where time is measured in nanoseconds, five minutes is an eternity. Instead of solving the problem, such circuit breakers actually make it worse. High-speed traders can game the system by causing delays in the trading of some stocks, thereby driving up their prices. As analysts in *Money and Speed* point out, "If you're the one who causes it [the price rise and hence delay], anytime you know what's going to happen before somebody else does. That's the opportunity." George Dyson proceeds to explain: "If we operated on this time scale of five minutes, you could go out for a cup of coffee, come back and find that you've lost a billion dollars. That would ruin your day and yet for these computers operating in micro-seconds it makes no difference so using circuit breakers is a case of imposing our timescale on computing timescale." The bottom line is that high-speed ECANs short-circuit the circuit breakers designed to control them.

Commenting on these developments, Henry Hu, a former SEC director of risk, strategy, and financial innovation and professor at the University of Texas, Austin, explains, "What is starting to become clear is that the costs in terms of these random shocks to the system are occurring in ways that people never anticipated."[32] The reason people did not anticipate destructive disruptions is that they have been blinded by their own presuppositions and theories and thus do not understand the structure and dynamics of emerging complex adaptive networks. In nonlinear, positive feedback systems, disruptive events are not outliers; to the contrary, fat tails are periodic, though their precise timing is unpredictable. Abrupt changes are not only being caused by external events or merely the aberrant behavior of individuals or particular institutions; rather, major changes are the result of the gradual buildup of factors internal to the system itself. The nonlinearity of self-reinforcing mechanisms and events creates positive feedback loops that strengthen inclinations and actions of interrelated agents. Expectations feed expectations at an accelerating rate, creating a network effect in which more becomes different. At a certain juncture, the market reaches a "tipping point," which results in something like a phase shift. Since investors—be they people or algorithms—are not simply independent individuals but are interactive agents, these decisions and actions become self-reinforcing.

Per Bak, who was a professor in the physics department at the Brookhaven National Laboratories, draws on his understanding of natural systems to explain how the gradual change leads to abrupt disruptions in social, political, and economic ECANs. "Complex behavior in nature," he explains, "reflects the tendency of large systems with many components to evolve into a poised, 'critical' state, way out of balance, where minor disturbances may lead to events, called avalanches, of all sizes. Most of the changes take place through catastrophic events rather than by following a smooth gradual path. The evolution of this very delicate state occurs without design from any outside agent. The state is established solely because of the dynamical interactions among individual elements of the state: the critical state is *self-organized*. Self-organized criticality is so far the only known general mechanism of complexity."[33] The example Bak uses to illustrate his point is a pile of sand. As the pile grows grain by grain, it approaches a critical point at which one more grain will cause an avalanche. While it is possible to know with certainty that the pile will collapse, it is not possible to know precisely which grain of sand will cause the avalanche.

With greater connectivity and higher speeds, disruptive effects cascade through networks faster and faster. For theorists and traders committed to the notions of equilibrium and rationality embedded in the efficient market hypothesis, investors poised at the tipping point appear to be acting irrationally. Instead of carefully assessing their situation and making independent judgments, they go with the accelerating flow. Rather than being merely the result of decisions made by single individuals, market movements are subject to dynamics that are a function of the networks as a whole.

In order to understand the extraordinary range of factors that have contributed to the emergence of extreme finance in these networks, it is necessary to add a final factor to this volatile mix—the fungibility of information and data. In a digital environment, data become fungible and thus the networks that transmit different data can interact in ways that previously were not possible. I have insisted that ECANs have the same structure and work the same way regardless of the medium in which they operate. This means that their coevolution follows the same trajectory—natural, social, political, religious, cultural, economic, or financial networks all tend to become more complex and accelerate in ways that make them more unstable. Since these networks are open rather than closed and the information and data circulating through them are fungible, they form a network of networks or a worldwide web that functions by the same principles as each subnetwork. And because the boundaries of networks are porous, data can migrate among networks, making it impossible to distinguish inside from outside. From this point of view, disruption is neither precisely endogenous nor exogenous. The flow of information explodes as prices of commodities; consumer products; financial assets; media; entertainment; news about local, national, and international events; and even the weather circulate through inter-operative networks at an accelerating rate. Lines of influence are multidirectional rather than one-way. News influences financial markets, which, in turn, have an effect on the news. For example, the weather influences crop prices, which are reflected on primary, secondary, and tertiary global futures and options markets, and the price of these financial assets influences the amount of capital available for agricultural producers. While this is going on, half a world away, religious beliefs fuel political rebellions that drive up the price of oil, which, in turn, rattles worldwide commodity and security markets.

This interlocking network of networks has expanded and accelerated considerably over the past two decades. During the 1980s and 1990s, traditional print publications that investors depended on began to give way to burgeoning television networks like CNBC, FNN (Financial News Network), and Fox Business, which were devoted to financial markets. With the dot-com boom in full swing, finance became a new form of entertainment. Programs like *Squawk Box, Street Signs, Market Week,* and *Market Wrap* were broadcast from NASDAQ headquarters in Times Square. One of the most important features of these new networks and shows was the invention of celebrity financial journalists —Ron Insana, co-anchor of CNBC's *Street Signs* and *Business Center,* who is long gone; Louis Rukeyser, host of PBS's *Wall Street Week,* who is dead; Maria Bartiromo, dubbed the "Money Honey," co-anchor of CNBC's *Street Signs* and *Money Wrap* who now anchors Fox Business's *Opening Bell;* and Lou Dobbs, formerly anchor of CNN's *Moneyline* and now on the Fox Business Network. With the growth of cable networks in the past two decades, there has been a steady increase in the number of TV shows devoted to financial markets. This avalanche of information has gained further momentum from countless websites devoted to the economy and financial markets. Financial markets and news outlets form yet another self-reinforcing loop—news outlets provide information that drives markets whose movements are then reported by the news outlets.

No company embodies the intersection of financial markets, news, and entertainment more than the $16 billion global conglomerate Bloomberg. Founded in 1981 by Michael R. Bloomberg, the company has more than two hundred offices and offers a global news service, worldwide television programming, radio, and publications on the Internet and in print. With 145 bureaus around the world, Bloomberg Television provides over 5,000 news stories daily to approximately 350 newspapers and magazines. While these services continue to expand, the company's most influential innovation has been the Bloomberg Terminal, which enables users to analyze real-time financial market data changes and place trades on its electronic trading platform. What makes the system unique is that it provides news, price quotes, and messaging across all parts of its proprietary network. The desktop terminals have a ridiculous 30,146 functions and have between two and six displays. Most major financial firms have subscriptions to Bloomberg terminals and services for a monthly fee of $2,400, and some exchanges charge clients additional fees to access their real-time price quotes on the terminals. As of May 2010, there were 310,000 Bloomberg Terminal subscribers worldwide.[34] The Bloomberg Terminal transforms every trader's desk into a node in a worldwide web that provides a constant flow of information and data and facilitates transactions anywhere, any time.

While the Bloomberg network is for big players, recent technological innovations are also changing how individuals consume information for investment purposes. The emergence of social media and mobile devices like iPhones and tablets add additional layers that further complicate interactive networks. The amount of data carried on mobile networks continues to expand. According to the most recent estimate by Cisco Systems, it will rise about 66 percent this year. Just as there was a shift from mass communications to mass customization in consumer products and advertising, so too there has been a shift from mass communications to mass customization in financial news and products. With high-speed mobile devices and wireless networks more widely available, individualized news feeds and personalized financial data are available anywhere, anytime.

As each network as well as the network of these networks continues to accelerate, the entire system approaches the tipping point. Systems, structures, and networks, I have argued, have as a condition of their own possibility that which eventually undoes them. For the financial economy to continue to grow, many investors believe it must accelerate further, but there are speed limits even in virtual reality. In the world of extreme finance, as in the world of extreme weather, catastrophic events are becoming more common and, as we will see in Chapter 10, for precisely the same reasons. At a certain point, the speed of virtual networks, on the one hand, and real people and natural systems, on the other, diverge, creating a gap that cannot be bridged. The consequences of this turn of events are as disastrous for individuals as for the multiple interconnected networks in which their lives are entangled. In this high-speed world, neither people nor money ever sleep. And yet the faster they rush to catch up, the less time people have and the further behind they fall.

Fungibility in economics
Fungible assets simplify exchange + trade

9. Reprogramming Life— Deprogramming Minds

· ·

Misleading intro
— not really about Life
but individual reflections
of life

Lessons of a Teacher

Explore

To be an effective teacher, it is necessary to listen to and learn from students. The lessons students have taught me over the past four decades are often surprising and sometimes disturbing. The last year I was at Williams College, I taught a course with a colleague in the Chemistry Department, Chip Lovett, entitled "What Is Life?" This was not a course about the pressing existential questions of young adults, but an examination of the philosophical implications of how biologists and chemists understand life today. Chip is an extraordinarily talented teacher and led the students and me through complex biological and chemical theories, models, and formulas with the utmost clarity. I was responsible for leading a discussion about philosophers who have written about recent developments in biology.

Uses this Science to give credence

My motivation for proposing this course grew out of my own research and writing. For the previous several years, I had been studying emergent complex adaptive networks in the economic, social, political, and cultural systems and had concluded that they have the same structure and work in virtually the same way in all media. I was curious to see if this analysis could be applied to biological organisms and systems.

Chip Lovett :— expertise
DNA/ SOS in bacteria — B. subtilis
Chem 321 Biedensky

266

With the decoding of the genome and the increasingly sophisticated understanding of chemical interactions as rudimentary coding mechanisms, I had begun to suspect that biochemical processes functioned something like information processes. If this were so, then the fungibility of data had to be extended to biological organisms and chemical processes. This, in turn, would mean that the network of networks would include social, cultural, economic, financial, political, chemical, biological, and ecological networks and systems.

The course was very successful and the students' response was overwhelmingly positive. But the experience was memorable for another, more personal reason: it was the first time I had students whose parents I had taught. Late in the semester, one of these students came to see me to discuss her final paper assignment. I had taught both her mother and father and had been close to them during their undergraduate years but, as so often happens, had lost touch with them. As their daughter and I talked, she told me about growing up on the Upper East Side and attending a posh girls' school where social pressures were surpassed only by academic pressure. She said that she wanted to do her paper on the problem of attention deficit disorder. Rather than limiting her discussion to the social issues, she wanted to study the biochemical basis of the condition. When I asked her why she was interested in this subject, she replied that during high school her parents had forced her to go to a psychological counselor who diagnosed her as having ADD and prescribed Ritalin. She insisted that she did not have the condition and resisted taking the drug but the counselor persisted. When she arrived at college, she stopped taking Ritalin and started giving it to her friends, who used it to help them concentrate when writing papers or taking exams. I asked her how many Williams students she thought took speed and she replied that over 50 percent used the drug. She also reported that many students both at her prep school and in college go to counselors known for prescribing Ritalin freely so they can get the drug and use it to give themselves a competitive advantage in their schoolwork. I asked her if their parents knew what is going on and she said, yes, and many approve of it. As a member of the generation for whom speed had meant LSD, a quite different chemical fix, this news was a revelation to me.

Not in UK — speed always amphetamie?

The second lesson grew out of my experiments with technology in the classroom. In the early 1990s, I realized that the same technologies that were changing media, communications, and financial networks were going to transform higher education. In the fall of 1992, I taught the first global tele-seminar with my Finnish colleague Esa Saarinen. Ten students at Williams College met weekly with ten students at the University of Helsinki in a seminar entitled "Imagologies: Media Philosophy," where we discussed the philosophical, social, psychological, political, and economic implications of rapid technological change. It is easy to forget how fast technology changes; none of the students in the seminar had used email—nor had Esa or I. The course was an enormous success and received considerable national and international attention.

e-mail

Having confirmed my suspicions about the transformative effect of emerging media, I began regularly teaching classes that required students both to study demanding philosophical works and to analyze critically the issues we were exploring in a multimedia format. In terms of my own research, these courses have been among the most productive I have offered because students have taught me about cutting-edge technologies and their interests have given me a very good sense about which way the winds of change are blowing.

A few years ago, I became intrigued by the burgeoning interest in video games and decided to teach a course on massive multiuser online games entitled "Gods, Games, and Play." I was not only interested in learning about the world of video games, but also wanted to consider the ways that technology and changing economic and financial conditions are transforming attitudes about work and play. Predictably, the

LSD — hallucogen
Ritalin — stimulant; methylphenidate : attention/behavior
Not sure it is 'Adderall is: it is amphetamine like

course had eighteen men, some of whom were playing video games like *World of Warcraft* forty hours a week, and two women. Since it was not possible for students to create a video game in one semester, the final project required teams of students to design a video game and develop a business plan to pitch to venture capitalists who might fund its development. The plan had to include a description of the game, an analysis of the technical requirements, a budget for the project, a market analysis, and a timetable for production. The only requirement was that the game had to have some socially redeeming value; I left it up to the students to determine what "socially redeeming" meant. At the end of the semester I brought in two people with considerable investment experience and each team pitched their project to them. The investors evaluated both the viability of the games and the effectiveness of the presentations.

The course was in many ways very successful and I learned at least as much from the students as I hope they learned from me. I was amazed by what I discovered about video games and how involved so many students were in them. The more I learned about this new world, the more relevant these games seemed to be for the future of these students. Many of them will spend their lives in front of computer screens manipulating images and data at very high speeds in extremely competitive environments. Indeed, I began to realize that hedge funds, where many of the students hoped to get jobs, are actually massive multiuser online games.

But in spite of the involvement with gaming and interest in the readings and issues we were considering, something was missing in our discussions. There was no energy, passion, and enthusiasm. While this happens sometimes in courses, I had always known what buttons to push to vitalize discussions; this time everything I tried failed. One day, I said, "We are going to take a time out. Something's wrong. You are totally into video games and seem interested in the readings, but there is no energy in our discussions. You seem timid and cautious. What's going on?" I gave them as long as they needed to talk among themselves and in a rather short time, they came to a consensus about the reasons for the problem. They explained that even before they entered kindergarten, they had been programmed to do well so they could take the next step required on the long path that eventually would lead to college. One of the lessons they had learned along the way was that failure is not an option because a single B in a course can be the difference between getting into or not getting into your top choice college. What depressed me even more is that they were right about the insane admissions system that has been created. Though it was never stated explicitly, students had figured out that it was better to play it safe and not take risks that might be judged negatively. Much to my astonishment, they were afraid to let their imaginations roam freely. Furthermore, they faced a dilemma they never anticipated—having been successful in their lifelong quest to get into the college that *U.S. News and World Reports* annually ranks the number one liberal arts college in the country, they really did not know why they were there and had no idea where they were heading after graduation.

Two years later the memory of that class returned. My son Aaron, who was living on the Upper West Side at the time, called.

"Hey, I have good news! Selma [who was two and a half at the time] got an interview for the preschool on 81st Street."

"Great! How many others are there?"

"Fourteen kids are interviewing for two places. Her interview is next Tuesday. We can take her but not be in the room for the interview."

"What kind of questions will they ask her?"

"I have no idea."

The final lesson that is relevant in this context comes from my own experience as a student. With college looming on the horizon, my parents, who both taught at the public high school I attended, decided I should take a course in speed reading, offered by a newly hired instructor. I wanted to take auto mechanics, but they insisted that being able to read faster would be a big help when I got to college. In those pre-computer days, the teacher used films and workbooks to try to teach students how to read in phrases rather than word-by-word. Like an athlete beginning slow and building up his strength, the films of written texts started by highlighting short groups of words and gradually lengthening them until you were supposed to be reading whole sentences in a single glance. After viewing each film, we were given a multiple-choice test to check our comprehension. The course did not help me much and my reading remained rather slow. I had been a reluctant student but the real problem was that most of the books that interested me could not be read quickly.

I thought about this course often during my final year of graduate school at Harvard. A visiting professor from the University of Heidelberg, Dieter Henrich, was teaching an undergraduate philosophy course entitled "Between Kant and Hegel." Because Harvard, like most other American universities, was so deeply committed to Anglo-American analytic philosophy, no one had taught major continental figures like Kant, Hegel, Kierkegaard, and Nietzsche for many years. A group of graduate students from different departments audited the course and found it so helpful that we recorded the lectures and hired someone to transcribe them. The single-spaced, three-hundred-page manuscript circulated for many years until one of the students edited and published the lectures as a book. Professor Henrich ran a concurrent reading seminar on Hegel's notoriously difficult *Science of Logic* for graduate students. The text we studied for the entire semester consisted of just fourteen of the 844 pages in Hegel's weighty tome. Henrich explained that since Hegel's system is fractal, if you understood one part of it, you would understand the whole. I soon discovered that there is no more difficult work in the entire history of Western philosophy. Week after week, we engaged in a word-by-word, line-by-line analysis of the text until the structure of Hegel's entire system gradually began to emerge. This seminar proved to be a unique educational experience for me and has profoundly influenced everything I have taught and written ever since. Indeed, I could not have written this book without what I learned in that seminar. It was in Henrich's slow, patient interpretation of those few pages that I began to appreciate the far-reaching importance of the central issues that lie at the heart of this book: the one and the many, unity and plurality, community and individuality, identity and difference, simplicity and complexity, whole and part, synthesis and analysis, integration and fragmentation, linear and nonlinear systems. But the most lasting lesson was one whose importance extended far beyond Hegel's *Logic*—I learned that truly important works must be read slowly and the thinking that really matters takes time, sometimes an entire lifetime.

obvious!

F-Reading

In 1882, Albert Robida wrote an astonishingly prescient science-fiction novel entitled *The Twentieth Century,* which is set in 1950s France. The innovative interplay of image and text creates a hypertextual effect that enacts the developments Robida presents. The world he describes bears an uncanny similarity to life today. New media erode the boundary between news and entertainment, telecommunications collapse distance, multinational corporations dominate politics and create societies and cultures that are increasingly homogeneous. As global financial networks spread, France is transformed into a limited corporation and voters become shareholders in the nation. Public and private authorities maintain control through telephonescopes that are hidden in schools, offices, and bedrooms and connected in vast surveillance networks. This hyper-connected world takes a toll on its citizens.

Modern science is somewhat responsible for the general bad health of the public. Overwrought, wired up, frightfully busy and

Technology Ad science

nervous, life in the electrical age, we must admit, has overtaxed the human race and brought about a kind of universal degeneration. . . . Muscles have gone lax. . . . The brain, being the only organ at work, absorbs the vital influx to the detriment of the rest of the body, which in turn atrophies and degenerates. The man of the future, if we do not intervene, will end up as an enormous brain within a skull like a dome mounted on most fragile limbs! . . . Not to mention a thousand other ailments, such as the general nervousness produced by this omnipresent electricity, by this fluid that circulates all around us and soaks through us.

Parents and teachers are continually devising new strategies to help children keep up in this increasingly fast-paced world. A recent college graduate in the humanities explains the logic of the school's "efficient" curriculum.

"Oh! Of course, you realize that the curriculum in literature is not a very demanding one. Concentrated literature courses have been invented to both facilitate and abbreviate literary studies. Not too taxing for the brain. . . . The old classics are now condensed into three pages!"

"Excellent! Those old classics, those Greek and Roman rascals, made life difficult for generations of students."

"The transformation they underwent made it easy to study, completely painless. Each author has been summed up in a mnemonic quatrain, easy to learn, effortless to memorize."[1]

Robida's novel uncannily anticipates concerns of a growing number of people today. The recent deluge of articles and books expressing concern about the effects of the Internet, World Wide Web, iPads, iPods, smartphones, and an ever-growing list of other electronic devices borders on hysteria: "Is Google Making Us Stupid?"; "Is the Internet Making Us Crazy?"; *iDisorder: Understanding Our Obsession with*

Technology and Overcoming Its Hold on Us; iBrain: Surviving the Technological Alteration of the Modern Mind; Distracted: The Erosion of Attention and the Coming Dark Age; Data Smog: Surviving the Information Glut; The Shallows: What the Internet Is Doing to Our Brains. Such anxious responses to new technologies are not, of course, new. We have seen that in the early twentieth century, trains, telephones, telegraphs, photography, and cinema created grave concerns about the physical and psychological effects of technology. Scientific and medical research at the time led to procedures and prescriptions for cures that today seem misguided, if not downright foolish. What makes the situation today different is that new technologies have become both more pervasive and invasive and are proliferating and operating faster and faster. At the same time, scientific advances in neuroscience and brain research now make it possible to understand how technology changes the way our minds work as it transforms the physical structure and operation of the brain.

The facts about the accelerating use of technology are sobering. Nicholas Carr reports that in 2009 the average American, regardless of age, was spending an average of twelve hours a week online, which was twice the average in 2005. The iPhone, which was introduced in 2007, has only made the situation worse since then. Today the average person sends or receives four hundred texts a month, four times the number in 2007, and the average teen processes 3,700 texts a month.[2] Rather than reducing work and increasing leisure, as technology enthusiasts had long promised, mobile and wireless devices extend the working day beyond all reasonable limits. For harried workers chained to their iPhones and Blackberries, Henry Ford's formula of eight hours work, eight hours leisure, and eight hours rest seems a quaint memory for a bygone era. A recent international survey of 27,500 people between the ages of eighteen and fifty-five found that respondents on average spent 30 percent of their so-called leisure time online.[3] Moreover, in today's overly competitive environment, a growing number of Americans do not feel free to take all the vacation to which they are entitled. Even when taking time off, they are afraid to disconnect and thus remain on call 24/7/365.

As technology continues to invade our lives, the list of maladies attributed to its use has grown. Research studies by respected scientists have established a plausible correlation between Internet use and anxiety, depression, boredom, distraction, cardiovascular stress, and poor vision. The most troubling finding is the growing evidence that this new medium is actually addictive. Peter Whybrow, director of the Semel Institute for Neuroscience and Human Behavior at UCLA, goes so far as to argue that "the computer is like electronic cocaine."[4] Psychologist Larry Rosen sums up the research results: "Recent reviews of the non-substance or behavioral addictions that have been studied run the gamut from well-investigated ones like gambling addiction to less studied ones like sugar addiction and pornography addiction. The evidence that a behavioral addiction is the same as a drug addiction, as far as the brain is concerned, appears to be strongest for gambling addictions; however, there is some evidence that Internet addiction might function like a drug addiction. Bradford Regional Medical in Pennsylvania recently launched the country's first inpatient treatment program for Internet addiction. Dr. Kimberly Young, who founded the program, claims that Internet addiction 'in this country can be more pervasive than alcoholism.'"[5] The ten-day program costs $14,000, which is not covered by health insurance. Modeled on the well-established approach of Alcoholics Anonymous, this program includes a seventy-two-hour "digital detox," during which patients are cut off from the Internet and any use of computers, as well as a psychological evaluation and group therapy.

A recent study of brain tissue in adolescents afflicted with Internet addiction leaves no doubt that there are differences between addicts and non-addicts in terms of their brain systems. The researchers found that there were "significant differences in the gray matter and white matter—measures related to the structure and functions of neurons

—between the addicted adolescents and their 'healthy' counterparts."[6] While the evidence is not yet conclusive, the next edition of the standard *Diagnostic and Statistical Manual of Mental Disorders* will specify Internet addiction as an area for further research.

These studies confirm suspicions that many people have about the deleterious effects of digital media and technology on children and young people. Nowhere are these concerns more evident than in the worried responses to what can only be described as the epidemic of attention-deficit hyperactivity disorder (ADHD). The Centers for Disease Control and Prevention recently reported that approximately 6.4 million children ages four to seventeen have been diagnosed with ADHD. This represents a 16 percent increase since 2007 and a 53 percent increase in the past decade. The condition is more common in school-age boys (15 percent) than girls (7 percent). With this increase in diagnoses, there has been a correlative increase in the use of drugs like Ritalin, Adderall, Concerta, and Vyvanse for treating the condition. From 2004 to 2012, sales of stimulants to treat ADHD rose from $4 billion to $9 billion. The report provoked an alarmed response on the part of parents, physicians, and the news media. Many critics who were eager to criticize pharmaceutical companies for pushing their drugs raised the specter of doctors over-diagnosing the condition, perhaps even as part of an unethical partnership with the drug companies.

While these criticisms are not necessarily misguided, simply blaming drug companies and doctors oversimplifies an extremely complex problem. To understand the actual or perceived increase in ADHD, it is necessary to place the problem in the context of the multiple intersecting trajectories I have been tracing. The most pressing questions are not only what we are doing with technology, but also what technology is doing to us. There is a recurrent feedback loop in which human beings produce technologies that turn back on them and recreate their creators in their (that is, the technologies') own image. Just as industrial technologies standardize and industrialize bodies and minds, so do digital

In lockdown is this bad?

You find what you look for

technologies customize and reprogram bodies and minds. Postmodern digitization and mediatization have extended and radicalized the privatization, dematerialization, acceleration, and fragmentation that modern industrialization began through a process of internalization that rewires the brain, reprograms the mind, and transforms the very structure of human selfhood.

To understand how these dynamics work, I would like to return to a question I am often asked: How have students changed since you have been teaching? I have suggested that to answer this question, it is necessary to consider how the world around them has changed. The most important change I have seen is that students read differently now than they did when I started teaching. The following remarks are not based on academic research but grow out of my own experience and reflections over four decades of teaching. It is, however, important to note that much research currently being done confirms my personal observations.

In matters of technology, I have stressed, I have learned by becoming a student of students. I realized the world-transforming effect of information, communications, and media technologies earlier than most people in the academy, but knew early on that I would never be a native in this new territory. One of the students who has been my teacher for more than twenty years is José Márquez, who now creates scripted programs that are distributed to TV and online channels for Telemundo. In the mid-1990s, he was helping me set up a new computer in my office. I was irritated and complained to him that my office was too small and I needed more space for my books. José smiled, gestured to the cramped space and said, "Mark, this is not your office anymore." Turning to the monitor, he said, "This is, and it is bigger than you will ever need." That was an "Aha!" moment for me because suddenly I realized that José related to the computer completely differently than I did. He did not look at the screen confronting him but saw it as a window he could pass through. As he entered the computer, the computer entered him until it inhabited him and actually changed his mind. Watching José navigate this new territory for which I had no map, I began to understand that he and his generation reads, creates, and even thinks differently than I do.

While thought clearly has a neurological foundation, the mind is not hardwired but is extremely plastic and changes throughout a person's lifetime. The ways the mind functions, thinking operates, and knowledge is structured coevolve with the modes of production and reproduction. The transition from oral language to written and then printed text involved a shift of disciplinary regimes every bit as disruptive as the change from book to screen. When Gutenberg's press replaced handwritten scrolls with printed books, the substance as well as the form of texts changed. Standardization imposed structures and rules that transformed writing and by extension, reading. Prior to print, words were not separated, there was no punctuation, and there were no sentences or paragraphs. In addition, handwritten and copied manuscripts were highly irregular and filled with errors. Since scrolls had to be rerolled as they were unrolled, they could never be grasped as a whole and, thus, were strictly linear.

With the advent of printing, all this changed. Standardized punctuation, pagination, and fonts regularized production and regulated writing and reading. In addition to this, textual codes like title pages, tables of content, indices, and bibliographies functioned as proto-search engines that helped readers find materials for which they were looking. The invention of footnotes introduced something like a hyper-textual web that wove together disparate texts. The logic of print imposes itself on writers and readers in ways that create new possibilities and impose new restrictions on thought and expression. Like other technologies considered in this book, print harbors contradictory tendencies—it not only standardizes production and consumption, but also individualizes and privatizes them. In this way, print culture contributes to the erosion of the communalism of oral culture by cultivating solitary writing and reading.

Most of the writers I have taught over the years write long books that are very demanding: Hegel, Kierkegaard, Marx, Nietzsche, Freud, Melville, Poe, Heidegger, Derrida, Lacan, Blanchot, Gaddis, Auster, Powers, Danielewski, DeLillo, to name the most important. Their books cannot be read quickly. They take time—sometimes an entire lifetime—to begin to understand. Most of my career I have taught undergraduates, and I have never hesitated to assign a work because I thought it would be too difficult for them. I tell students that you have to live with important works long enough for them to live in you. The more demanding the text, the greater the pedagogical challenge and the higher the reward for students as well as the teacher. Over the years, this strategy has served me well—several generations of students have taken genuine pleasure in engaging with truly demanding writers. Though few went into academia, I receive notes from time to time that suggest that many lives were changed by the works we read together. In the past decade, however, there have been fewer students interested in, or willing to read, these demanding authors. It is not that students are less intelligent; rather, their interests have changed. Furthermore, the way they read, write, and think is not adapted to many of the authors I believe they should study. Having tracked these changes, I have no doubt that they are the result of the extensive use of electronic and digital media.

Many people lament the fact that young people do not read or write as much as they once did. But this is wrong—the issue is not how much they are reading and writing; indeed they are, arguably, reading and writing more than ever before. The problem is *how* they are reading and writing. There is a growing body of evidence that people really do read and write differently online. The crucial variable once again is speed. The claim that faster is always better is nowhere more questionable than when reading, writing, and thinking. Throughout history philosophers and scientists have used different metaphors for understanding the human brain. The most popular metaphor today is the computer. But when the brain is understood as a computer, thinking appears to be little more than information processing. And while there appear to be algorithmic aspects of human intelligence, it is a mistake to reduce thinking and, by extension, writing and reading, to computational processes.

All too often reading online resembles rapid information processing rather than slow, careful, deliberate reflection. Long, complicated works give way to brief texts that can be comprehended quickly or grasped at a glance. When speed is essential, the shorter, the better; complexity gives way to simplicity, and depth of meaning is dissipated in a play of surfaces over which fickle eyes surf. Obscurity, ambiguity, and uncertainty, which are the lifeblood of art, literature, and philosophy, become coding problems to be resolved by the reductive either-or of digital logic. It is, however, possible that reality is to some extent analog and not merely digital. Speed reading fosters impatience, which leads readers to skip over anything that is not immediately obvious or relevant. As with other media, there are advantages and disadvantages to reading and writing online. The fungibility of data opens the possibility of creating new kinds of work in multiple media. No longer limited to the use of words, authors can create texts that include images, videos, animations, and sounds. Electronic media also afford novel opportunities for design and interactivity. Finally, online writing and reading break down barriers that previously isolated works from each other by establishing hypertextual networks that are immediately searchable. No longer separate books with their own numbers in the Dewey Decimal System, works become nodes in constantly morphing and expanding webs.

Changes in readers' behavior online are no longer a matter of speculation. In 2006, the Nielsen Norman Group used eye-tracking visualizations to conduct a study of 232 people who were asked to look at thousands of Web pages. Researchers discovered what they described as an "F-shaped pattern for reading web content" that is surprisingly consistent across all websites. Reporting on this study, Jakob Nielsen writes, "F for *fast*. That's how users read your precious content. In a few

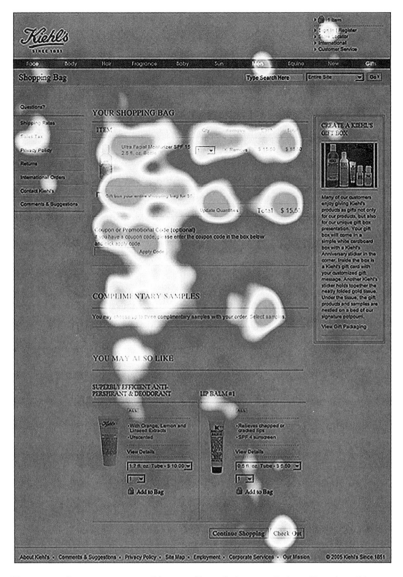

Heatmaps from user eyetracking studies of three websites. Reprinted by permission from the Nielsen Norman Group from http://www.nngroup.com /articles/f-shaped-pattern-reading-web-content.

seconds, their eyes move at amazing speeds across your websites' words in a pattern that's very different from what you learned in school." Heatmaps of eye movements while reading reveal the F-pattern, whereby, as Nielsen explains:

- Users first read in a **horizontal movement**, usually across the upper part of the content area. This initial element forms the F's top bar.
- Next, users move down the page a bit and then read across in a **second horizontal movement** that typically covers a shorter area than the previous movement. This additional element forms the F's lower bar.
- Finally, users scan the content's left side in a **vertical movement.** Sometimes this is a fairly slow and systematic scan that appears as a solid stripe on an eyetracking heatmap. Other times users move faster, creating a spottier heatmap. This last element forms the F's stem.[7]

Fingers not used!

The results of this study are now widely accepted and are influencing the design of websites. In a high-speed world, word placement is as important as product placement. When TiVo and time-shifting gave TV viewers the ability to fast-forward and skip ads, the most expensive advertising spot or time became the last seconds before the program began again. With the discovery of the F-shaped pattern of speed reading, the most valuable location on the website for grabbing attention is on the upper left side of the screen. The rest of the text fades from the field of vision and does not catch readers' attention.

Rapid browsing is not the only problem with online reading; there are other disadvantages to hyperlinks and hypertexts. As Nicholas Carr points out, "When the Net absorbs a medium, it re-creates that medium in its own image. It not only dissolves the medium's physical form; it injects the medium's content with hyperlinks, breaks up the content into searchable chunks, and surrounds the content with the content of all other media it has absorbed. All these changes in the form of the content also change the way we use, experience and even understand the content."[8] Here we discover the connection-disconnection pattern we have seen in other networks—as connectivity increases, fragmentation grows. In online multimedia hypertexts, this fragmentation is a function of methods of both composition and search. Hypertexts are hybrids created by assembling, but not always integrating, materials from different sources and media. The result is a collage in which meaning, if there is any, emerges through juxtaposition and association. This hybridity encourages associative reading that skips quickly from source to source and text to text, rather than sustained analysis and reflection of single texts. Multitasking further compounds this problem. Screens with multiple windows open allow users to jump back and forth from one website or text to another. It is not only texts that are fragmented, but the consciousness and unconsciousness of readers are as well. It is important to stress that this difference is not reducible to linear and nonlinear ways of writing and reading. Contrary to a common assumption, the screen is actually more linear than the book. Like handwritten scrolls, the screen text is never present all at once but must be navigated sequentially in a linear fashion. The book, by contrast, is present all at once and allows readers to move back and forth freely and easily.

The current state of search technology further fragments our experience of reading. Carr correctly argues that "searches also lead to the fragmentation of online works. A search engine often draws our attention to a particular snippet of text, a few words or sentences that have strong relevance to whatever we're searching for at the moment, while providing little incentive for taking in the work as a whole. We don't see the forest when we search the Web. We don't even see the trees. We see twigs and leaves. As companies like Google and Microsoft perfect search engines for video and audio content, more products are undergoing the fragmentation that already characterizes written works."[9] As I have already noted, semantic search, which takes context into account, has not yet been perfected, so searches target isolated words. Part of the problem with current search technology is that machines cannot index what does not explicitly appear on the page. Not only is context missing, but ideas that are implied or suggested, but not explicitly stated, cannot be recorded and stored. Computerized indexing and searching are definitely faster but they are not always better than previous technologies and methods in avoiding the pitfalls of today's overly literal search technology.

Just as printing transformed text production, so the Internet and the World Wide Web are transforming how people read as well as how they write. In the past two decades, there has been an intriguing reversal. Whereas software programs began by imitating print media with metaphors of desktop, file folders, and page numbers, print media have now started imitating the screen: magazines, newspapers, and books increasingly resemble websites. As form changes, so does content. Writing becomes shorter and faster, so that it includes not only tweets but "books" with 140 characters, cell phone "novels," e-"novels," constantly updated customized news, and digests of entertainment updates (also sometimes called "news"). These developments make the traditional *Reader's Digest* or *Moby-Dick for Dummies* look like high literature. As reading habits change, even established publishers have begun encouraging shorter, more accessible books. A well-respected editor recently said to me, "Write shorter, easier books; nobody has time to read long, demanding works anymore."

The speed of online publication has another negative effect that is rarely noticed—responsible editing and revision have virtually vanished. If, as is often said, journalism is the first draft of history, then that is all we seem to have today. As any serious author knows, the amount of work required on a manuscript between its "completion" and its appearance in print is time consuming and often takes as long as a year. But the revisions and refinements involved with fact checking, revising, and copy editing greatly improve the work and increase its value. When all of the people involved in this process are disintermediated, the end result suffers. Longtime technology writer Ken Auletta profiled Henry Blodget, an erstwhile securities analyst who was charged with securities fraud, permanently banned from the securities industry, and now is a media mogul. Commenting on his new online publication *Business Insider,* Blodget explains, "It's half way between broadcast and print. . . . It's controversial. There's a real element of being on air when you're at your desk." Auletta points out the implications of Blodget's venture. "Intrinsic to this conversation is speed; if the facts or conclusions turn out to be wrong, they can be fixed later."[10] When this is the accepted practice of the day, how can I insist that my students write accurately and responsibly?

While it is true that many young people are writing more today than ever before, their writing has been transformed by the technologies to which they are addicted. They might be able to tweet effectively or post engaging messages on their Facebook page, but far too many do not know how to write long, rigorous papers that present a clear thesis and coherent argument. In advanced undergraduate courses, I often require students to write twenty- to twenty-five-page research term papers. As I have noted, these courses usually focus on very demanding artists, writers, and philosophers. Students must read additional primary sources and survey secondary sources to get a sense of the different ways these works have been interpreted by analysts and critics. The final papers must have footnotes and a bibliography, and can have no spelling or grammatical errors. I explain that a research *term* paper means just that—a semester-long project that culminates in a polished finished product. I stress that this kind of reading and writing takes time and cannot be rushed; students cannot, therefore, write the paper at the last minute and expect a satisfactory grade. For many students today, this is the first time they have been required to write such a paper, and they have no idea how to go about it. They do not know how to conduct research and many rarely go to the library; rather, they do everything online. No matter how many times I tell them to outline their argument before they start writing, few follow my suggestion. And no matter how often I tell them they have to finish the paper at least two days before it is due so someone else can proofread it and they can revise it, what they usually hand in is a first draft. I stress that these are very good students who are attending an elite liberal arts college and leading research university, and still many do not know how to write well.

The fault does not lie entirely with students but must be shared by teachers. When I was in high school in the 1960s, during my junior and senior years, I had to write the kind of term papers I require of my college students. We also had to read books over the summer, and during the first week of school we wrote book reports in class. I had always done well in English courses, but junior year I received a C on my beginning-of-the-year book report and was crushed. Over the course of that year, Mrs. Sutherland tore down and built up my writing. It was a painful process but a great gift—by the end of the year, I truly knew how to write. Today, secondary-school teachers work under multiple pressures that make it difficult to devote adequate time to writing. In addition, the cultural obsession with assessment and results has led to an increased reliance on standardized tests to measure educational success. With their own jobs depending on student test performance, teachers understandably teach to the test and do not devote adequate attention to slow, careful instruction in writing. Recognizing the importance of writing and acknowledging the inadequacy of instruction in school, I decided years ago to teach my own children, Aaron and Kirsten, how to write. From the summer after their sixth grade year through the summer before they went to college, I made them write a three-page paper every week on any subject they chose. The only requirement was that it could not be creative writing but had to present a thesis and construct an argument to support it. This too was a long (seven-year) and painful process involving many tears and much conflict. But they both can write and that probably is the most valuable inheritance I will leave them.

The situation is not much better in college. Far too many students arrive at college without being able to write and never have the time to catch up. Working with students on research papers, reading and responding to what they produce, takes time that many faculty members think they do not have. Some schools require students to take writing-intensive courses but this is the exception rather than the rule. With the increasing demands for publication and, correlatively, the decreasing value placed on teaching, there is very little incentive for faculty members to require students to produce time-consuming papers. As a result, in recent years writing assignments in far too many courses have shifted from long to short papers or even periodic blog posts. While shorter forms of writing serve certain practical purposes, much is lost when students do not learn how to conduct research and write long papers that present a sustained argument. As the world continues to accelerate and becomes more complex, careful, deliberate reflection and analysis are needed more than ever. And yet these are precisely the skills that we are failing to cultivate.

Attention Management Disorder

For many years I have said that there are two things you cannot improve—you can't get faster and you can't get smarter. But technological innovation has proven me wrong. Consider the case of Lance Armstrong, seven-time winner of the Tour de France, arguably the best cyclist in history and a cancer survivor who suffered a dramatic fall from grace. In June 2012, both the U.S. and world anti-doping agencies accused Armstrong of using illicit performance-enhancing drugs, and two months later they imposed a lifetime ban from competition and stripped him of all the titles he had won since 1998. While Armstrong eventually publicly admitted to doping, he never explained his methods or confessed to the extent of his deceit. The only reason he gave for doping was to gain a competitive advantage by biking faster. Even in

Conflicted   Armstrong took drugs. Period

the era of steroids and performance-enhancing drugs, Armstrong was widely criticized by fellow athletes as well as the general public.

While Armstrong's actions should not be condoned, the issues his case raises are considerably more complex than the debate it triggered. Technological innovations, including *You can see this* genetic engineering, hormonal treatments, sex-change operations, increasingly effective drug therapies, *interesting but wrong* implants, and transplants make it impossible to distinguish the natural from the artificial. What drugs, procedures, and operations are not performance enhancing? The most radical development in this area is the extension of performance-enhancing technology from the body to the mind. In an article on President Obama's recent brain-mapping project, Philip Boffey writes, "Recent advances in nanotechnology, microelectronics, optics, data compression and storage, cloud computing, information theory and synthetic biology could make possible investigations unimaginable before. For instance, scientists might extend the value of traditional brain scans by implanting neurosensors, wireless fiber-optic probes or genetically engineered living cells to penetrate brain tissue and report which neurons are firing in response to various stimuli."[11] *Not successful* This research has already yielded important results that are being used to treat patients with brain trauma as well as conditions like Parkinson's disease. But these technologies are also being used for more questionable purposes.

We have seen that the Industrial Revolution required a new disciplinary regime. By applying Taylor's principles to workers' bodies and minds, managers attempted to increase the speed and efficiency of production. The newly emerging advertising industry at the time took advantage of mass media to promote mass consumption by stimulating and managing people's desires. Neuroscience, neuropharmacology, and neurosurgery extend scientific management first to the brain and then to the mind. With more and more information, media, images, and data being processed faster and faster, the management of attention

Pg 72 Retrains body (+mind) to rate of machine   Workers Body Managers Mind

equates science to measurement

becomes both more difficult and increasingly valuable. When time is money, there are profits to be made by manipulating attention.

With these insights, let us return to the problem of ADHD. According to many critics, today's high-speed wired world creates a state of distraction that makes it almost impossible to focus the mind and sustain a state of concentration. While this condition began with the invention of speed at the beginning of modernity, it has become progressively worse over the past century, with a growing number of people turning to drugs to cope with the endless acceleration of life. Paradoxically, they believe that the cure for the problem of speed is speed. This drug therapy is one part of the emerging attention-management business that takes many forms. There are three primary reasons young people take Ritalin and Adderall: to control behavior deemed abnormal, to get thinner, and to get smarter. For many parents, teachers, administrators, and physicians with too many kids and too little time, drugs seem to be a quick fix. The government, as well as pharmaceutical and insurance companies, is an important part of this story as well. Just as insurance companies' refusal to pay for psychoanalysis and behavior modification therapy has led to an increase in pharmacological therapies for psychological disorders, so too cuts in school budgets have led to fewer advisers and counselors and an increase in the use of drugs to manage "disruptive" student behavior. Dr. Jerome Groopman, a professor at Harvard Medical School, underscores the dangerous side effects of these drugs and warns of their overuse. "There's a tremendous push where if the kid's behavior is thought to be quote-unquote abnormal— if they're not sitting quietly at their desk—that's pathological, instead of just childhood."[12]

While the use of Ritalin and Adderall for behavior management is often involuntary on the part of the patient, many people take the drugs either to lose weight, which is most common among girls, or to increase mental functioning and enhance one's academic or professional performance. Like athletes, these people take drugs to gain a competitive advantage. When understood in this way, Ritalin and Adderall, as well as other mental-performance-enhancing drugs, are steroids for the brain. Roger Cohen, who has dubbed Adderall "the competition drug," reports the experience of a twenty-four-year-old University of Massachusetts student: "I started taking it [Adderall] my first year in college. My performance had always fluctuated a lot. It was hard to pay attention, even in classes I was interested in. I was getting D's. I felt something had to change. Adderall flies around campus. The first time I took it I wrote a paper for an astronomy class that was out of this world. I could not believe it—I was so inspired it made me want to be a doctor!"[13] As we saw in the case of the daughter of my former students, parents often encourage or even force their kids to take these drugs. Indeed, many of the same people who trashed Lance and called for Barry Bonds and Roger Clemens to be banned from membership in the Baseball Hall of Fame either look the other way or tell their kids to pop pills to improve their grades and increase their SAT scores.

2014 (Published)

interest point

There are mechanical and electronic prostheses as well as chemical supplements that are already enhancing both physical and mental functions. One of the most ambitious projects in this area is BrainGate, which is being developed by scientists at Brown University, Massachusetts General Hospital, and the U.S. Department of Veterans Affairs. Brain-Gate is an implant to help people who have lost control of limbs or bodily functions. A sensor is implanted in the brain and an external decoder connects a prosthesis to external objects. The sensor uses electrodes that conform to the electromagnetic function of the brain's neurons that fire in the areas of the brain responsible for motor control. The sensor transforms the activity into electrical signals that are sent to the external decoder, which uses the brain signals to move a robotic arm or move a cursor. BrainGate enables a person to move his or her body and manipulate physical objects through nothing more than mental activity.[14] But not all the time

BrainGate sold — Guardian article 2011

Though this technology is still in its infancy, it is not difficult to imagine where it will lead. When the brain is more accurately mapped, it will be possible to develop much more sophisticated enhancements that will radically transform the way the mind works. The Kavli Foundation, in cooperation with major research universities, sponsors the Innovative Neurotechnology Initiatives, whose goal is to enable researchers to produce dynamic pictures of the brain that can "show how individual brain cells and complex neural circuits interact at the speed of thought. These technologies will open new doors to explore how the brain records, processes, uses, stores, and retrieves vast quantities of information, and shed light on the complex links between brain function and behavior."[15] Miyoung Chun, the foundation's vice president for science programs, predicts that the completion of the proposed brain activity map will "revolutionize everything from robotic implants and neural prosthetics, to remote controls" that allow a person to "change the channel by thinking about it."[16] This advanced wireless technology will create unprecedented privacy issues by making it possible to hack remotely into brains as well as computers. According to John Donoghue, a neuroscientist and director of the Brown Institute for Brain Science, current technology already makes it possible to read people's brains. A program named P300 "can determine which letter of the alphabet someone is thinking about based on the area of the brain that is activated when she sees a full screen of letters. But even when advances in brain-reading technologies speed up, there will be new challenges, as scientists will have to determine if the person wants to search the Web for something in particular, or if he is just thinking about a random topic."[17] At that point it will be impossible to know whether the Web is a prosthesis of the brain or the brain is a prosthesis of the Web.

Since technology has a logic of its own, it inevitably has unanticipated and unintended effects. Historically, the same technologies that liberate often enslave, and sometimes even do both simultaneously. The extraordinary advances in computational power, data processing, nanotechnology, and neuroscience that are expanding our understanding of the human brain and mind and creating the possibility of unprecedented medical breakthroughs are also being used for less noble purposes. What David Shenk aptly describes as "data smog" creates a condition in which the competition for people's attention becomes fierce. In his instructive article "Toward a History of Attention in Culture and Science," Michael Hanger writes:

> As a direct effect of the omnipresence of new media, attention has become a central focus of interest. Since the spectrum of visual stimuli and entertainment has become so broad, curiosity, pleasure and admiration are no longer regarded as virtues and passions to be stimulated and satisfied. The problem is rather how to acquire and manage more and more information in shorter and shorter periods of time. In this situation, attention is so precious and expensive, because it cannot be increased at one's discretion and it is a target for anyone who wants to "sell" goods, ideas, knowledge, or ideology. Authors such as Georg Frank speak of an "economy of attention" and regard it as a currency that makes it necessary to decide how to invest one's attention and how to evoke attention in others.[18] *like the mating of birds*

I have already considered the ways in which information, media, and communications technologies are being used to target people with customized information and advertisements. Neuroscience and brain research are creating new technologies that are powerful tools in the arsenals of companies, governments, and institutions that want to manage people's attention. While this development is not new, scientific research and technological innovations have increased the effectiveness and efficiency of mental manipulation. These new methods take subliminal advertising to another level. The most extreme forms of attention management to have been developed so far are neuromarketing and neuroadvertising. These techniques attempt to program human behavior by hacking the brain's neural networks. Researchers study customers' sensorimotor, cognitive, and affective responses to advertising stimuli by using magnetic resonance imaging (MRI) and electroencephalography (EEG) to measure changes in the activity of specific parts of the brain. They also map physiological changes by measuring heart rate, respiratory rate, and galvanic skin responses. The most successful neuromarketing firm is NeuroFocus, Inc., which is a global company with offices in Berkeley, New York, Dallas, London, Tokyo, Tel Aviv, Seoul, and Bogotá. Now Neilsen Holdings

In 2011, the information, measurement, and analytics company Nielsen acquired NeuroFocus for $5 billion. A. K. Pradeep, a pioneer in neuromarketing and the CEO of NeuroFocus, explains that he developed his advertising technique by appropriating results from studies of the brains of people with ADHD. He figured that the neurological effects of advertising could be calculated by extending the methods used by neuroscientists studying ADHD. "We put a cap on your head that measures your brain impulses," he explains. "We measure all parts of your brain continuously. Second by second, we measure how much attention you're paying. We get [to learn] what emotions you're experiencing and what memories you are memorizing."[19] Each ad is graded on a scale from one (completely ineffective) to ten (sure bet). The neuromarketing business is currently growing at a rate of more than 100 percent a year and NeuroFocus's expanding list of clients includes major companies like Google, Microsoft, Yahoo, Intel, PayPal, Hewlett-Packard, Disney, PepsiCo, Frito-Lay, Chevron, McDonalds, Unilever, Procter & Gamble, and Citigroup. Sensitive to mounting criticism of the company's techniques, the leadership of NeuroFocus has asked respected academics to show their support by serving on the company's advisory board.

Not limited to the commercial sphere, neuromarketing is also beginning to transform the political process as well. Just as political operatives are using the advertising technique of mass customization to

Flashy Focus groups

No Metrics or Peer review

Yis No Peer review

target potential voters, so too are they using neuroscience to manage voters' attitudes. In the months leading up to the 2008 presidential election, Marco Iacoboni, Joshua Freedman, and Jonas Kaplan from the Semel Institute for Neuroscience and Human Behavior at UCLA conducted a study in which subjects were placed in a brain scanner for one hour. "While in the scanner," researchers explain, "the subjects viewed political pictures through a pair of goggles; first a series of still photos of each candidate was presented in random order, then video excerpts from speeches. Then we showed them the set of photos again. On the before and after questionnaires, subjects were asked to rate candidates on the kind of 0–10 thermometer scale frequently used in polling, ranging from 'very unfavorable' to 'very favorable.'" The results were somewhat surprising. "When we showed the words 'Democrat,' 'Republican' and 'independent,' they exhibited high levels of activity in the part of the brain called the amygdala, indicating anxiety. The two areas in the brain associated with anxiety and disgust—the amygdala and the insula—were especially active when men viewed 'Republican.' But all three labels also elicited some activity in the brain area associated with reward, the ventral striatum, as well as other regions related to desire and feeling connected. There was only one exception: men showed little response, positive or negative, when viewing 'independent.'"[20] A more recent study conducted at the Medical University of South Carolina's Brain Stimulation Laboratory confirmed these results. Lead researcher Roger Newman-Norlund concluded that "the brains of self-identified Democrats and Republicans are hard-wired differently." He reports: "The results found more neural activity in areas believed to be linked with broad social connectedness in Democrats (friends, the world at-large) and more activity in areas linked with tight social connectedness in Republicans (family, country). In some ways the study confirms a stereotype about members of the two parties—Democrats tend to be more global and Republicans more American-centric—but it actually runs counter to other recent research indicating that Democrats enjoyed a virtual biological lock on caring for others."[21]

The results of this research can be interpreted in two opposite but equally troubling ways: on the one hand, that the brain is hardwired and cannot be changed, and on the other hand, that the brain is highly plastic and can be manipulated without people being aware of it. I have argued that nature and culture or, in this case, brain and mind, are codependent because they are bound in mutually influential feedback loops. The brain conditions the mind, whose activities, in turn, reconfigure the brain. Advertisers and political operatives are interested in understanding the dynamics of mind-brain interaction so they can manage attention, manipulate preferences, and program decisions. The preoccupation with attention-deficit hyperactivity disorder has led to what might best be described as attention management disorder. In today's overloaded, high-speed attention economy, competitors will stop at nothing to program people's minds. These developments are having a transformative effect on society and culture by programming decisions that once were personal. In a strange way, Timothy Leary was right when he claimed that it's not only speed (that is, LSD), but also computers that transform minds. Fifty years ago, however, no one could have imagined the ways that neuromarketing and neuroadvertising are programming people's attention and attitudes—how we are being channeled into action by algorithms that circulate through the cloud and are transmitted to our brains' neural circuits. While Marx might not have been right when he declared that the first draft of history is tragedy, he surely was right when he insisted that the second draft is farce.

There is a profound irony in these developments. We have seen that during the past four decades, the ideology of individual choice has been the cornerstone of neoconservative politics and neoliberal economics. Moreover, the conviction "the more choices the better" has been the unquestioned assumption driving consumer as well as financial capital-

Says nothing

Comment on this

?

Libet 2006

The mind represents subjective experience is no physical (?)

ism. But as Kierkegaard taught us two centuries ago, genuinely free choice inevitably involves uncertainty and risk. And nothing makes financial markets more anxious than uncertainty and risk. In a high-speed, hyper-connected world, the question for major players seeking profitable returns becomes how to manage risk. With the stakes rising faster and faster, investors have concluded that human beings cannot be trusted and, therefore, the safest strategy is to get them out of the loop. Thus financial markets, consumer markets, and political campaigns are controlled by algorithms running on global networks of high-speed computers that interact, through vast resources of data, directly and indirectly with our brains.

Deprogramming Minds

Kierkegaard, as much as any other thinker in history, understood the structure of individual selfhood and dynamics of personal decision. Individuals, he argues, are radically free and completely responsible for their lives. While people are conditioned by their natural abilities; the circumstances of their birth; and the social, political, and economic conditions of their time, they must nonetheless self-consciously acknowledge who they are and take full responsibility for the person they become through their own decisions. The present moment of decision is poised on the cusp of a past that extends beyond the individual and an approaching future rich with possibility but fraught with danger. Responsible decisions require individuals to accept the constraints that their past imposes as they move self-consciously toward an open future.

Kierkegaard develops this interpretation of selfhood in a series of pseudonymous writings he published between 1842 and 1855 in which he plots the progression from less to more authentic forms of selfhood. He identifies three basic forms of human life: aesthetic, ethical, and religious. While the details of his analysis need not concern us here, his account of aesthetic life illuminates the implications of the trajectory

Consuses "being used to" — with change

I have been charting. The aesthetic stage, which is the least authentic form of existence, is characterized by what Kierkegaard describes as "immediacy." Aesthetic immediacy takes two seemingly different forms —sensuality and reflection. On the one hand, a person can be completely controlled by desires and sensuous inclinations over which he has no control, and on the other hand, a person can be shaped by abstract ideas and attitudes of others transmitted through upbringing, historical tradition, and most important, public opinion as mediated through the newly emerging mass media of the time. In neither case does the person become a self-conscious individual capable of making his or her own free decisions. One is either programmed by desires however they are stimulated (sensuality), or programmed by impersonal customs and mass media (reflection). Rather than a coherent self with a personal past and open future, aesthetes are driven hither and yon by forces they neither comprehend nor control. Like Bruce Springsteen's "drunk in an alley . . . stumbling blind with no destination at an unholy speed," they have no sense of order, direction, or meaning.

Though written over two centuries ago, Kierkegaard might well be describing lives of many people today. To understand the relevance of his analysis, it is necessary to recall the long arc of history dating back to the beginning of modernity, modernization, and modernism. The processes of speed, dematerialization, privatization, and fragmentation that began in the nineteenth century reach their limit at the beginning of the twenty-first century. The acceleration of life created by the intersection of technological change and financial exigencies has resulted in a culture of distraction that makes it virtually impossible for people to concentrate or sustain their focused attention. Drugs and neural intervention are only the most extreme form of attention management disorder—and as discussed earlier, these techniques exacerbate the very problems they are intended to cure. But the common diagnosis of distraction as the definitive condition of life today misses the most significant point about what is going on. The problem is not so much that distraction scatters attention but that excessive intrusions on attention splinter consciousness and fragment the self. The structural dispersion of decentralized, deregulated, and privatized networks is mirrored in the existential scattering of the self. This point is not only philosophical but biological as well. Gary Small, director of both the Memory Clinic and the Center on Aging at UCLA's Semel Institute for Neuroscience and Human Behavior, and his co-author Gigi Vorgan, maintain that "multitasking allows Digital Natives to instantly gratify themselves and put off long-term goals. The competing simultaneous tasks often provide a superficial view of the information being presented rather than an in-depth understanding. Educators complain that young people in this multitasking generation are less efficient in their school work. Chronic and intense multitasking may also delay any and adequate development of the frontal cortex, the area of the brain that helps us see the big picture, delay gratification, reason abstractly, and plan ahead. If a teenager has the tools and know-how to gain immediate mental gratification from instant messaging or playing a video game, when will that teen learn to delay satisfying every pressing whim or urge in order to completely finish a tedious project or dull task?"[22]

Lest we think that this condition is limited to teenagers playing video games, it is important to recall that hedge funds are in effect massive multiuser online games. High-speed, high-volume traders can no more delay gratification by making responsible long-term investments than adolescent gamers can grasp the long-term consequences of their actions. The screen creates something like an electromagnetic field that draws users into its orbit and immerses them in the fleeting moment, thereby sealing them off from the rest of the world. When long-term collapses into the short-term, the simultaneity of so-called real time makes authentic real time unreal. This is the instant the fusion of connectivity leads to fission, in which the whole explodes into countless parts that are infinitely fragmented. When this occurs, Schiller's words describing the fragmentation of both society and individuals brought about by the Industrial Revolution once again echo through the centuries to describe our condition: "Everlastingly chained to a single little fragment of the whole, man himself develops into nothing but a fragment; everlastingly in his ear the monotonous sound that he turns, he never develops the harmony of his being, and instead of putting the stamp of humanity upon his own nature, he becomes nothing more than the imprint of his occupation or of his specialized knowledge."[23] The machine is now digital rather than mechanical, but the pattern remains the same.

As time contracts, it speeds up, and as time speeds up, it contracts. People in the thrall of these technologies cannot be deprogrammed until the tension of time is restored, and the fleeting present is expanded to include an accumulating past as well as a future full of possibilities. This process can occur only by saving time—not by speeding up, but by slowing down enough for there to be time for reflection, deliberation, perhaps even meditation.

10. Meltdowns

....

Losing Time

In 1928, with unemployment rising, social unrest stirring, and the Great Depression looming, John Maynard Keynes delivered a lecture at Cambridge University intended to persuade impressionable undergraduates that capitalism was a more viable, and every bit as idealistic, economic system than communism. Two years later he published the lecture with the title "Economic Possibilities for Our Grandchildren." Keynes acknowledged temporary economic problems but insisted that they were the result of the difficulties of adjusting to the speed of technological change. "We are suffering, not from the rheumatics of old age, but from the growing-pains of over-rapid changes, from the painfulness of readjustment between one economic period and another. The increase of technical efficiency has been taking place faster than we can deal with the problem of labor absorption; the improvement in the standard of life has been a little too quick." Taking the long view, he briefly traced economic development from the Middle Ages, through the Industrial Revolution, to the twentieth century. Noting that factory output in the United States increased 40 percent between 1919 and 1925, Keynes argued, "We may be on the eve of improvements in the efficiency of food production as great as those which have al-

300

ready taken place in mining, manufacture, and transport. In quite a few years—in our own lifetimes I mean—we may be able to perform all the operations of agriculture, mining, and manufacture with a quarter of the human effort to which we have been accustomed." The rapidity of these changes had created what he labeled "technological unemployment," which had occurred due to the "means of economizing the use of labor outrunning the pace at which we find new uses for labor." Keynes was convinced that this was a temporary problem and went so far as to predict that in the long run "mankind is solving its economic problem." The success of capitalism, he believed, would usher in an era of leisure in which people would need to work only fifteen hours a week to satisfy their needs.

> Thus for the first time since his creation man will be faced with his real, his permanent problem—how to use his freedom from pressing economic cares, how to occupy the leisure, which science and compound interest will have won for him, to live wisely and agreeably and well.
>
> Thus the strenuous, purposeful money-makers may carry all of us along with them into the lap of economic abundance. But it will be those peoples, who can keep alive, and cultivate into a fuller perfection, the art of life itself and do not sell themselves for the means of life, who will be able to enjoy the abundance when it comes.[1]

Freed from the utilitarian struggle of making money, people would have sufficient time to devote themselves to the so-called finer things in life.

As an active member of the Bloomsbury group, Keynes's commitments were always divided between art and money. His appreciation for the impracticalities of the aesthetic life reflected an appreciation for the value and social status of leisure that has long since faded. In his influential 1899 book *The Theory of the Leisure Class*, Thorstein Veblen ar-

The Last Iceberg/Stranded Iceberg II, Cape Bird, Antarctica, 2006. Courtesy of Camille Seaman Photography.

gues that in the early twentieth century, social status was measured by how little rather than by how much a person worked. "A life of leisure," he argues, "is the readiest and most conclusive evidence of pecuniary strength, and therefore, of superior force; provided always that a gentleman of leisure can live in manifest ease and comfort. . . . Conspicuous abstention from labor therefore becomes the conventional mark of superior pecuniary achievement and the conventional index of reputability; and conversely, since application to productive labor is a mark of poverty and subjection, it becomes inconsistent with a reputable standing in the community." The foundational principle of the leisure class is the "sense of the unworthiness of productive work."[2] Keynes and Veblen's agreement about the virtues of leisure should not obscure their important differences. Unlike Veblen, Keynes's predictions about a coming leisure society are not class bound; capitalism, he suggests, is far more revolutionary than communism because it will lead to the democratization of leisure.

Keynes was not alone in his insistence on the importance of leisure. In a 1932 essay entitled "In Praise of Idleness," Bertrand Russell confesses that he, like many others in his generation, was raised to believe that "Satan finds some mischief for idle hands to do." Or, as my Protestant grandmother always used to say, "Idleness is the devil's workshop." Russell proceeds to explain: "Although my conscience has controlled my actions, my opinions have undergone a revolution. I think that there is far too much work done in the world, that immense harm is caused by the belief that work is virtuous, and what needs to be preached in modern industrial countries is quite different from what always has been preached." Recalling Max Weber's notion of the Protestant principle of "inner worldly asceticism," Russell insists that "only a foolish asceticism, usually vicarious, makes us continue to insist on work in excessive quantities now that the need no longer exists." Then, as now, the choice many people faced was time or money—more leisure or more goods. Russell chooses time over money. "In a world where no one is compelled to work more than four hours a day, every person possessed of scientific curiosity will be able to indulge it, and every painter will be able to paint without starving, however excellent his pictures may be. Young writers will not be obliged to draw attention to themselves by sensational pot-boilers, with a view to acquiring the economic independence needed for monumental works, for which, when the time at last comes, they have lost the taste and the capacity. . . . Above all, there will be happiness and joy of life instead of frayed nerves, weariness, and dyspepsia."[3] Russell's vision of the coming capitalist utopia sounds suspiciously like Marx's description of the life in a realized socialist society. The question was less about the goal than the means by which it could be achieved—capitalism or communism.

With the advent of the Cold War, this debate heated up. We have seen that after the end of World War II, the conflict between capitalism and communism expanded from the battleground to the economy. With each side claiming to be able to deliver the goods faster and more efficiently than the other, economic growth became the measure of human well-being. Carl Horne reports that "in 1956, Richard Nixon told Americans to prepare for a four-day workweek in the 'not too distant future.' A decade later, a U.S. Senate subcommittee heard that by 2000 Americans would be working as little as fourteen hours per week."[4] Throughout the 1960s, philosophers, sociologists, and theologians as well as the counter culture's hippies and yippies confidently predicted the dawning Age of Aquarius would be an era of leisure, when the pace of life would slow down and play would displace work as people's primary occupation.

Needless to say, this is not how things have worked out. Even though productivity in the United States has doubled since 1948, leisure time has been declining and the number of hours worked has steadily increased. In her landmark book *The Overworked American: The Unexpected Decline of Leisure,* Juliet Schor observes that "beginning in the late 1960s, the United States had entered an era of rising worktime."

In other words, at the precise moment that social commentators were predicting the coming age of leisure, people were beginning to work longer hours and thus have less free time. "The decline in Americans' leisure time," Schor explains, "is in sharp contrast to the potential provided by the growth of productivity. . . . When productivity rises, a worker can either produce the current output in less time, or remain at work the same number of hours and produce more. Every time productivity increases, we are presented with the possibility of either more free time or more money. That's the productivity dividend."[5] By the early 1990s, advances in technology made it possible for many people to work four days a week or even six months a year. But when faced with the choice—your time or your money—most Americans consistently choose more money and less time. In this new financial calculus, you are wasting time if you are not working productively. People in other countries—most notably Europe—have made other choices. U.S. manufacturing employees currently work 320 hours per year more than their counterparts in Germany and France. The obsession with work has been accompanied by an increasing suspicion of leisure. In the early twenty-first century, the average American failed to take 20 percent of his or her paid vacation.

Why were the predictions of Keynes and many others so wrong? There is no simple answer to this question; cultural, technological, economic, and political factors are involved. While confidently predicting decreasing work and increasing leisure, Keynes nevertheless hedged his bet. "Yet there is no country and no people," he admits, "who can look forward to the age of leisure and of abundance without a dread. For we have been trained too long to strive and not to enjoy. It is a fearful problem for the ordinary person, with no special talents, to occupy himself, especially if he no longer has roots in the soil or in custom or in the beloved conventions of a traditional society."[6] Too much free time leads to boredom, which breeds discontent. But Keynes hints at a deeper issue when he writes, "We have been trained too long to strive and not to enjoy." Once again the ghost of Protestantism haunts capitalism. Protestantism, we have seen, not only encouraged privatization, decentralization, and deregulation of religious and economic structures and promoted literacy and numeracy, but also imposed a disciplinary regime without which capitalism as we know it would have been impossible. Within this tradition, hard work and worldly prosperity are signs of divine election; leisure and pleasure, by contrast, are temptations that threaten to lead people astray. Rather than enjoying the fruits of their labors, disciplined workers are counseled to save their money and invest it with the hope for profitable worldly and otherworldly returns.

With the rise of neoliberal economics, this latent Protestantism has led to a change in the social status of leisure. Far from a virtue and mark of social superiority, leisure has come to be regarded as a vice characteristic of lower social classes, less accomplished people, and less prosperous societies. In the secularized Protestantism of today's wired world, status is measured by how much, rather than how little, a person works. If you are not connected 24/7/365, you must not be very important. This new attitude toward work represents a complete reversal of Veblen's analysis in which the leisure class enjoys social status. It is important to note, however, that there remains a class dynamic. The new non-leisure class for whom long hours are a sign of success consists of primarily aspiring professionals whose Blackberries, iPhones, and Bloomberg terminals keep them constantly connected. The situation has become so bad that not even the bedroom is off-limits. A *Wall Street Journal* article entitled "More Work Goes 'Undercover': Bringing the Office to Bed for 3 a.m. Emails to China; Wi-Fi Mattress," reports that as many as 80 percent of young New York City professionals work regularly from bed. To accommodate changing patterns of work, Reverie, a maker of adjustable beds, now "offers a built-in power outlet in the base of its beds to plug in lamps, televisions or laptops. Both the outlet and the bed's movement can be operated with a hand-held remote, or with the user's smartphone or tablet via built-in Wi-Fi and

Bluetooth." Luxury-bed manufacturer E. S. Kluft & Co. offers a seven-by-seven-foot bed, 16 percent bigger than a standard king bed, for working couples. "One split model features separate adjustments for each side, partly to allow couples to spread out papers and work from bed, says chief executive Earl Kluft. A recent ad shows a couple eyeing a laptop side-by-side, portraying the bed as 'a gathering place, a work-place, a comfort zone for the couple,' says Mr. Kluft."[7]

At this point, the absurdity of the situation becomes transparent. As Schor correctly stresses, "The time squeeze surfaced with the young urban professional. These high achievers had jobs that required sixty, eighty, even a hundred hours a week. On Wall Street, they would regularly stay at the office until midnight or go months without a single day off. Work consumed their lives. And if they weren't working, they were networking. They power-lunched, power-exercised, and power-married. As the pace of life accelerated, time became an ever scarcer commodity, so they used their money to buy more of it. . . . They cut back on sleep and postponed having children. ('Can you carry a baby in a briefcase?' queried one Wall Street executive when she was asked about having kids)."[8]

As work has become a virtue and leisure a vice, European socialism has become the target of growing criticism. While Americans were increasing the length of the workweek, European countries were decreasing the hours people were permitted to work. In 1993, the European Union mandated a maximum workweek of forty-eight hours and by 2000, the French had implemented a thirty-five hour workweek, with guaranteed vacation ranging from six to nine weeks. With the collapse of the Soviet Union and the rise of neoliberalism in the United States and the United Kingdom, however, European socialism has come to epitomize the problems with centralized planning and government regulation. To underscore this point, many American executives have started casting economic criticisms in moralistic terms. In early 2013, French industry minister Arnaud Montebourg approached Maurice Taylor, chairman of Titan International and a former Republican presidential hopeful, with a proposal to save 1,173 French jobs at a failing Goodyear tire plant. This request came after five years of fruitless negotiation with France's largest communist-backed union. An article entitled "U.S. CEO Goes Off on France's Work Ethic in Epic Letter: 'Lazy' Union Workers Who Talk Too Much," reports Taylor's response to the proposed purchase of the factory:

> And like most things American, Taylor's response to Montebourg was blunt and to the point: "Do you think we're stupid?"
>
> No, really, in a letter published Wednesday by *Les Echos,* Taylor —whose bearish negotiating style earned him the nickname "The Grizz"—had nothing but criticism for France's work ethic. "I have visited that factory a couple of times. The French workforce gets paid high wages but work only three hours," the turnaround artist said in a letter dated Feb 8.
>
> "They get one hour for breaks and lunch, talk for three and work for three. I told the French union workers to their faces. They told me that's the French way!"[9]

Taylor's comments reflect a widespread attitude today on Main Street as well as Wall Street. The French way versus the American way—not only two versions of capitalism, but also two sets of values and two different ways of life.

It would be a mistake, however, to conclude that the increase in the number of hours that people are working is simply the result of individuals' choices. Larger technological and economic factors are forcing some people to work more and others to work less. In the past several decades, economic recession, technological innovation, and globalization have combined to create increasing pressure for longer working hours for some, and unemployment or underemployment for others. During the 1970s, the rise in oil prices as well as the cost of social welfare programs led to a slowdown in productivity and growth, which in turn created deeper and longer recessions. Schor points out that "businesses were under increasing pressure to cut costs and improve profit margins. Predictably, a large portion of the burden was 'downloaded' onto employees—particularly during the 1980s, when the squeeze on many U. S. corporations hit hardest. Their strategy has been to require workers to do more for less."[10] Since it was cheaper to require workers to work longer hours than to hire more people, overtime increased and vacation time decreased. In the current system, there is no economic incentive for reducing the number of hours that employees work in order to distribute the work more evenly among more people. Hard-pressed workers do not resist longer hours because they need the income; even if these people want to work less, many cannot afford to do so.

At the same time, new manufacturing, transportation, and communications technologies have made it possible to outsource work to countries where wages are lower. Globalization has resulted in an increasingly competitive environment in which companies have to produce more faster, but with fewer people and less resources. Since 1973, global competition has led to a decrease in pay for hourly workers. With the decline in the power of unions, a decline that accelerated with Reagan's breaking of the Professional Air Traffic Controllers Organization (PATCO) in 1981, labor has been unable to resist the pressure to work longer hours for less money. In addition, growing economic insecurity makes workers more likely to comply with the demands of management for fear of losing their jobs. In a highly competitive job market, employees have little leverage and are compelled to work longer hours, leaving them with less time for other pursuits. Today's turbo-financial capitalism creates a catch-22 for many workers—the more they work, the further behind they fall, and the further behind they fall, the more they have to work.

The increase in work time and the decrease in leisure time cannot be attributed solely to the demands of growing competitive production. No less important is the rapid spread of competitive consumption since the 1960s. Keynes made another assumption that suggests why many people tend to choose more money over more time.

> Now it is true that the needs of human beings may seem to be insatiable. But they fall into two classes—those needs which are absolute in the sense that we feel them whatever the situation of our fellow human beings may be, and those which are relative in the sense that we feel them only if their satisfaction lifts us above, makes us feel superior to, our fellows. Needs of the second class, those which satisfy the desire for superiority, may indeed be insatiable; for the higher the general level, the higher still are they. But this is not so true of the absolute needs—a point may soon be reached, much sooner perhaps than we are all of us aware of, when these needs are satisfied in the sense that we prefer to devote our further energies to non-economic purposes.[11]

While absolute needs like food, clothing, and shelter are limited and can be satisfied, relative needs or, more precisely, desires, which can be endlessly manipulated, are potentially infinite. From the time of primitive potlatch ceremonies, the ostentatious display of wealth has provided a way to signal social superiority. Social status is marked by the excessive expenditure of resources on luxury items like art, jewelry, and fashion that have little or no practical value. As soaring prices in the art market make clear, today's Wall Street titans continue to stage ancient potlatch ceremonies to secure as much prestige as money can buy. As we have seen, it is not enough for Steve Cohen to run one of the biggest hedge funds or to have the largest estate in Greenwich, Connecticut; he must also dominate the art market by paying exorbitant prices for a decaying shark floating in formaldehyde and a shiny party balloon on a string.

But something else is going on with competitive consumption as well. While the theory of trickle-down economics is questionable, trickle-down competitive consumption is an undeniable fact of contemporary life. Conspicuous consumption is not, of course, new; mass consumption, we have seen, is a product of mass production, which was introduced during the Industrial Revolution. Capitalism has always traded on the insatiability of human desire. In contemporary capitalist society, competitive consumption is more necessary than ever. The only way for the economy to continue growing, I have argued, is for people to spend money they don't really have for stuff they don't need. There is a fundamental contradiction at the heart of capitalism—on the one hand, for capitalism to prosper people must work hard, save money, and invest wisely; on the other hand, for the economy to expand people must spend money even if they cannot afford to do so. As competition and the demand for economic growth increase, it becomes essential for the rate of consumption to accelerate. Information and communications technologies are creating ever more sophisticated marketing techniques that transform what once were considered luxuries into what less affluent people consider necessities. This dynamic gives rise to what Schor describes as "the cycle of work-and-spend."[12] Consider, for example, the purchases of houses, which led to the global financial disaster. When William Levitt built his Levittowns in the 1950s, the standard house was 750 square feet; by 1970, the average home size in the United States was 1,400 square feet; by 2009, it had grown to an astonishing 2,700 square feet. To buy houses bigger than they needed, people took out loans bigger than they could afford until they were as overleveraged as the banks that were offering them the funny money. In this world of competitive high-speed production and consumption, enough is never enough—until it is.

Ever prescient, Nietzsche foresaw more than a century ago that the scales would tip in favor of money over time. Commenting on "the American lust for gold" in *The Gay Science* (1882), he writes,

> *Leisure and Idleness*. . . . the breathless haste with which they work —the distinctive vice of the new world—is already beginning to infect old Europe with its ferocity and is spreading a lack of

spirituality like a blanket. Even now one is ashamed of resting, and prolonged reflection almost gives people a bad conscience. One thinks with a watch in one's hand, even as one eats one's midday meal while reading the latest news of the stock market; one lives as if one always "might miss out on something." Rather do anything than nothing. . . . Living in a constant chase after gain compels people to expend their spirit to the point of exhaustion in the continual preens of overreaching and anticipating others. Virtue has come to consist in doing something in less time than someone else.[13]

Speed was supposed to save time and make life better by leaving people with more leisure, but the faster we go, the less time we seem to have and the more fragmented and frenzied life becomes. If life is time, then to lose time is to lose life. Speed has a cost, a high cost—sometimes it even kills.

As acceleration accelerates, individuals, societies, economies, and even the earth that sustains us approach meltdown. Faster is not always better. We have been conned into worshipping speed and craving the new by a financial system that teeters on the edge of collapse. Rather than improving life, acceleration creates a pervasive sense of anxiety. Anxiety, unlike fear, has no definite object or source; it reflects a profound unease that results from insecurities that cannot be precisely identified and can never be mastered. When caught in the throes of anxiety, the future seems threatening rather than promising. The distraction of busyness becomes a temporary coping mechanism, but ultimately fails to solve the problem because that which is repressed always returns to haunt those who attempt to flee it.

When multitasking becomes a way of life, people are torn in many directions. And time is not all that is lost in the rush of daily life. With little or no time to spare, people lose touch with what once seemed to matter most—family, friends, and the simple pleasures. With life spinning out of control, perhaps it is not surprising that a growing number of people have declared that enough is enough and are attempting to slow down.

In 1986, Carlo Petrini's protest against the opening of fast-food giant McDonald's newest restaurant in the Piazza di Spangna, Rome, led to the creation of the Slow Food organization. Over the following years, the Slow Movement, which encourages a slowing down of the pace of life, evolved. The most ambitious initiative of this reform movement to date is Cittaslow (Slow City), founded in Italy in October 1999. Inspired by the Slow Food movement, Cittaslow has established an international charter that participating cities and towns must formally accept. The aim of the organization is to "improve the quality of life in towns by slowing down its overall pace, especially in a city's use of spaces and the flow of life and traffic through them." Since its founding, Cittaslow has expanded beyond Italy—by 2009, fourteen countries had at least one official Cittaslow community.[14] Other initiatives have taken up the cause of slowness. The World Institute of Slowness was also founded in 1999 by Geir Berthelsen. The banner on the institute's websites cites Kierkegaard: "Most men pursue pleasure with such breathless haste that they hurry past it." In the past decade, the Slow Movement has continued to expand until it encompasses many aspects of life: Slow Gardening, Slow Money, Slow Coffee, Slow Beer, Slow Parenting, Slow Travel, Slow Art, Slow Media, Slow Fashion, Slow Software, Slow Science, Slow Goods, Slow Church, Slow Counseling, Slow Education, Slow Revolution. While the interests and aims of each of these movements differ, they are united by their resistance to what they describe as "the cult of speed." The Slow Manifesto, published on the website of the International Institute of Not Doing Much (www.slowdownnow.org), effectively captures the shared sensibility of the slow movement.

There are those who urge us to speed. We resist!

We shall not flag or fail. We shall slow down in the office, and on the roads. We shall slow down with growing confidence when all those around us are in a shrill state of hyperactivity (signifying nothing). We shall defend our state of calm, whatever the cost may be. We shall slow down in the fields and in the streets, we shall slow down in the hills, we shall never surrender!

If you can slow down when all around you are speeding up, then you're one of us. Be proud that you are one of us and not one of them. For they are fast, and we are slow. If a thing is worth doing, it is worth doing slowly. Some are born to slowness—others have it thrust upon them. And still others know that lying in bed with a morning cup of tea is the supreme state for mankind.[15]

But lying in bed with a morning cup of tea will not solve the pressing problems we face; nor will the slow movement with its dedication to creating places where it is possible to retreat from the frenzy of the world. Slowness alone is no cure for the addiction to speed. As complex systems and networks expand and connectivity increases, the rate of change will continue to accelerate and the frequency of major meltdowns will increase. Disasters already occurring signal looming catastrophes that are realistic possibilities rather than apocalyptic fantasies. If major disasters from which there may be no recovery are to be avoided, it is necessary to act quickly. But time is short—the addiction to speed must be broken with speed.

Ground Zeroes

Disaster 1—September 11, 2001.

In a world that appears to be increasingly virtual, place still matters —perhaps more than ever. Not once, not twice, but three times. The site of the disasters was neither arbitrary nor accidental. In today's networked world, some hubs are more important than others. For half a century, the hub of hubs for global capitalism has been southern Manhattan. The symbol for this financial empire was the World Trade Center (WTC), or Twin Towers. Initially proposed by Governor Thomas E. Dewey in 1943, the WTC opened on April 4, 1973. Joining the industrial past with the post-industrial future, the project was designed by the Port Authority to revive rail service between New York and New Jersey. At the time of its completion, the WTC was the tallest building in the world. When the Twin Towers failed to attract companies and organizations taking part in world trade, big financial companies like Morgan Stanley, Salomon Brothers, and Cantor Fitzgerald moved in. The complex also served as a telecommunications center. On top of the 110th floor of the North Tower, there was a 360-foot antenna that television and radio networks used to broadcast their programs. Caught up in the financial frenzy sweeping Wall Street, the Port Authority decided in 1998 to privatize the World Trade Center. The deal did not close until July 2001, when Silverstein Properties took possession of the complex less than two months before 9/11.

There were warning signs, but they were ignored. On February 26, 1993, at 12:27 p.m., a truck filled with 1,500 pounds of explosives exploded in an underground garage of the North Tower. The blast tore a hundred-foot hole through five sublevels of the building, killing six people. The attack was planned by Ramzi Yousef, who fled to Pakistan and was arrested in Islamabad in 1995. Two years later, Yousef and Eyad Ismoil were convicted of carrying out the attack. The judge in the trial concluded that their intention had been to topple both towers.

Disaster 2—August 7, 2007.

The worst financial crisis since the Great Depression started on August 7, 2007, when BNP Paribas ended withdrawals from three hedge funds because of a total evaporation of liquidity. Incongruously, two months later on October 9, 2007, the Dow Jones Industrial Average closed at 14,164, which was then an all-time high. As the implications of the financial crisis began to register, questions regarding the solvency of banks, financial firms, and eventually even countries shattered investor confidence and global financial markets linked by high-speed networks plummeted. By January 2, 2009, the Dow had fallen to 6,594, down 50 percent in just 17 months.

In the aftermath of the crisis, so-called experts could not agree on its causes—overleveraged banks, over-extended consumers, a shadow banking system running out of control, new complex high-risk financial products that were widely used but little understood, undisclosed conflicts of interest, the failure of regulators and credit rating agencies, irrational exuberance, the madness of crowds. There was, however, agreement that the transformation of the financial markets and the advent of high-speed, high-volume trading in globally wired markets during the previous decade had played a major role in the severity of the crisis and the speed with which it spread.

There were warning signs, but they were ignored. The Russian debt crisis and Asian financial crisis in 1997–98; the collapse of Long-Term Capital Management and its bailout in 1998; the dot-com bubble in 1997–2000; Enron, 2001; the U.S. housing bubble in 2006.

Disaster 3—October 28, 2012.

Hurricane Sandy hit southern Manhattan, flooding streets, tunnels, and the subway, and plunging the entire city south of 34th Street into darkness. With damages estimated at more than $75 billion, "Superstorm Sandy" was the second costliest hurricane in U.S. history. The year 2012 had already been an expensive one: the year-long drought in the Midwest and plains had taken a $35 billion toll. Sandy was responsible for at least 285 deaths in seven countries. Air and rail service throughout the Northeast were suspended and power was not restored to southern Manhattan for several days. This was the second time in fourteen months that the entire subway system had been shut down because of a hurricane. Trading on the U.S. stock market was suspended October 29–30.

There were warning signs, but they were ignored. In recent years, extreme weather events have been increasing worldwide and the intensity of storms has been growing. While it is impossible to attribute any particular storm to climate change, there is a growing consensus that shifts in global weather patterns have an important influence on weather events. In 2012, the winter was considerably warmer in the United States and much colder in Europe. Scientists believe that this temperature change was one of the factors that contributed to the severity of Hurricane Sandy. The other seemingly unlikely factor was melting Arctic sea ice. In an article entitled "Did Climate Change Cause Hurricane Sandy?" Mark Fischetti explains that the reason Sandy got so strong was "because it wandered north along the U.S. coast, where ocean water is still warm this time of year, pumping energy into the swirling system. But it got even larger when a cold Jet Stream made a sharp dip southward from Canada down into the eastern U.S. The cold air, positioned against the warm Atlantic air, added energy to the atmosphere and therefore to Sandy, just as it moved into that region, expanding the storm even further." What is even more interesting is the reason for these colliding currents:

> Here's where climate change comes in. The atmospheric pattern that sent the Jet Stream south is colloquially known as a "blocking high"—a big pressure center stuck over the very northern Atlantic Ocean and southern Arctic Ocean. And what led to that? A climate phenomenon called the North Atlantic Oscillation (NAO)—essentially, the state of atmospheric pressure in that region. This state can be positive or negative, and it had changed from positive to negative two weeks before Sandy arrived. The climate kicker? Recent research by Charles Greene at Cornell University and other climate scientists has shown that as more Arctic sea ice melts in the summer—because of global warming—the NAO is more likely to be negative during the autumn and winter. A negative NAO makes the Jet Stream more likely to move in a

big, wavy pattern across the U.S., Canada and the Atlantic, causing the kind of big southward dip that occurred during Sandy.[16]

When glaciers melt in the Arctic, the lights go out on Wall Street and financial markets shut down.

Fishy Markets

May 11, 2013. Reykjavík, Iceland.

I was visiting Reykjavík at the invitation of an organization of Lutheran pastors to deliver a lecture at the Icelandic Institute of Religion and Reconciliation entitled "Meltdowns: Perils of Extreme Finance." Iceland is a small country with a population of only 318,000 living in an area roughly the size of Iowa. Located just south of the Arctic Circle, Reykjavík is the northernmost capital in the world. From 1262 to 1918, Iceland was part of the Norwegian and later the Danish monarchies. Though the country gained its independence in 1918, it did not become a republic until 1944. The first known permanent settlers in Iceland were Celtic monks who came from Ireland. In the ninth century, an influx of immigrants from Norway and later other Scandinavian countries began to arrive. The early history of Iceland was dominated by Norse paganism and Catholicism, but in the middle of the sixteenth century, King Christian III of Denmark began to impose Lutheranism on the entire population. While the constitution of 1874 guarantees religious freedom, it also specifies that the "Evangelical Lutheran Church is a national church and as such it is protected and supported by the State." During the modern era, Iceland, like the rest of northern Europe, has become very secular but approximately 85 percent of the population still belongs to the national Lutheran Church.

Having lived in Denmark for several years and begun my academic journey by learning Danish to study Kierkegaard, I had long wanted to visit Iceland. The country's unique geology and stunning natural beauty were also a draw. The real reason I wanted to come to Iceland, however, was not to learn more about theology or philosophy but to explore the collision between financial capitalism and climate change. In Iceland you can see how the immaterial and material flows fueling the global economy intersect, creating rapidly shifting financial and physical landscapes. In 2001, the National Research Council issued a report entitled *Abrupt Climate Change: Inevitable Surprises* that begins, "Recent scientific evidence shows that major and widespread climate changes have occurred with startling speed. For example, roughly half the north Atlantic warming since the last ice age was achieved in only a decade, and it was accompanied by significant climatic changes across most of the globe. . . . Developing theoretical and empirical models to understand abrupt climate changes and the interaction of such changes with ecological and economic systems is a high priority."[17] More than a decade later, this challenge has not been met, and with each passing year, the task of understanding the relationship between economic growth and climate change becomes more urgent. Nowhere are the deleterious effects of speed more evident than in changes occurring in the world's climate and ecosystems. Glacial change is accelerating at an alarming rate, and though the effects are beginning to be felt worldwide, economic interests and political ideology continue to block every effort to address the problem before it is too late. Protestantism, financial crisis, and climate crisis converge in Iceland, making it ground zero for the disasters threatening the future of human life on earth.

In the fall of 2008, the economy of Iceland collapsed, sending shockwaves throughout the financial world. The disproportionate effect of Iceland's banking failure and subsequent economic crisis were the result of the network effect of wired global financial systems. What makes the Icelandic financial crisis so puzzling is how contrary the speculative frenzy was to the country's entire economic and cultural history. From the time of its founding until the early twenty-first century, the economy of Iceland was based on farming and its natural resources—sheep, wool, hydroelectric and geothermal energy, and especially fishing. Like other Scandinavian countries, the deep commitment to social equality led to an extensive social welfare system that provided universal healthcare, education through the university level, social security for retirees, and even support for the national church. By American standards, tax rates are quite high to support these services: 37.32 percent for incomes less than $24,000; 40.22 percent for incomes between $24,000 and $74,000; and 46.22 percent for incomes above $74,000. In addition, there is a value added tax of 25.5 percent. Additional taxes drive the price of gasoline above $9.00 a gallon. But the system worked well—so well that in 2008, Iceland was ranked number one on the United Nations' Human Development Index.

All of this changed abruptly when Davíð Oddsson, who was prime minister from 1991 to 2004, drew the country into the frenzy of global financial capitalism. "Back in the 1980s," Michael Lewis reports, "Oddsson had fallen under the spell of Milton Friedman, the brilliant economist who was able to persuade even those who spent their lives working for the government that government was a waste of life. So Oddsson went on a quest to give Icelandic people their freedom, by which he meant freedom from government controls of any sort. As prime minister he lowered taxes, privatized industry, freed up trade, and, finally, in 2002, privatized the banks. At length, weary of prime-ministering, he got himself appointed governor of the Central Bank—even though he had no experience in banking and was, by training, a poet."[18] It is difficult to convey just how fast these changes occurred. Within the brief span of a few years, the country went from being a nation best known for its fish and wool with virtually no financial industry to an economy based largely on financial services and investment banking. Lifelong fishermen docked their boats and started trading currencies and speculating in exotic financial instruments they did not understand. Following a pattern that is familiar by now, Icelanders borrowed excessively and invested in highly speculative financial products as well as real estate. Unknowledgeable investors went so far as to buy significant shares in foreign banks as well as in companies ranging from airlines to soccer teams. With annual returns approaching 14 percent, major European banks started investing in Icelandic banks, expanding the web of eventual destruction. In addition to borrowing and investing, people borrowed excessively to buy stuff they did not need. As if awakening from a centuries-long slumber, a country long known for its Protestant frugality and caution went on a spending spree—lavish parties, jewelry, private jets, and second and third homes in Iceland as well as foreign countries. For many young people, the symbol for newfound prosperity was the Range Rover; Reykjavík's narrow streets became crowded with oversized SUVs. Throwing belief in the equality of its citizens to the wind, which is always blowing in Iceland, banks and investment firms provided black Range Rover Sports SUVs with white leather interiors to young stock brokers and mid-level executives, and larger black Range Rover Vogues, also with white leather interiors, for top-level executives. For a brief period, social status was measured by the size and the model of the vehicle a person drove. When everything fell apart a few years later, Range Rovers were dubbed "Game Overs," and most of them were repossessed or simply abandoned and shipped to other countries, where they were recycled like other toxic assets.

Though not everyone drove a black Range Rover, the number of people who benefited from the growth in virtual capital was more widespread than many Icelanders now looking back like to admit. During the halcyon days of the financial industry, the more people borrowed and spent, the faster the economy grew and the higher stock prices soared, and the faster the economy grew and the higher stock prices rose, the more people spent and invested. For a few years, it seemed the bet had paid off. "From 2003 to 2007, while the value of the U.S. stock market was doubling, the value of the Icelandic stock market multiplied nine times. Reykjavík real estate prices tripled. In 2006 the average Icelandic family was three times as wealthy as the average Icelandic family had been in 2003, and virtually all of this new wealth was, in one way or another, tied to the new investment banking system."[19]

But the fantasy of this high-speed virtual economy soon was forced to confront reality. It is equally difficult to convey just how fast the party ended. With analysts becoming increasingly wary of Iceland's banking system, lenders became more cautious. When the crisis hit, the three largest banks (Glitnir, Landsbanki, and Kaupthing) had a combined debt that was six times the nation's gross domestic product. In 2008, all of these privately owned commercial banks had trouble refinancing their short-term debt, setting off a run on deposits in the Netherlands and the United Kingdom. This bank run triggered a positive feedback loop in which losses rapidly accelerated until the entire banking system was on the brink of collapse. Since major banks from other countries were heavily invested in Icelandic banks, Iceland's crisis was the world's crisis. What went on in Iceland did not stay in Iceland but spread across the globe with increasing speed. The more money people in Iceland withdrew from their local banks, the more precarious the international banking system became, and the more precarious the banking system became, the more money people withdrew.

Iceland's response to this crisis differed significantly from actions taken in the United States and much of Europe. While Iceland is not formally a member of the European Union, prior to 2008, the krona was pegged to the euro, making it effectively a member. When the crisis hit, this link was broken and there was a huge devaluation of its currency. The three largest banks were put into receivership (that is, allowed to fail) and domestic depositors were protected (the government guaranteed all domestic depositors). Foreign creditors and depositors were not protected and suffered significant losses. In other words, unlike other countries, Iceland let its banks fail and allowed foreign leaders and depositors to take losses. While this strategy is controversial, it was effective, and at least one economic policy consultant and analyst, Jeff Madrick, sees lessons for other countries in Iceland's handling of the crisis. Relative to the size of its overall economy, Iceland experienced the largest banking collapse of any country in history. Banks lost over $100 billion, which amounted to roughly $330,000 for every Icelandic person.[20]

Today the streets of Reykjavík seem relatively unchanged; few shops are empty and business, if no longer booming, is at least recovering. But appearances are deceiving. Five years after the crisis, many people remain obsessed with trying to understand what happened and how so many people allowed themselves to be duped by a financial confidence game that betrayed so many of their traditional values. They are hungry for explanations that extend beyond mathematical formulas, charts, and graphs.

Glacial Change

The two days before my lecture, my wife and I traveled along the southern coast of Iceland. Our destination was Jökulsárlón, where Breiðamerkur-jökull, Iceland's largest glacier, meets the sea. Here the ravaging effects of climate change are undeniable for anyone willing to take the time to understand what is happening. Iceland is a young land that was formed by volcanic eruptions, and the island, with its numerous hot springs, gey-sers, and volcanoes, remains geologically very active. Iceland's location marks the intersection of multiple vectors that shape global currents. The world's eighteenth largest island, Iceland is situated at the junc-ture of the North Atlantic and Arctic oceans. It also lies along the Mid-Atlantic Ridge, which separates North America and Eurasia in the Northern Hemisphere, and South America and Africa in the Southern Hemisphere. In Þingvellir, where the country's first General Assembly was established in 930, the fault where the North American and Eur-asian plates are drifting apart is exposed.

The austere, rugged beauty of the countryside is memorable. The narrow two-lane coastal road threads its way between endless black-sand beaches and high cliffs that rise abruptly along fields of lava. The island's abundant streams and rivers create numerous dazzling water-falls. The blackness of the sand, lava, and mountains occasionally is punctuated by verdant fields with sheep grazing and lambs frolicking. Finally finding a turnoff, I stopped to take a photograph of one of the typical pristine white farmhouses with a colorful red roof. I was sur-prised to discover a roadside sign explaining that the steep cliff rising immediately behind the farm was the infamous Eyjafjallajökull volcano, which erupted for the first time since 1821 on March 21, 2010. Ad-ditional eruptions on April 14 brought air travel to a halt throughout Europe and some of North America. An even more powerful eruption occurred on May 21, 2011, when the powerful Grímsvötn volcano ex-ploded and thrust lava and ash twenty kilometers into the atmosphere, posing a danger to jet aircraft across the northern Atlantic and in all of Europe. At the same moment the Icelandic banking crisis was threaten-ing global financial networks, a distant Icelandic volcano was disrupting global transportation networks.

Between Eyjafjallajökull and Jökulsárlón there are vast lava fields interrupted by only a few very small villages. Some of the lava fields are composed of fine sand, others are covered with pebbles and small stones worn smooth by water and wind, and still others feature large rocks and boulders covered by soft grayish-green moss. The farther north we drove, the stronger the wind became and by the time we reached the largest lava field, the wind was blowing so hard that I had to use two hands on the wheel to keep the car from blowing off the road. The wind swept the lava into a vast cloud that pelted the car and obscured the road until I could see no more than a few feet in front of me. There was no one else on the road and no place to pull over; even though we were terrified, there was no choice but to continue to drive. Eventually the wind subsided and the lava cloud dispersed; nature once again had made its point to anyone willing to listen.

The Jökulsárlón lagoon is a small inlet where the seawater of the

Jökulsárlón Lagoon, Iceland, 2013

North Atlantic and Arctic oceans mixes with fresh water from melting glaciers. Glaciers throughout the world are melting faster and faster and nowhere more so than the Breiðamerkurjökull glacier, which is disappearing more quickly than any other glacier in Europe. In the early twentieth century, the glacier extended all the way to the sea; since 1932, it has retreated 7.1 kilometers and continues to melt at an alarming rate of a hundred meters a year or almost a foot a day. As the ice melts, glaciers calve, sending icebergs into the waters of the lagoon. Strong winds shift the ice, creating a vista that changes hour by hour. We took a boat ride through the lagoon. Weaving among blue, gray, black, and white forms more intricate than any human sculptor could create, it was impossible not to be awed by nature's beauty. Seals lie on the ice and occasionally an Arctic Tern, whose migration from South Africa to

Iceland is longer than any other bird's, soars overhead. The pilot stopped the boat and scooped from the water a chunk of ice that looked like Georg Jensen crystal. Breaking off chunks and offering them to passengers to suck, he said, "This is older than anything you have ever touched—it is at least 1,000 to 5,000 years old." Immersed in an otherworldly beauty whose ageless rhythms dwarf human time, I had to remind myself that the reason I had come to this distant corner of the earth was to see the natural currents that are being shaped by, and now are threatening, global economic and financial networks. My grandchildren will not be able to experience this beauty because by the time they are my age, the glaciers will be long gone. The urgent question is whether the disappearance of the glaciers will result in the dissolution of other networks as well.

Matter Matters

In the spring of 2013, Huang Nubo, a former official in the Chinese Communist Party's Propaganda Department and now a property developer in Beijing, proposed building a luxury hotel and "eco golf course" for wealthy Chinese in Grímsstaðir, Iceland. At the same time, the Zhongkun Group submitted a proposal to renovate a small landing strip in the Grímsstaðir area and to purchase ten new aircraft to service the facility. In an article entitled "Teeing Off at the Edge of the Arctic? A Chinese Plan Baffles Iceland," Andrew Higgins reports, "Struggling to stand upright against a howling wind, Bragi Benediktsson looked out over his family's land—a barren expanse of snow and ice that a Chinese billionaire wants to buy to turn into a golf course—and laughed. 'Golf here is difficult,' said Mr. Benediktsson, a 75-year-old sheep farmer."[21] To sweeten his offer, Huang announced a contribution of $1 million to create a China-Iceland cultural fund. At the same time, the state-owned China Development Bank and Huang's company reached an agreement worth $800 million for development projects in Iceland.

Though some people in Iceland might be baffled, it is not hard to figure out what the Chinese, as well as many other countries, are up to. On August 2, 2007, a Russian submarine planted a titanium flag four kilometers beneath the North Pole. The Arctic is melting faster and faster, opening new territory with significant oil, gas, and mineral reserves for drilling and mining. Iceland has an estimated 13 percent of the world's undiscovered oil resources and almost a third of its undiscovered natural gas. The proposed airport in Grímsstaðir is close to the region richest in oil. Chris Krenz, senior scientist at Oceana, an international ocean conservation organization based in Washington, observed, "The Arctic is inextricably linked to the world. As we're seeing with climate change, what happens in the rest of the world affects the Arctic. Importantly for the rest of the world, the opposite is true too."[22]

We have seen that since the early days of the Industrial Revolution, material and immaterial flows have been inextricably interrelated. The virtual realities of financial capitalism are grounded in real cables and wires that are located in real places; computers, tablets, devices, and the batteries and chips that run them require increasingly rare precious metals that are mined by real people under desperate conditions in some of the world's poorest countries; and, most important, high-speed networks require energy, which is still largely provided by the consumption of natural resources and the burning of fossil fuels. Andrew Blum points out that "according to a 2010 Greenpeace report, 2 percent of the world's electricity usage can now be traced to data centers, and that usage is growing at a rate of 12 percent a year. By today's standards, a very large data center might be a 500,000-square-foot building demanding fifty megawatts of power, which is about how much it takes to light a small city. But the largest data center 'campus' might contain four of those buildings, totaling more than a million square feet—twice the size of the Javits Center in New York, the same as ten Walmarts. We've only just begun building data centers, and already their accumulated impact is enormous."[23] From 1998 to 2004, the number of federal data centers grew from 432 to 2,094, but government officials cannot determine how much energy they consume. According to the article "Power, Pollution and the Internet," published in the *New York Times,* "Worldwide, the digital warehouses use about 30 billion watts of electricity, roughly equivalent to the output of 30 nuclear power plants. . . . Data centers in the United States account for one-quarter to one-third of that load."[24]

As troubling as the vast amounts of energy that data centers consume is the fact that 90 percent of this energy is wasted. In a world where speed is a premium, and everything must be available instantaneously 24/7/365, any delay is unacceptable, and excessive redundancy is the accepted price of doing business. Indeed, companies spare no expense in their attempt to insure against even the slightest interruption in service to their customers. A recent analysis by McKinsey Associates concluded that data centers on average use "only six per cent to 12 percent of the electricity powering their servers to perform computations. The rest is essentially used to keep servers idling and ready in case of a surge in activity that could slow or crash their operations." David Cappuccio, a managing vice president and chief of research at the technology firm Gartner explains, "What's driving the massive growth—the end-user expectation of anything, anytime, anywhere. . . . We're what's causing the problem."[25] This problem is rapidly getting worse. Eli Pariser reports that "the National Security Agency, which copies a lot of the Internet traffic that flows through AT&T's main hub in San Francisco, is building two new stadium-sized complexes in the Southwest to process all that data. The biggest problem they face is a lack of power: There literally is not enough electricity on the grid to support that much computing."[26]

Competition for scarce energy is already fueling conflicts between local communities and major Internet companies. In 2006, Microsoft bought seventy-six acres in the farming community of Quincy, Washington; Dell and Yahoo followed shortly thereafter. The attraction of this small town in the desert was cheap energy supplied by hydroelectric plants along the Columbia River. While Internet companies have carefully crafted the image of being a clean industry, the dirty secret is not only their increasing energy use but also the pollution that the dedication to growth and speed creates. To guard against disruptions as brief as a few hundredths of a second, which might be caused by the interruption in service by a power grid, companies use massive backup generators with thousands of lead-acid batteries run by diesel fuel. The large number of generators required for big data warehouses causes so much air pollution that many of the data centers in Silicon Valley "are on the state government's Toxic Air Contaminant Inventory, which lists the area's top stationary diesel polluters."[27] In today's competitive markets, profits trump the environment and, in some cases, even the well-being of children. Local officials in Quincy who were concerned about pollution, especially by generators located close to an elementary school, were critical of Microsoft's low-balling of its estimated energy use and imposed a $210,000 penalty on the company. In response, Microsoft "proceeded to simply waste millions of watts of electricity. . . . Then it threatened to continue burning power in what it acknowledged was an 'unnecessarily wasteful' way until the fine was substantially cut."[28]

What drives this wasteful consumption of energy is the continuing addiction to speed, which in turn results from the unquestioned commitment to economic growth. Economist William Baumol maintains that "under capitalism, innovative activity—which in other types of economy is fortuitous and optional—becomes mandatory, a life-and-death matter for the firm. And the spread of new technology, which in other economies has proceeded at a stately pace, often requiring decades or even centuries, under capitalism is speeded up remarkably because, quite simply, time is money. That, in short, is the . . . explanation of the incredible growth of the free-market economies. The capitalist economy can usefully be viewed as a machine whose primary product is economic growth. Indeed, its effectiveness in this role is unparalleled."[29] But this very success harbors the prospect of systemic failure.

Just as there are spatial limits to market expansion, so too are there temporal limits. The growth and speed required to maintain growth are fast approaching the tipping point, which threatens not only economic and financial systems but also the conditions of human life on earth.

Nowhere are speed limits more obvious than in Jökulsárlón lagoon. The Arctic is melting faster and faster every year and, as the melting accelerates, the possibility for abrupt climate change increases dramatically. The immaterial flows of today's financial markets and the material flows of matter and energy affect the environment and climate through the nonlinear dynamics characteristic of complex emergent complex adaptive networks (see Chapter 8). More specifically, financial bubbles and abrupt climate change follow identical patterns. The recognition of the similarity between financial and climactic systems points to the beginning of a response to the question of their interaction that was posed by the National Academy of Sciences. The academy's report defines abrupt climate change as occurring "when the climate is forced to cross some threshold, triggering a transition to a new state determined by the climate system itself and faster than that cause. Chaotic processes in the climate system may allow the cause of such an abrupt climate change to be undetectably small."[30] Such hair triggers also occur in high-speed, high-volume financial markets. In these complex networks, the rate of change gradually accelerates until a seemingly insignificant event can set off a cascade that may cause the system to spin out of control. In financial systems, the nonlinearity of self-reinforcing mechanisms and events creates positive feedback loops that strengthen the inclinations and actions of interrelated agents, which can be either human or, increasingly, algorithmic. If these interactions continue to accelerate, there is a network effect in which the system crosses the threshold, leading to an abrupt phase shift. Stampeding herds can be either bulls or bears, driving prices up or down. With greater connectivity and higher speeds, disruptive effects ripple through networks faster and faster and outliers become more and more common.

To see how this dynamic works in ecological systems, consider the dynamics of melting sea ice and glaciers. James Hansen, formerly director of NASA's Goddard Institute for Space Studies and now with Columbia University's Earth Institute, has gone so far as to claim that "the dominant issue in global warming is sea level change and the question of how fast ice sheets can disintegrate."[31] Though other factors were also at work in Hurricane Sandy, the effects of sea level change contributed to the flooding of southern Manhattan. The effects of melting sea ice are less evident but no less important. Sea ice, which plays a critical role in regulating the global climate system, is disappearing at an alarming rate. In 1979, Arctic sea ice covered an area approximately the size of the United States; since then, it has shrunk 40 percent, or an area equivalent to New York, Georgia, and Texas combined. During the same period, the average thickness of the ice has decreased by a third and, according to reliable estimates, sea ice could be completely gone by 2016. The melting of sea ice and glaciers is the direct result of global warming. Through what is known as the albedo effect, sea ice helps to regulate the planet's temperature by reflecting incoming sunlight away from the earth and preventing the warmth of the water from escaping into the atmosphere. A report from scientists with the National Center for Atmospheric Research explains that "sea ice is both ocean sunscreen and blanket, preventing solar rays from warming the waters beneath and thwarting ocean heat from escaping to warm the air above. But if gradually warming temperatures melt sea ice over time . . . fewer bright surfaces are available to reflect sunlight, more heat escapes from the ocean to warm the atmosphere and the ice melts further. Thus, even a small increase in temperature can lead to greater warming over time, making the polar regions the most sensitive areas to climate change on earth—global warming is amplified in the polar regions."[32]

The melting of sea ice is another example of a positive feedback system analogous to what we have discovered in financial markets. Recall the example of the overleveraged financial firm whose investments turn bad. If investors have borrowed too much money to gamble in speculative markets and have used the assets purchased to secure the loan, they do not have sufficient liquid capital to meet a margin call when the value of their collateral declines. They will then have to sell the securities to generate the required capital, but this drives down prices even further, thereby leading to an additional margin call. This process continues to accelerate until a threshold is passed and the investment firm collapses.

The same dynamic is at work in the melting of sea ice. Since sea ice helps to regulate the climate by reflecting sunlight and preventing the heat of oceans from radiating into the atmosphere, when sea ice melts, there is less insulating material and reflective surface and the water gets warmer. As the temperature of the water increases, more ice melts, and the more ice melts, the faster the temperature of the water increases. This process continues to accelerate until a threshold is crossed and all the sea ice disappears—and in the absence of sea ice, the increase in atmospheric temperature accelerates. The important point to underscore is that both financial and natural networks are emergent complex adaptive networks in which a single, minor event can ripple through the system, creating catastrophic change. The same dynamic that leads to increasing speed in global financial networks is driving the acceleration of change in global climate systems. For example, just as the collapse of banks in the small country of Iceland can trigger a global financial crisis, so too can a gradually rising atmospheric temperature create interrelated changes that can lead to abrupt shifts in climate over a very short, critical time interval.

This dynamic is also at work in the melting of permafrost. The term "permafrost" designates ground that has remained frozen for at least two years. The depth of permafrost can vary from a few feet to a mile. Most of today's permafrost dates back to the last glacial period 120,000 years ago. The outermost layer of permafrost thaws in the summer and thus can support plant life and even small trees. Arctic life cycles, how-

ever, differ from those in more temperate zones. Due to low temperatures, plants and trees do not completely decompose when they die. As
this organic material settles and freezes over the centuries, permafrost
becomes a storage receptacle for vast amounts of carbon. When
permafrost melts, it releases carbon dioxide and methane, which are
greenhouse gases that increase global temperature. A 2012 report issued by the UN Environmental Program entitled "Policy Implications
of Warming Permafrost" summarizes the significance of this development. "The release of CO_2 and methane from thawing permafrost will
amplify the rate of global warming and further accelerate permafrost
degradation. This amplification of surface warming due to CO_2 and
methane emissions from thawing permafrost is called *permafrost carbon feedback*. The permafrost feedback is irreversible on human time
scales."[33]

As I saw in Jökulsárlón lagoon, the effects of climate change are
most dramatically evident in what is happening to glaciers. Rapid glacial melting, known as deglaciation, is not limited to Iceland but has
been evident throughout the world since the 1960s. In Glacier National
Park, for example, there were 150 glaciers in the 1800s; today there are
only thirty-five, and computer models predict that by 2030 there will
be none. In Switzerland, melting glaciers are threatening villages, and
from Peru to the Himalayas, deglaciation is contributing to the increasing severity of tsunamis. Though accelerated melting did not begin in
Iceland until the 1990s, it is now progressing so rapidly that scientists
calculate that by the end of this century Iceland will have no ice. The
effects of glacial meltdown are even more complex than the melting of
permafrost and sea ice. Recent discoveries in Iceland suggest that the
melting of glaciers can actually lead to an increase in volcanic activity.
As the weight of ice is reduced, it is easier for magma to surface.[34] Volcanic eruptions spew polluting ash into the air and further contribute
to global warming, which in turn causes glaciers to melt even faster.

The most obvious result of Arctic melting, however, can be seen in rising sea levels with all the related problems this will bring. If the entire Greenland ice sheet melted, the level of seas throughout the world would rise by twenty-three feet. But the more serious problems created by melting glaciers are even more complex. It is not only financial markets that are connected in global networks; global climate is also an emergent complex adaptive network. Furthermore, financial and climate networks are not only functionally and operationally similar, but also interconnected in a way that makes them mutually dependent. Economic policies and actions have direct and indirect effects on climate systems, and global climate change, in turn, influences the economy in ways that drive markets either up or down.

One of the most important natural networks is what is known as the "conveyor," which joins the currents of the world's oceans in a great global loop that moves water from the Arctic to the Antarctica and that joins the Atlantic, Pacific, and Indian oceans. The conveyor, which was discovered by Columbia University geologist Wallace Broecker in 1952, refers to the Atlantic Ocean portion of this system. "Surface waters, including those of the Gulf Stream, carry tropical heat to the Atlantic's northern reaches where during the winter heat is sucked out of the water and into the atmosphere. So, just as conveyor belts carry coal to furnaces of electrical power plants, the Great Ocean Conveyor delivers heat to the northern reaches of the Atlantic."[35] The circulation of ocean currents influences the circulation of air currents, which brings changes in the climate that influence ocean currents. Glacial melting, in other words, changes ocean currents, and thereby affects weather patterns. This is because glaciers are made of fresh water, which differs in density from salt water. When glaciers melt, they change the mix of fresh and salt water in oceans—salt water sinks, and fresh water remains closer to the surface. This, in turn, can lead to a shift in both water and air currents. As University of Colorado geographer Konrad Steffan explains, the conveyor system "is the energy engine for the world climate.

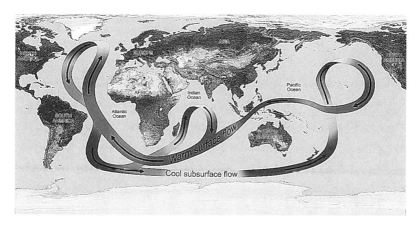

Global ocean conveyor belt, illustrating the circulation of the global ocean waters. Throughout the Atlantic Ocean, the circulation carries warm waters northward near the surface and cold deep waters southward. Courtesy of NASA's Jet Propulsion Laboratory.

And it has one source: the water that sinks down. And if you just turn the knob a little bit . . . we can expect significant temperature changes based on the redistribution of energy."[36]

There are two ways to turn this knob: increase the heat of the oceans, or increase the amount of fresh water in polar seas. Both processes are already occurring. Greenland's ice cap is losing approximately two hundred gigatons (or two hundred billion tons) of ice each year and the rate of melting continues to increase throughout the Arctic. What makes such trends so deceptive is that the changes can be so gradual that they go undetected until it is too late to stop them. We have seen repeatedly that complex systems can drift toward a critical point where even a minor shift can result in abrupt, even catastrophic change. There is a growing fear among many scientists that rising temperatures and increased melting could overturn the global circulation among the world's oceans. This is not idle speculation—there are precedents for the conveyor system shutting down; over the past 60,000 years, this has occurred at least seven times. While another shutdown does not appear to be imminent, few responsible scientists doubt that the Arctic meltdown is already influencing global weather patterns. It is possible, perhaps even likely, that melting of sea ice, permafrost, and glaciers led to the altered weather patterns that intensified Hurricane Sandy. When cold air from the north blocked the movement of warm air from the south, the Atlantic Ocean continued to heat up and the storm intensified until it crashed into the Eastern Seaboard, flooding southern Manhattan, shutting down the New York Stock Exchange, and disrupting global financial markets.

In the spring of 2013, carbon dioxide levels in the atmosphere, measured atop the Mauna Loa volcano on the big island of Hawaii, reached an average daily level above four hundred parts per million, which scientists have long feared could be the tipping point for abrupt climate changes. This amount of gas in the air has not been seen since three million years before humans evolved. Throughout the eight-thousand-year history of human civilization, levels of carbon dioxide have remained relatively stable. But the increased use of fossil fuels that began with the Industrial Revolution has changed the situation dramatically. Since then, there has been a 41 percent increase in heat-trapping gases in the atmosphere, and amounts of these gases continue to grow. Commenting on the implications of this trajectory, Maureen Raymo of the Lamont-Doherty Earth Observatory has gone so far as to warn, "It feels like the inevitable march toward disaster."[37] Increasingly violent weather across the globe—hurricanes, cyclones, drought, severe thunderstorms, tornadoes—are early signs of this looming catastrophe.

Despite this stark reality, countries throughout the world remain unwilling to address the escalating problem of climate change. As the economies of China and India continue to grow, and the United States and Europe refuse to curb their energy use, the situation will only get worse. Edward Wong reports,

> There is consensus now that China's decades of double-digit economic growth exacted an enormous environmental cost. But growth still remains the priority; the Communist Party's legitimacy is based largely on rapidly expanding the economy, and China officially estimates that its G.D.P., which was $8.3 trillion in 2012, will grow at a rate of 7.5 percent this year and at an average of 7 percent in the five-year plan that runs to 2015. A Deutsche Bank report released last month [in February 2013] said that the current growth policies would lead to a continuing steep decline of the environment for the next decade, especially given the expected coal consumption and boom in automobile sales.[38]

The effort to meet the anticipated demand for energy is what led to a Chinese businessman's absurd proposal to create a golf course on Iceland's frigid, barren lava fields.

China is not the sole, indeed perhaps not even the primary, source of the problem; the United States is also at fault. In the United States, economic self-interest and political ideology have made it nearly impossible to persuade public and private officials to take corrective actions. Climate change has been recognized as a serious threat in this country for almost half a century. On February 8, 1965, President Lyndon Johnson sent a "Special Message to the Congress on Conservation and Restoration of Natural Beauty," in which he observed, "This generation has altered the composition of the atmosphere on a global scale through . . . a steady increase in carbon dioxide from the burning of fossil fuels." During this era, when a fragmented political system makes reasonable debate all but impossible, it is difficult to remember that not so long ago the environment and climate change were bipartisan issues. Not only

Kennedy and Johnson but also Nixon supported legislation to protect the environment. Indeed, it was during Nixon's presidency that the National Environmental Policy Act (1970), important amendments to the Clean Air Act (1970), as well as the Clean Water Act (1972) and the Endangered Species Act (1973), were passed and the Environmental Protection Agency (1970) was created.

Nixon's support of these measures met with resistance from the Republican Party's traditional base of business leaders, whose dedication to the free market made them suspicious of any government regulation. When Ronald Reagan's neoconservative political program and Milton Friedman's neoliberal economic agenda took root, debates about the environment and climate change became caught up in the politics of the Cold War. In their illuminating and disturbing book *Merchants of Doubt: How a Handful of Scientists Obscured the Truth on Issues from Tobacco Smoke to Global Warming,* Naomi Oreskes and Erik M. Conway demonstrate that conservative think tanks like the George C. Marshall Institute, American Enterprise Institute, Cato Institute, and the Cosmos Club, all funded by corporations with much to gain from deregulation, have been backing the efforts of scientists to create doubt about climate change. Two of the most influential scientists in this campaign are Frederick Singer and Frederick Seitz. Singer was the first director of the National Weather Bureau's Satellite Service Center and chief scientist at the Department of Transportation in the Reagan administration. Seitz worked on the atomic bomb and later was president of the National Academy of Sciences, lending further credibility to his opinions. Singer and Seitz were vehemently anti-communist and recruited like-minded colleagues to form a lobbying group to support Reagan's Strategic Defense Initiative (known rather derisively as the "Star Wars" initiative). Oreskes and Conway maintain that "when the Cold War ended, these men looked for a new great threat. They found it in environmentalism. Environmentalists, they implied, were 'watermelons': green on the outside, red on the inside." Each of the most pressing environmental threats, they insist, represents "a market failure, a domain in which the free market had created serious 'neighborhood' effects that are 'potentially deadly'—and global in reach. To address them, governments would have to step in with regulations, in some cases very significant ones, to remedy the market failure. And this was precisely what these men most feared and loathed, for they viewed regulation as the slippery slope to Socialism, a form of creeping Communism."[39]

This was not the first time that Singer and Seitz had been recruited to provide "scientific" evidence on behalf of companies that opposed government regulation. During the 1970s, they were involved with efforts to create doubt about acid rain, the ozone hole, and most notoriously, the health risks of smoking. Over the years, they refined their tactics but their strategy remained the same: publish articles in seemingly legitimate journals, many of which were not peer reviewed, about research that purportedly contradicts the results of legitimate scientific investigations, and then attack the reputations of accomplished scientists. This experience made these "merchants of doubt" media savvy. Business, industry, and political-interest groups provided the financial resources necessary to make these campaigns extremely effective. When senators Robert Byrd and Charles Hagel introduced a bill in July 1997 to block the Kyoto Protocol to the U.N. Framework Convention on Climate Change, which set binding obligations on industrialized countries to reduce emissions of greenhouse gases, it passed by a vote of 97–0. More than a decade later, noted conservative columnist George Will declared that environmentalism is "green with red roots." Will's colleague Charles Krauthammer went even further in denouncing responsible efforts to deal with the rapidly deteriorating environment. Oreskes and Conway report that in 2009, when world leaders again tried to reach agreement on controlling greenhouse gases, Krauthammer "declaimed in the *Washington Post* that environmentalism was socialism by other means, a brazen attempt to transfer wealth from rich to poor. With socialism dead, the gigantic heist is now proposed as a scare service in the newest religion: environmentalism . . . the Left was adrift until it struck a brilliant gambit: the metamorphosis from red to green. . . . Since we operate an overwhelmingly carbon-based economy, the EPA will [soon] be regulating everything. . . . Not since the creation of the Internal Revenue Service has a federal agency been given more intrusive power over every aspect of economic life. . . . Big Brother isn't lurking in CIA cloak. He is knocking on your door, smiling under the EPA cap."[40] Unbelievably, all of this is enough to make one long for the return of Nixon.

While neoliberals and neoconservatives continue to rant and rave, the situation continues to worsen at an accelerating rate. Rather than recognizing the increasing speed with which the Arctic ice cap is melting as a harbinger of global disaster, many business leaders and politicians obsessed with market expansion and economic growth are taking actions that make the problem worse. As the ice recedes, the United States, along with China, Russia, and Europe, are engaged in an oil rush in the Arctic. In addition, new fracking technologies now make it possible to extract vast amounts of oil and natural gas, which will further increase dependence on fossil fuels and spell the death of the clean energy industry in this country for at least a century. The growth in fossil fuel consumption will result in more carbon emissions that will contribute to greater climate change, which, in turn, will create economic instability and financial insecurity. Legislators are either unable or unwilling to understand the magnitude and the urgency of the problem. As the rate of climate change is speeding up, the rate of responsible political action in Washington is slowing down or even grinding to a halt. On the rare occasions when Congress does pass legislation, as often as not it is counterproductive. Consider, for example, that the summer of 2012 was the hottest on record in the United States, with the worst drought in fifty years. Yet at this precise moment, Congress passed a farm bill that would not only "accelerate global warming by encouraging more greenhouse gas emissions, it would make the nation's farms more vulnerable to the impacts of those emissions." To make matters worse, subsidies increase with production and thus encourage farmers to use excessive amounts of fertilizers and pesticides to increase output. Many of these products, which are made from petrochemicals, also increase emissions of heat-trapping gases.[41]

Such policies are not only ignorant and foolhardy; they are destructive. In the relentless effort to promote economic growth, countries as well as companies are not only doing irreparable environmental harm, but also increasing the cost of doing business everywhere in the world. In 2005, damages from Katrina cost an estimated $81 billion, and this was only one of 484 reported natural disasters worldwide whose cost totaled $176 billion. In 2011, the cost of natural disasters had risen to over $350 billion. That same year thunderstorms in the United States caused $25 billion in damages, more than twice the previous record, and a year later, Hurricane Sandy cost an additional $78 billion.[42] Even in economic terms, policies that promote such destruction make no sense. In the long run, however, the cost will not be calculated by money alone but will be measured by the quality or even the very viability of human life.

Recovering Time

Language is not only descriptive; it is also prescriptive. Metaphors matter because they both shape how we understand ourselves and guide personal, social, political, and economic decisions and policies. Thomas Friedman has popularized the idea that in the brave new world of global capitalism, the earth is flat. This image suggests that in today's hyper-competitive world, the horizon is infinite and endless expansion in every direction is a realistic possibility. But of course the world is not flat; it is both physically and metaphorically round. Rather than expanding infinitely, material and immaterial currents intersect and bend back on themselves to create circuits of exchange that have unavoidable limits. Within these complex networks, expansion cannot be infinite and growth cannot be endless. There are physical, environmental, economic, and speed limits that constitute the constraining parameters within which we are destined to live. When we transgress these limits, we threaten the very systems that sustain life.

It is not clear whether there is time to recover. Finding solutions to problems that have been emerging for several centuries requires time— lots of time, which we might not have. Speed eventually kills—not always suddenly, sometimes gradually. The world that speed continues to create is unsustainable; the pressing question is whether processes that have been set in motion have already passed the tipping point and cannot be reversed. What is clear is that we are fast approaching the end of a trajectory that began with the Protestant Reformation, continued during the Industrial Revolution, accelerated with consumer capitalism, and has reached warp speed in today's financial capitalism. Speed is tearing apart bodies, minds, countries, communities—even the earth itself. As networks expand and connectivity increases, speed approaches its limit and it becomes necessary either to slow down or face systemic collapse. The slowing down required to delay or even avoid disaster does not merely involve pausing to smell the roses or taking more time with one's family, though doing so is important; rather, it is necessary to devote considerable time and significant resources to understanding the intersecting vectors that have brought us to this tipping point. Only then might it be possible to develop tactics and strategies to adjust interactive networks in ways that make it possible for them to function effectively within unavoidable limitations. Short-term measures are necessary but not sufficient to deal with accelerating problems; the deeper issue is the need for what Nietzsche aptly described as a "transvaluation of values." The values that have allowed Western capitalism to thrive now threaten its collapse: commitment to parts, divisions, individualism, competition, utility, efficiency, simplicity, choice, consumption, busyness, excess, growth, and speed—above all, speed. And the values this regime has repressed now need to be cultivated: commitment to the whole, relationships, community, cooperation, generosity, patience, subtlety, deliberation, analysis, complexity, uncertainty, leisure, and reflection—above all, reflection.

The increasing fragmentation that connectivity imposes makes it difficult even to comprehend the nature and magnitude of the challenges that will only become more urgent in coming years. With more and more people trapped in ideological bubbles and silos of self-interest, a sense of the whole upon which life depends disappears. The inward turn to the subject, which began with the Protestant Reformation, has degenerated into a competitive individualism that has turned destructive. In today's networked world, where all is co-dependent, it is more urgent than ever to recover not only the awareness, but also the detailed understanding of the comprehensive whole in and through which everything is constituted and sustained. Economic, social, political, psychological, and ecological problems know no boundaries. When confronted with unavoidable limits to growth and market expansion, cooperation becomes more important than competition. The planet simply cannot sustain a further extension of the levels of global consumption and financial speculation practiced by today's so-called advanced economies. Everything is inextricably interrelated; expansion in one area eventually results in contraction somewhere else. It follows, then, that some form of redistribution of resources and wealth among the nations and peoples of the world is neither a free option nor a socialist dream; rather, it is a practical necessity forced on us by unavoidable parameters of constraint.

While these constraints impose limits, they can also create the conditions needed for new forms of creativity to emerge. If this creativity is to flourish, it will be necessary to shatter the silos and the filter bubbles that nourish today's repressive monocultures. In natural, social, or cultural systems, creativity comes about when what is usually held apart is brought together to generate unexpected combinations, collaborations, and syntheses. When people, nations, and organizations remain confined within their own echo chambers, the result is the eternal repetition of the same in self-reinforcing loops that lead to even deeper divisions. Creativity requires being open to those whose understanding of the world differs from one's own. Conversation, not chatter; response, not reaction; negotiation, not confrontation. It is precisely in dangerous moments of critical transition that the possibility for such creativity often is the greatest.

The future depends not only on openness to other people, but also on openness to the natural world in all its complexity, ambiguity, and obscurity. For many true believers, matter, body, and earth are burdens that shackle the mind. When wealthy Silicon Valley entrepreneurs commercialize space travel to escape the gravity of earth and fantasize about leaving the body by uploading their minds into some cosmic computer, they are as nihilistic as religious fanatics who long for the end of the world so they can enter the immaterial and eternal realm of heaven. The challenge today is not to escape but to save time by saving the earth. "Human," after all, derives from the word "humus"—the organic material from which life emerges and to which it returns. To lose touch with earth is to become inhuman.

The sense of the whole is temporal as well as spatial. So-called real time is unreal; in this high-tech, networked age, past and future frequently collapse into momentary fragments of time that eternally return but are never truly present. Truly real time is tensed—past and future intersect in a present that is always passing. At this late date, the new has become old and the past once again becomes a resource rather than a burden. Milan Kundera is right: "There is a secret bond between slowness and memory, between speed and forgetting. . . . In existential mathematics, that experience takes the form of two basic equations: the degree of slowness is directly proportional to the intensity of memory; the degree of speed is directly proportional to the intensity of forgetting."[43] The faster we go, the more we forget, and the more we forget, the less we know who we are or where we are going. The past is never dead and gone because it always forms the horizon that defines the constraints within which the future emerges. When we lose our memory or download it in the cloud, we are no longer human.

The future, of course, is not completely within our control, even when we struggle to plot it. Google's vision of planned serendipity represents the lingering belief in a tired modernism that extends the will to power and the will to mastery by attempting to program the future to produce automatons who no longer know how to think for themselves. To be open to the future is to be open to the unexpected and the unprogrammable, which lend life its irrepressible uncertainty and latent mystery and vitality. The risks involved in this uncertainty cannot be managed and the attempt to do so usually makes matters much worse. The problems confronting us are complex and do not yield to quick and simple solutions. When memory and expectation meet in the present of truly real time, it becomes possible to shift from a short-term to a long-term perspective—not years, not decades, not even centuries, but a duration that extends from the ancient geological time of Iceland's volcanoes and glaciers beyond the virtual realities of Wall Street to a future we cannot imagine. Only within this long arc of history can the cost of our actions be calculated.

The future approaches us as much as we approach it, and the most effective response we can have is not anticipatory control but patient waiting. Waiting bestows the gift of time, which is nothing less than life itself. When life slows down, it becomes possible to reflect thoughtfully on what usually rushes by too fast for us to notice. To managers and investors obsessed with efficiency, productivity, and profitable returns, such idle reflection appears to be a useless waste of time. But what is really useless and what really is useful, what is really productive and what is really wasteful, what is really profitable and what is really unprofitable, when life hangs in the balance? In his "Reflections," Franz Kafka writes, "Remain sitting at your table. Do not even listen, simply wait. Do not even wait, be quite still and solitary. The world will freely offer itself to you to be unmasked, it has no choice, it will roll in ecstasy at your feet."[44] The ecstasy of reflection arrests the ecstasy of speed.

The table at which I have written this book is in a converted barn overlooking the Berkshire Mountains in Massachusetts. These days, my life is divided between two places—country and city—and two speeds—slow and fast. I can read in the city but cannot write there. The problem is not just the noise, the rush, the distraction—the issue is more a matter of rhythm. Reflection and writing have rhythms of their own, which are not completely within one's control and, thus, cannot be rushed. Thoughts and ideas appear when they will and often disappear before they can be written down. But their halo remains and when the next thought arrives, it is shadowed by what has already slipped away. Though I have written many books, all of this remains as mysterious today as when I began writing years ago.

In many ways, the process of writing this book has enacted the complex interplay of speed and slowness I have been exploring. I had been considering the problem of speed for several years and had read well over a hundred books and countless articles on the subject. The more I read, the more I came to understand the relation of speed and the problems it creates to questions I have been pondering for more than four decades. Far from simple opposites, speed and slowness, I have gradually learned, are profoundly interconnected. On the one hand, increasing acceleration inevitably leads to systemic failure, which leads to an abrupt slowdown; on the other hand, slow accumulation over an extended period of time sometimes leads to a sudden emergence that brings about a phase shift in increasingly diverse and connected networks. On an individual level, stress created by the accelerating pace of life can reach the tipping point, where pills no longer work and a person falls apart both physically and mentally; alternatively, years of study and reflection can lead to a moment of illumination when things come together and suddenly make sense.

My reading and reflection on the subject of speed took more time than I expected. Having read so much over such a long period of time, last January I decided to spend the break between semesters going back over pages and pages of my notes and trying to organize my thoughts. The second semester promised to be extremely busy and I knew I would not have time to do much more reading and surely no writing. My plan was to be in a position to begin writing by the summer, when the pace of life would be slower. Then something unexpected but not unprecedented happened—in an instantaneous flash I saw this book. This is not the first time I have had this experience; it has happened often over the course of my career. Once a book appears, I cannot avoid writing no matter how little time I think I have. This way of describing the situation is not, however, precisely accurate because, having passed the tipping point, I do not really write the book; rather, the book writes itself through me and the rhythm and pace of the writing are not really my own. Indeed, many days my pencil and keyboard have trouble keeping up with the rush of thoughts. Against all expectations, I began writing at the beginning of February and six weeks later this book was basically written. While many refinements, revisions, additions, and subtractions would of course be necessary, the book was substantially finished.

No matter how many times this happens, the process always remains mysterious. As I have reflected on how my investigation of speed might be related to the speed with which I wrote about it, I have come to realize that the creative process of writing is governed by the same dynamics of emergent complex adaptive systems that I have been investigating. Creativity, I have suggested, occurs by bringing together what is usually held apart. Through a long and slow process, something like a primal soup of thoughts and ideas gradually accumulates. After these ideas reach a certain density and diversity, the soup must be allowed to simmer. During this time, which might be days, weeks, months, or even years, ideas bump and collide until one day all of a sudden they self-organize and the book emerges. This emergence is as sudden and can be as disruptive as the collapse of financial markets or the disappearance of sea ice and glaciers.

In *Four Quartets,* T. S. Eliot writes,

We shall not cease from exploration
And the end of all exploring
Will be to arrive where we started
And know the place for the first time.

In writing as in life, the beginning becomes clear, if at all, only at the end. Kierkegaard was right when he insisted that life can only be understood backward even if it must be lived forward. As I now look back, I still wonder whether my father would agree that the world changed more during his lifetime than during mine. In the course of researching and writing this book, I have discovered that our worlds and lives have not been as different as I once thought. The lessons he learned on that Gettysburg farm more than one hundred years ago have shaped the way I understand life, and they now create the sense of urgency that time might be running out because the speed of life is approaching its limit. My father's greatest lesson was not in the classroom—where he tried, not very successfully, to teach me physics—but out of doors, where he made me cut lawns, dig gardens, and shovel snow. Though he never explained what he was doing, I now understand that he was teaching me that matter truly does matter, and that we forget this lesson at our own peril. Regardless of how virtual the world becomes, there is no life without the material matrix that supports and sustains it.

The windows in the barn where I am writing these words are not limited to Microsoft's disciplinary operating system; beyond the computer screen, the barn's windows open onto gardens, ponds, and streams that I have been designing and cultivating for years. More recently, I have added sculptures that I have created from metal, stone, and bone. This

Stone Hill, Williamstown, Massachusetts

material realm balances the immaterial world in which I spend much of my life. It has a gravity that is refreshingly liberating, so liberating that by comparison the lightness of the immaterial world sometimes seems almost unbearable. When you slow down long enough to cultivate reflection by cultivating earth, the axis of reality sometimes shifts, even if ever so slightly. In this moment, it becomes possible to hope that the recovery of an appreciation for time will allow time for all of us, and our planet, to recover.

I often do my best thinking not when sitting at my desk or staring at the computer, but when moving rocks, turning soil, bending metal, and drilling bones. Dig deep enough and you discover that everything really is connected. While recently digging in a field where I have often worked, I uncovered a large outcropping that was hiding in plain sight. The more I uncovered, the more astonished I became. Rich burnt umber on the surface and brilliant white within, this massive rock was a work of art no human hand could craft. The striated layers of rock look like pages from a long-lost book. When I asked a geologist friend what kind of stone it was, he said it is Stockbridge Marble that millions of years ago lay two hundred miles to the east, off the coast of Nantucket on the floor of the ocean where Herman Melville once roamed. The marble is etched with fossils that form cryptic hieroglyphs. In today's fast-paced world, too few people consider such weighty volumes. But for readers who are patient enough to allow time to decipher these lines, there are important lessons to be learned. Not all reality is virtual, and the quick might not inherit the earth. After all these years, it seems that the wager remains the same: your time or your money? Given the choice, who would not choose time?

Appendix

Final Exams, Spring 1922
Arendtsville High School
Arendtsville, Pennsylvania

HISTORY.

1. Name the first two permanent Spanish settlements in the United States.
2. Give an account of the settlement of Georgia, telling of the purpose, by whom founded, the classes of settlers, and the date of settlement.
3. What were the Intercolonial Wars?
4. What was the influence of the Allegheny Mountains on the settlement of the English?
5. Give the cause of the French and Indian War.
6. Name four great American inventors and their inventions. When was Adams County organized? Of what county was it a part?
7. What were the Alien and Sedition Laws?
8. Where was the seat of government when Washington was inaugurated? When was it removed to the present location?
9. Connect with each of the following some event in American History: DeSoto, Magellan, Drake, Raleigh.

READING.

1. Recite to the committee one or more of the poems studied this winter.

2. Write a short biography of Henry W. Longfellow.

3. Tell the poem from which these lines are taken:

   (a) "Do you think, O blue-eyed banditti."

   (b) "The splendor falls on castle walls."

   (c) "Rest, rest, on mother's breast."

   (d) "The sky is ruddy in the east."

4. Define and use in good sentences the following words: smithy, painting, breeze, commerce, toiling.

GEOGRAPHY.

1. (a) Name five rivers of North America and the body of water into which each flows.

   (b) Name and locate the principal mountain systems of North America and state in what direction each extends.

   (c) Locate three seaports.

2. Name the countries of Europe that border the Mediterranean Sea and give the capital of each.

3. What and where are the following: Amazon, Sydney, Hawaii, Gibraltar, The Golden Gate?

4. Define Equator, poles, meridian, strait, isthmus, peninsula, cape and river.

5. Name the rivers and largest cities of Pennsylvania.

6. Name the different zones of climate. Give a characteristic plant and animal for each zone.

HISTORY.

1. (a) Give a brief account of the settlement of Virginia.

   (b) What exploration or discoveries did the following make and what nation did each represent: Columbus, De Soto, Champlain, Hudson and Drake?

2. What important laws were passed during Wilson's Administration?

3. What was the Missouri Compromise?

4. Give the various causes that led up to the Revolutionary War. How long did the war last? What was gained by it?

5. From whom did we purchase Alaska? When? Amount? For what is Alaska valuable?

6. Tell about the discovery of gold in California.

GRAMMAR.

1. What is case? Name, define and illustrate the different cases.

2. What is declension? Decline these words: Mr. Hope, who, she, bell.

3. What properties or modifications do verbs have? Adjectives?

4. What do we give as the principal parts of a verb? Give the principal parts of these verbs: Do, be, have, burst, choose.

5. What is number? Write the plural of these words: Entry, radius, analysis, piano, tooth, Miss Jewel, son-in-law, Mr. Kemp.

6. What is a phrase? A clause?

7. In what must a verb agree with its subject?

8. Give four uses of nouns in sentences, writing sentences to illustrate.

9. Name the relative pronouns. The interrogative pronouns.

FINAL EXAMINATIONS For April 15, 1922
ARITHMETIC.

1. Multiply .006134 by 80.32 and divide the result by .0032.

2. Divide the sum of 1/2 and 1/3 by their difference.

3. What will 3240 feet of lumber cost @ $22.50 per thousand feet?

4. Find the interest on $850 for 3 years, 3 months, 3 days at 5 per cent.

5. Mr. Upkeep is assessed at $10,000 on which he pays annual taxes amounting to $250. On the same basis, how much tax should Mr. Equal pay on property assessed at $7225?

6. Find the area of a circular flower bed 12 feet in diameter.

7. I, C, and R engage in business. I furnishes $1200, C furnishes $1000, and R furnishes $800. They clear $3250. What is each one's share of the gain? What is the rate of gain?

8. Two soldiers travel, one 120 miles due north and the other 90 miles due west. How far are they apart by direct line?

9. A man sold a carriage for $234, and by so doing lost 10%. What should we have sold it for in order to gain 10%?

GEOGRAPHY.

1. Mention an important export of Cuba, Australia, Alaska, South Africa.

2. Explain the following terms: metropolis, equinox, and earth's orbit.

3. Describe the ownership, location and government of Cuba and Porto Rico.

4. Name and locate a city famous for the manufacture of each of the following: Paper, lace, toys, shoes and silk.

5. Name and locate the city which is suggested to you by the following names: Kaiser, Sultan, Parliament.

6. Describe the vegetation of the torrid zone; the animals; the inhabitants; and the climate.

7. In what state is each of the following cities located: Rochester, Memphis, Kansas City, Cincinnati?

8. Name the principal rivers that empty into the Mississippi.

9. Locate the following cities and tell by what nation each is controlled: Hong Kong, Manila, Calcutta, and Singapore.

SPELLING.

hoping	shovel	rascal
repel	trellis	misspell
bureau	eligible	occasion
pigeon	raisin	lizard
athlete	panel	judgment
villain	division	deceit
parallel	fugitive	alien
deceive	parable	corps
artery	heifer	saucy
compel	deficit	onion
zincky	edible	auricle
succeed	frontier	distil
zealous	luxury	liege
tenable	civilian	secrecy
pretzels	citadel	compost
estuary	chattel	accretion
adjunct	monopoly	

PHYSIOLOGY.

1. Trace a particle of food from the mouth to the blood.
2. Name the respiratory organs.
3. What first aid would you render in a case of fainting? In a case of apparent drowning?
4. Discuss the lungs with reference to location, size, structure, use and care of them.
5. How are broken bones healed?
6. Give uses of muscles.
7. Name the organs of digestion.
8. What are some good forms of exercise? How frequently should exercise be taken?
9. What are adenoid growths?

GRAMMAR.

1. Classify sentences according to use. Define and illustrate each.
2. Write the present tense, the past tense, and the perfect participle of the verbs *do* and *see*. Use each correctly in a sentence.
3. (a) Decline: I, he, man, lady.
   (b) Compare: big, little, beautiful.
   (c) Write the possessive singular and the possessive plural of dog, child, Mr. Smith.
4. Write a business letter to L. B. Herr & Son, Lancaster, Pa., ordering a dictionary.
5. Define a verb. Name the properties of verbs.
6. Diagram: General Reynolds, who was killed at Gettysburg, was a native of Lancaster County.

PHYSIOLOGY.

1. Define the following: femur, periosteum, antitoxin, cerebrum, appendicitis.
2. Name a contagious disease, give its symptoms and its effects, and tell how it may be kept from spreading.
3. Why is all blood sent to the lungs?
4. What are the digesting juices? How many kinds are there?
5. What is an organ? Mention a number of organs of the human body.
6. Describe the heart, telling its shape, its parts, its work.

WRITING.

1. Copy neatly to show your best hand-writing, this:
   "We are not worst at once; the course of evil
   Begins so slowly and from such slight source,
   An infant's hands might stem the breach with clay;
   But let the stream grow wider, and philosophy
   Age and religion, too, may strive in vain
   To stem the headlong current."

ARITHMETIC.

1. Which is the better salary, 16 2/3c per hour or $9 per week? You are to work 9 hours a day on Monday, Tuesday, Wednesday, Thursday and Friday, and 4 hours on Saturday.

2. Divide .001809 by 9000.

3. A brick wall contains 29700 bricks. Find the cost at $18.50 per thousand bricks.

4. If a dealer makes $15 on a horse which he sells for $195.00, what per cent does he gain?

5. The sum of two fractions is 1 1/11; one of them is 1/3, what is the other?

6. What will it cost to lay a cement walk, 150 ft. long, 1 ft. 6 in. wide, at 50c a square yard?

7. What is the interest of $3600 for 4 years, 7 months and 15 days at 5 per cent?

Notes

Chapter 1. Addiction to Speed

1. Milan Kundera, *Slowness,* trans. Linda Asher (New York: Harper, 1996), 2.
2. Michael Crichton, *Prey* (New York: Harper, 2002), 103–4.
3. J. R. McNeill, *Something New under the Sun: An Environmental History of the Twentieth Century* (New York: Norton, 2000), 297–98.
4. I will return to the implications of the continuing effects of the Industrial Revolution throughout the book, but especially in Chapter 10.
5. Alan Trachtenberg, foreword to Wolfgang Schivelbusch, *The Railway Journey: The Industrialization of Time and Space in the 19th Century* (Berkeley: University of California Press, 1986), xvi. In developing my account of the railway industry in Great Britain and the United States, I have followed the insightful analysis of Schivelbusch and the informative study by George Taylor, *The Transportation Revolution, 1815–1860* (New York: Rinehart, 1951).
6. Ibid., 33–34, 7, 37.
7. Ralph Waldo Emerson, "The Young American," 1844, available at http://www.emersoncentral.com/youngam.htm (accessed February 3, 2014).
8. Rebecca Solnit, *River of Shadows: Eadweard Muybridge and the Technological Wild West* (New York: Viking, 2003), 58.
9. I will consider ADHD and its treatment with Ritalin, that is, speed, in Chapter 9.
10. Stephen Kern, *The Culture of Time and Space, 1880–1918* (Cambridge, MA: Harvard University Press, 2003), 125. The Crichton-Browne and Nordau references are cited by Kern.
11. Ibid., 129, 130.
12. Ibid., 52, 56.
13. Henry David Thoreau, *Walden* (Princeton, NJ: Princeton University Press, 1988), 117–18.

14. William Wordsworth, *The Prelude*, 7.725–8, available at http://www.bartleby .com/145/ww293.html; and Georg Simmel, "The Metropolis and Mental Life," available at http://periplurban.org/blog/wp-content/uploads/ 2008/06/simmel_metropolisandmentallife.pdf (both accessed February 3, 2014).
15. Simmel, "Metropolis and Mental Life," 11–12.
16. Quoted in Solnit, *River of Shadows*, 21–22.
17. For a discussion of the continuing impact of these developments, see my books *Disfiguring: Art, Architecture, Religion* (Chicago: University of Chicago Press, 1992), chaps. 5 and 6; *Confidence Games: Money and Markets in a World without Redemption* (Chicago: University of Chicago Press, 2004), chap. 6; and *About Religion: Economies of Faith in Virtual Culture* (Chicago: University of Chicago Press, 1999), chap. 7.
18. Filippo Marinetti and Umberto Boccioni, *The Futurist Manifesto*, quoted in Stephen Kern, *The Culture of Time and Space, 1880–1918* (Cambridge, MA: Harvard University Press, 2003), 119.
19. Rebecca Solnit presents a detailed and illuminating discussion of Muybridge's photography and its implications in *River of Shadows*.
20. Kern, *Culture of Time and Space*, 118. The Léger quotes are cited by Kern.
21. Ibid., 120.
22. Jonathan Crary, *Suspensions of Perception: Attention, Spectacle, and Modern Culture* (Cambridge, MA: MIT Press, 1999), 310. Crary points out that during the latter half of the nineteenth century, there was considerable scientific interest in perception. Elaborate mechanical devices were constructed to measure reaction time. As early as 1850, Hermann von Helmholtz had successfully measured the speed of nerve transmission. In Crary's books *Suspensions of Perception* and *Techniques of the Observer: On Vision and Modernity in the 19th Century* (Cambridge, MA: MIT Press, 1993), he presents a very helpful analysis of the ways in which different technologies have shaped perception. His discussion of Manet, Seurat, and Cézanne is unusually insightful. Though my focus is somewhat different, I have benefited from Crary's work.
23. Herschel B. Chipp, ed., *Theories of Modern Art: A Source Book by Artists and Critics* (Berkeley: University of California Press, 1986), 260.
24. Quoted in Roland Penrose, *Picasso: His Life and Work* (Berkeley: University of California Press, 1981), 153.
25. Quoted in George Hamilton, *Painting and Sculpture in Europe, 1880–1940* (New York: Penguin Books, 1981), 15.
26. Chipp, *Theories of Modern Art*, 227, 214.

27. "Georges Seurat," a Wikipedia article available at http://en.wikipedia.org/wiki/Georges_Seurat (accessed February 3, 2014).

28. I will return to Warhol in Chapter 4. We will see that in his Factory, Warhol adapted the methods of industrial production to commodify art in ways that reinforced consumer capitalism.

Chapter 2. Invisible Hands

1. Quoted in Patrick Collison, *The Reformation: A History* (New York: Modern Library, 2004), 6–7.

2. "In fact, Germany's *revolutionary* past is theoretical—it is the *Reformation*. In that period the revolution originated in the brain of a monk, today in the brain of the philosopher [i.e., Hegel] . . . Luther . . . shattered the faith in authority by restoring the authority of faith. He transformed the priests into laymen by turning laymen into priests. He liberated man from external religiosity by making religiosity the inner most essence of man." Karl Marx, "Contribution to the Critique of Hegel's Philosophy of Right," in *The Marx-Engels Reader,* ed. Robert Tucker (New York: W.W. Norton, 1972), 60.

3. Some historians and sociologists have recently raised questions about the significance that Weber attributes to Calvinism in the emergence of capitalism and democracy. Summarizing his survey of critical responses to Weber, André Biéler concludes, "Let us rest content with noting that between the eighteenth century, which Weber and Troeltsch analyzed, and the period of the Reformer were more than two centuries of history and nothing less than the Industrial Revolution. Thus the biggest thing we can hold against these authors is that they ignored that gap and allowed themselves to identify Calvin's influence with that of the religious movements that were of Calvinist origin but were already considerably distorted and secularized—despite their wish to distinguish between them." See André Biéler, *Calvin's Economic and Social Thought,* trans. James Greig (Geneva: World Council of Churches, 2005), 437. The undeniable importance of the Industrial Revolution, which I will consider further in the next chapters, and of doctrinal changes introduced in competing Protestant sects, in no way undercut the importance of Weber's account of the influence of Calvin's theology for today's world. For recent efforts to reclaim Weber's legacy, see Steve Bruce, *Religion in the Modern World: From Cathedrals to Cults* (Oxford, Eng.: Oxford University Press, 1996), and Peter Berger, "The Desecularization of the World: A Global Overview," in Peter Berger, *The*

Desecularization of the World: Resurgent Religion and World Politics (Grand Rapids, MI: William Eerdmans, 1999).

4. John Calvin, *Institutes of the Christian Religion,* ed. John McNeill (Philadelphia: Westminster Press, 1967), 1.

5. Thomas Aquinas, *Introduction to St. Thomas Aquinas,* ed. A. C. Pegis (New York: Random House, 1948), 193, 215.

6. Martin Luther, "Ninety-five Theses," in *Martin Luther: Selections from His Writings,* ed. John Dillenberger (New York: Doubleday, 1961), 495.

7. Joan Acocella, "The End of the World: Interpreting the Plague," *New Yorker* (March 21, 2005), 82.

8. Romans 1:17.

9. Biéler, *Calvin's Economic and Social Thought,* 340. See also George Huntson Williams, *The Radical Reformation* (Philadelphia: Westminster Press, 1962). For an elaboration of the relationship between notions of God and self, see my books *Kierkegaard's Pseudonymous Authorship: A Study of Time and the Self* (Princeton, NJ: Princeton University Press, 1975); *Journeys to Selfhood: Hegel and Kierkegaard* (Berkeley: University of California Press, 1980), esp. chaps. 4 and 5; and *After God,* esp. chaps. 2 and 3.

10. Cited in Norman O. Brown, *Life against Death: The Psychoanalytic Meaning of History* (New York: Random House, 1959), 226, 221, 228.

11. Calvin, *Institutes of the Christian Religion,* trans. Ford L. Battles (Philadelphia: Westminster, 1969), 1:197, 199, 201, 208.

12. Ibid., 1:721.

13. Adam Smith, *The Theory of Moral Sentiments,* ed. D. D. Raphael and A. L. Macfie (Oxford, Eng.: Clarendon Press, 1976). 185.

14. Adam Smith, *The Wealth of Nations* (New York: Modern Library, 2000), book 4, chap. 2, para. 9.

Chapter 3. Time Counts

1. Myron Gilmore, *The World of Humanism, 1453–1517* (New York: W. Langer, 1952), 186.

2. Arthur Geoffrey Dickens, *Reformation and Society in Sixteenth Century Europe* (New York, 1968), 51. This work is cited in Elizabeth Eisenstein's two-volume study *The Printing Press as an Agent of Change: Communications and Cultural Transformations in Early-Modern Europe* (New York: Cambridge University Press, 1979).

3. Eisenstein, *Printing Press.*

4. Mark Edwards, *Printing, Propaganda, and Martin Luther* (Berkeley: University of California Press, 1994), 39.

5. Rudolf Hirsch, *Printing, Selling, and Reading, 1450–1550,* 90, quoted in Eisenstein, *Printing Press,* 347.

6. Fernand Braudel, *Civilization and Capitalism: 15th–18th Century,* vol. 2: *The Wheels of Commerce,* trans. Sian Reynolds (Berkeley: University of California Press, 1992), 101–2, 495.

7. Edward S. Casey, *Getting Back into Place: Toward a Renewed Understanding of the Place-World* (Bloomington: Indiana University Press, 1997), 3.

8. Ibid.

9. Ibid., 4.

10. James R. Beniger, *The Control Revolution: Technological and Economic Origins of the Information Society* (Cambridge, MA: Harvard University Press, 1986), 221–23.

11. See the Wikipedia entries for "Greenwich Mean Time" and "Standard Time," available at http://en.wikipedia.org/wiki/Greenwich_Mean_Time and http://en.wikipedia.org/wiki/Standard_time, respectively (accessed February 3, 2014).

12. Daniel Boorstin, *The Americans: The Democratic Experience* (New York: Vintage, 1974), 362.

13. Friedrich Schiller, *On the Aesthetic Education of Man in a Series of Letters,* trans. E. M. Wilkinson and L. A. Willoughby (New York: Oxford University Press, 1967), 35.

14. Frederick Winslow Taylor, *The Principles of Scientific Management* (New York: Harper, 1929), 13.

15. Ibid., 117.

16. Ibid., 39, 40.

17. Boorstin, *The Americans,* 369.

18. Jonathan Crary, *Suspensions of Perception: Attention, Spectacle, and Modern Culture* (Cambridge, MA: MIT Press, 1999), 30, 4. Crary presents a very helpful detailed analysis of a vast array of little-known technological devices and psychological techniques developed during the modern period to investigate and control attention.

19. See "Eight-Hour Day," a Wikipedia article available at http://en.wikipedia.org/wiki/Eight-hour_day (accessed February 3, 2014).

20. See "Electrification," a Wikipedia article available at http://en.wikipedia.org/wiki/Electrification (accessed February 3, 2014).

21. Quoted in Boorstin, *The Americans,* 548.

22. Beniger, *Control Revolution,* 299.

23. Ibid., 298–99.

24. Ibid., 283; the dates for the inventions listed can be found on 281–84.

25. Ibid., 286.

26. JoAnne Yates, *Control through Communication: The Rise of System in American Management* (Baltimore: Johns Hopkins University Press, 1989), 41–43.

27. Ibid., 56.

28. See "Melvil Dewey," a Wikipedia article available at http://en.wikipedia .org/wiki/Melvil_Dewey (accessed February 3, 2014).

29. Quoted in Yates, *Control through Communication,* 14.

30. Ibid., 15.

31. I will consider department stores as well as electronic technologies and networks in Chapter 4.

32. Taylor, *Principles of Scientific Management,* 7, 12.

Chapter 4. Windows Shopping

1. Walter Isaacson, *Steve Jobs* (New York: Simon and Schuster, 2011), 45.

2. Ibid., 49.

3. Andy Warhol, *The Philosophy of Andy Warhol* (New York: Harcourt Brace, 1975), 92.

4. Misty White Sidell, "Modeling Scouts Hunt for Fresh Faces at Swedish Eating Disorder Clinic," *Daily Beast,* available at http://www.thedailybeast.com /articles/2013/04/19/modeling-scouts-hunt-for-fresh-faces-at-swedish -eating-disorder-clinic.html (accessed February 3, 2014).

5. See Centers for Disease Control, "Adult Obesity Facts," available at http:// www.cdc.gov/obesity/data/adult.html; and Centers for Disease Control, "Childhood Obesity Facts," available at http://www.cdc.gov/healthyyouth /obesity/facts.htm (both accessed February 3, 2014).

6. Dan Jones, "Britain's Weight Crisis Almost Hits U.S. Proportions," *Daily Beast,* February 21, 2013.

7. UPI International, "Americans Eat Out about Five Times a Week," available at http://www.upi.com/Health_News/2011/09/19/Americans-eat-out -about-5-times-a-week/UPI-54241316490172 (accessed February 3, 2014).

8. Quoted in Robert Hughes, *The Shock of the New* (New York: Alfred Knopf, 1967), 177–80.

9. Wolfgang Schivelbusch, *The Railway Journey: The Industrialization of Time and Space in the 19th Century* (Berkeley: University of California Press, 1986), 45, 47.

10. Quoted in William Leach, *Land of Desire: Merchants, Power, and the Rise of a New American Culture* (New York: Random House, 1993), 60.

11. Walter Benjamin, *The Arcades Project,* trans. Howard Eiland and Kevin McLaughlin (Cambridge, MA: Harvard University Press, 1999), 37.

12. Quoted in Mary Portas, *Windows: The Art of Retail Display* (New York: Thames and Hudson, 1999), 14.

13. Leach, *Land of Desire,* 136–37.

14. Quoted in Schivelbusch, *Railway Journey,* 192.

15. Nancy Stock-Allen, *A Short Introduction to Graphic Design History,* available at http://www.designhistory.org/Advertising_pages/FirstAd.html (accessed February 3, 2014).

16. James R. Beniger, *The Control Revolution: Technological and Economic Origins of the Information Society* (Cambridge, MA: Harvard University Press, 1986), 345, 349–50.

17. Daniel Boorstin, *The Americans: The Democratic Experience* (New York: Vintage, 1974), 127–28.

18. See "Rural Free Delivery," a Wikipedia article available at http://en.wikipedia.org/wiki/Rural_Free_Delivery (accessed February 3, 2014). The introduction of radio and eventually television also plays an important role in these developments, which I will consider later in this chapter.

19. Beniger, *Control Revolution,* 378–80.

20. Ben Woolsey and Emily Starbuck Gerson, "The History of Credit Cards," available at http://www.creditcards.com/credit-card-news/credit-cards-history-1264.php (accessed February 3, 2014).

21. Boorstin, *The Americans,* 424.

22. Beniger, *Control Revolution,* 331.

23. The association of transgression with debt, accountability, accounting, and balancing books runs deep in the Christian and Jewish traditions. Consider, for example, the Lord's Prayer (Matthew 6:9–13): Give us this day our daily bread, / and forgive us our debts / as we also have forgiven our debtors. In his illuminating book *Charity: The Place of the Poor in the Biblical Tradition,* Gary A. Anderson underscores the longstanding use of economic and financial metaphors to explain the relationship between believers and God. "I have contended that charity was construed as a loan to God, which was then converted into a form of spiritual currency and stored in an impregnable divine bank. This idea is first attested in books of the Second Temple period and continues through the rabbinic and patristic periods." Gary A. Anderson, *The Place of the Poor in the Biblical Tradition* (New Haven: Yale University Press, 2013), 182.

24. Robert Venturi, Denise Scott Brown, and Steven Izenour, *Learning from Las Vegas* (Cambridge, MA: MIT Press, 1988), 13.

25. Robert Venturi, *Complexity and Contradiction in Architecture* (New York: Museum of Modern Art, 1966), 16.

26. *Wall Street,* directed by Oliver Stone (Century City, CA: 21st Century Fox, 1987).

27. See "Black Monday (1987)," a Wikipedia article available at http://en.wikipedia.org/wiki/Black_Monday_(1987) (accessed February 3, 2014).

28. Horst Kurnitzky, "Das liebe Geld: Die wahre Liebe," in *Museum des Geldes* (Frankfurt: Museum des Geldes, 1978).

29. See "Electrum," a Wikipedia article available at http://en.wikipedia.org/wiki/Electrum (accessed February 3, 2014).

30. In recounting this history, I have followed the excellent summary published by the Federal Bank of San Francisco, part of a 1995 annual report available at http://www.frbsf.org/publications/federalreserve/annual/1995/history.html (accessed February 3, 2014).

31. See "Crane & Co.," a Wikipedia article available at http://en.wikipedia.org/wiki/Crane_%26_Co (accessed February 3, 2014).

32. Karl Marx, *Capital,* ed. Friedrich Engels (New York: International Publishers, 1967), 1:126.

33. Friedrich Nietzsche, "On Truth and Lie in an Extra-Moral Sense," *The Portable Nietzsche,* ed. Walter Kaufmann (New York: Penguin, 1980), 46–47.

Chapter 5. Net Working

1. Richard R. John, *Network Nation: Inventing American Telecommunications* (Cambridge, MA: Harvard University Press, 2010), 6.

2. Henry David Thoreau, *Walden* (Princeton, NJ: Princeton University Press, 1988), 52.

3. Tom Standage, *The Victorian Internet: The Remarkable Story of the Telegraph and the Nineteenth Century's On-line Pioneers* (New York: Berkeley Books, 1998), 168–69. Standage's book is excellent and I have drawn from it, as well as John's *Network Nation,* in charting the history of the telegraph.

4. Quoted in Standage, *Victorian Internet,* 90–91.

5. Quoted in John, *Network Nation,* 370.

6. See "Transatlantic Telegraph Cable," a Wikipedia article available at http://en.wikipedia.org/wiki/Transatlantic_telegraph_cable (accessed February 3, 2014). I have also drawn on the following Wikipedia articles in developing this part of the argument: "Cyrus West Field," at http://en.wikipedia

.org/wiki/Cyrus_West_Field; and "Electrical Telegraph," at http://
en.wikipedia.org/wiki/Electrical_telegraph (both accessed February 3,
2014).

7. Standage, *Victorian Internet,* 102.

8. Thomas Nonnenmacher, "History of the U.S. Telegraph Industry," available via Economic History Services at http://eh.net/encyclopedia/his
tory-of-the-u-s-telegraph-industry (accessed March 8, 2014).

9. Standage, *Victorian Internet,* 140.

10. Ibid., 128–29.

11. Ibid., 166.

12. Ibid., 94.

13. "Ticker Tape," a Wikipedia article available at http://en.wikipedia.org/
wiki/Ticker_tape (accessed February 3, 2014).

14. Standage, *Victorian Internet,* 119.

15. JoAnne Yates, "The Telegraph's Effect on Nineteenth-Century Markets
and Firms," *Business and Economic History* 15 (1986): 158.

16. John Marshall and Kenneth Kapner, *Understanding Swaps* (New York:
Wiley, 1993), 19–20.

17. In anticipation of issues to be considered in Chapter 10, it is important to
note that in today's financial markets, the seller does not necessarily have
to own the security or the commodity when the option or future is sold.
One can sell these contracts while owning nothing and gamble that the
direction of the market will make it profitable. If it becomes necessary
to close the deal, one can purchase the security or commodity at the time
the option is exercised or the futures contract matures. When investors are
literally buying and selling nothing, dematerialization reaches its endpoint.

18. Richard DuBoff, "The Telegraph and the Structure of Markets in the
United States, 1845–1890," *Research in Economic History* 8 (1983): 259. This
excellent article includes a wealth of valuable information that informs the
following discussion.

19. Ibid., 258.

20. Ibid., 259–61.

21. Ibid., 262.

22. Ibid., 261.

23. Thomas Bass, *The Predictors: How a Band of Maverick Physicists Used Chaos
Theory to Trade Their Way to a Fortune on Wall Street* (New York: Henry Holt,
1999), 13–14.

24. Standage, *Victorian Internet,* 151.

25. Serge Guilbaut, *How New York Stole the Idea of Modern Art: Abstract Expres-*

sionism, Freedom and the Cold War (Chicago: University of Chicago Press, 1984), 177.

26. Andy Warhol, "What Is Pop Art? Answers from Eight Painters," *ARTnews* 62 (November 1963): 123.

27. Quoted in David Galenson, *Painting Outside the Lines: Patterns of Creativity in Modern Art* (Cambridge, MA: Harvard University Press, 2001), 138.

28. Ibid., 139.

29. The statistics in this section were derived in part from Eileen Kinsella, "$25 Billion and Counting," *ARTnews,* May 2008, 122–31.

30. Quoted in Calvin Tompkins, "The Turnaround Artist: Jeff Koons, Up from Banality," *New Yorker* (April 23, 2007), 56–67.

31. Deepak Gopinath, "Picasso Lures Hedge-Fund-Type Investors to the Art Market," available at http://southasiaspeak.blogspot.com/2006/01/picasso-lures-hedge-fund-type.html (accessed March 8, 2014).

32. Robin Pogrebin and Kevin Flynn, "As Art Values Rise, so Do Concerns about Market Oversight," *New York Times,* January 27, 2013.

33. Bryan Burrough and Bethany McLean, "The Hunt for Steve Cohen," *Vanity Fair* (June 2013), available at http://www.vanityfair.com/business/2013/06/steve-cohen-insider-trading-case (accessed March 3, 2014).

Chapter 6. Inefficient Market Hypothesis

1. Richard A. Easterlin, "When Growth Outpaces Happiness," *New York Times,* September 27, 2012.

2. E. J. Mishan, *The Costs of Growth* (Westport, CT: Praeger, 1993), 12. Emphasis added.

3. It is important to note that the culture of debt that fuels both the consumer and financial economy creates further pressure for incessant growth. In their provocative book *Rethinking Money: How New Currencies Turn Scarcity into Prosperity* (San Francisco: Berrett-Koehler, 2013), Bernard Lietaer and Jacqui Dunne explain, "Debt-based money requires endless growth because borrowers must find additional money to pay back the interest on their debt. For better-rated debtors (e.g., in normal times, government debt), the interest is simply covered through additional debt, resulting in *compound interest:* paying interest on interest. Compound interest implies exponential growth in the long run, something mathematically impossible in a *finite* world" (42).

4. Jared Bernstein, "Raise the Economy's Speed Limit," *New York Times,* December 12, 2012.

5. Robert Skidelsky and Edward Skidelsky, *How Much Is Enough?: Money and the Good Life* (New York: Other Press, 2012), 182–83.

6. Edmund Phelps, "Equilibrium: Development of the Concept," in *New Palgrave: A Dictionary of Economics,* ed. John Eatwell, Murray Milgate, and Peter Newman (New York: Macmillan, 1987), 2:180.

7. Robert Schiller, *Irrational Exuberance* (Princeton, NJ: Princeton University Press, 2000), 173–74.

8. Francis Fukuyama, *The End of History and the Last Man* (New York: Free Press, 1992), xi.

9. Vance Packard, *The Waste Makers* (New York: David McKay Company, 1960), 89.

10. Quoted in ibid., 25.

11. Quoted in ibid., 232.

12. One such company offering thousands of dress options is Aria Dress Company; see http://www.ariadress.com (accessed March 3, 2014).

13. Elizabeth L. Cline, *Over-Dressed: The Shockingly High Cost of Cheap Fashion* (New York: Penguin, 2012), 96.

14. Kasra Ferdows, Michael A. Lewis, and José A. D. Machuca, "Zara's Secret for Fast Fashion," Harvard Business School online archive, 2005, available at http://hbswk.hbs.edu/archive/4652.html (accessed February 3, 2014).

15. The statistics are drawn from Cline, *Over-Dressed,* 21–24.

16. Paul Sims, "Britain's Bulging Closet: Growth of 'Fast Fashion' Means Women Are Buying HALF Their Body Weight in Clothes Each Year," available at http://www.dailymail.co.uk/femail/article-1389786/Britains-bulging-closets-Growth-fast-fashion-means-women-buying-HALF-body-weight-clothes-year.html (accessed February 3, 2014).

17. See Adeline Koh, "No Time to Shop for Clothes? Try Stitch Fix!," *Chronicle of Higher Education,* September 5, 2013, available at http://chronicle.com/blogs/profhacker/no-time-to-shop-for-clothes-try-stitch-fix/51977?cid=pm&utm_source=pm&utm_medium=en (accessed February 4, 2014).

18. Quoted in Hiroko Tabuchi, "Fad-Loving Japan May Derail a Sony Smartphone, *New York Times,* June 26, 3013.

19. Quoted in Mishan, *Costs of Economic Growth,* 152.

20. Cline, *Over-Dressed,* 122.

21. Ibid., 123. See chap. 5, "The After Life of Cheap Clothes," for an informative and disturbing analysis of these issues.

22. For a vivid presentation of the eWaste problem in Asia, see the documentary *Exporting Harm: The High-Tech Trashing of Asia,* available at http://www.youtube.com/watch?v=yDSWGV3jGek (accessed March 8, 2014).

Chapter 7. Dividing by Connecting

1. Friedrich Nietzsche, *The Gay Science,* trans. Walter Kaufmann (New York: Random House, 1974), 125.
2. Martin Heidegger, "The Question Concerning Technology," in *"The Question Concerning Technology" and Other Essays,* trans. William Lovitt (New York: Harper and Row, 1977), 27.
3. Friedrich Nietzsche, *Will to Power,* trans. Walter Kaufmann (New York: Random House, 1968), 267.
4. Ibid., 327, 326.
5. Quoted in Susan Jacoby, *Freethinkers: A History of American Secularism* (New York: Metropolitan Books, 2004), 316.
6. Ibid., 321.
7. Ibid.
8. Bill Bishop with Robert G. Cushing, *The Big Sort: Why the Clustering of Like-Minded America Is Tearing Us Apart* (New York: Mariner Books, 2008), 4, 130. Bishop's account is packed with vital statistics and information, which I have drawn on throughout this section.
9. Ibid., 12.
10. Quoted in ibid., 34.
11. Ibid., 82.
12. Ibid., 90.
13. Significantly, however, religious conservatives, unlike hippies, did not want to get government out of the business of regulating reproductive rights.
14. Nicholas Negroponte, *Being Digital* (New York: Knopf, 1995), 153.
15. John Cassidy, *Dot.Con: The Greatest Story Ever Sold* (New York: Harper-Collins, 2002), 52.
16. Joseph Turow, *The Daily You: How the New Advertising Industry Is Defining Your Identity and Your Worth* (New Haven: Yale University Press, 2011), 47, 32. Turow's valuable study provides a wealth of information about recent advertising policies and practices. I have drawn on his account in my discussion of Netscape's introduction of the cookie.
17. Quoted in ibid., 48.
18. Eli Pariser, *The Filter Bubble: How the New Personalized Web Is Changing What We Read and How We Think* (New York: Penguin Books, 2001), 6.
19. Quoted in Nicholas Carr, *The Shallows: What the Internet Is Doing to Our Brains* (New York: Norton, 2010), 158.
20. Quoted in Jeffrey Rosen, "Who Do Online Advertisers Think You Are?," *New York Times,* November 30, 2012.

21. Andrew McAfee and Erik Brynjolfsson, "Big Data: The Management Revolution," *Harvard Business Review* (October 2012): 62–63.

22. Turow, *Daily You,* 65.

23. Quoted in Pamela Jones Harbour, "The Emperor of All Identities," *New York Times,* December 19, 2012.

24. Cade Metz, "Inside Google Spanner, the Largest Single Database on Earth," available at http://www.wired.com/wiredenterprise/2012/11/google-spanner-time (accessed February 4, 2014).

25. Gregory Ferenstein, "Google's New Director of Engineering, Ray Kurzweil, Is Building Your 'Cybernetic Friend,'" available at http://techcrunch.com/2013/01/06/googles-director-of-engineering-ray-kurzweil-is-building-your-cybernetic-friend (accessed February 4, 2014).

26. David Segal, "This Man Is Not a Cyborg. Yet.," *New York Times,* June 1, 2013.

27. Natasha Singer, "You for Sale: Mapping, and Sharing, the Consumer Genome," *New York Times,* June 16, 2012.

28. Natasha Singer, "A Data Broker Offers a Peek behind the Curtain," *New York Times*, September 1, 2013, available at http://www.nytimes.com/2013/09/01/business/a-data-broker-offers-a-peek-behind-the-curtain.html (accessed February 4, 2014).

29. Siva Vaidhayanathan, *The Googlization of Everything (and Why We Should Worry)* (Berkeley: University of California Press, 2011), 3.

30. Bill Keller, "Invasion of the Data Snatchers," *New York Times,* January 14, 2013.

31. Bishop, *Big Sort,* 185–86.

32. Don Peppers and Martha Rogers, *The One to One Future: Building Relations One Customer at a Time* (New York: Doubleday), 384.

33. Søren Kierkegaard, *The Present Age,* trans. Howard Hong and Edna Hong (Princeton, NJ: Princeton University Press, 1978), 104.

34. Pariser, *Filter Bubble,* 61–62.

35. Bishop, *Big Sort,* 251–52.

36. Quoted in Sasha Issenberg, *The Victory Lab: The Secret Science of Winning Campaigns* (New York: Crown Publishers, 2012), 116, 246.

37. Jeffrey Rosen, "Who Do Online Advertisers Think You Are?" *New York Times,* November 30, 2012.

38. See the online profile of Affectiva and its "automated facial coding solution" Affdex at http://www.affectiva.com/company/about (accessed February 4, 2014).

39. Quoted on Beyond Verbal's website, http://www.beyondverbal.com/about (accessed March 1, 2014).

Chapter 8. Extreme Finance

1. See Kalin Nacheff, "Ducati Scene in *Wall Street 2*," available at http://blog.leatherup.com/2011/07/29/ducati-scene-in-wall-street-2 (accessed February 4, 2014).
2. See "Guggenheim Las Vegas," available at http://www.guggenheim.org/new-york/press-room/releases/press-release-archive/2000/695-october-20-guggenheim-las-vegas (accessed February 4, 2014).
3. Kristen Petersen, "Vegas, Say Goodbye to Guggenheim," *Las Vegas Sun,* April 10, 2008, available at http://www.lasvegassun.com/news/2008/apr/10/vegas-say-goodbye-guggenheim (accessed February 4, 2014).
4. Tom Daniell, "Nothing Serious," *Log* (Winter/Spring 2013): 21.
5. James Owen Weatherall presents a very helpful account of the relationship between Shannon and Thorpe. In this section, I have been guided by his account. See Weatherall, *The Physics of Wall Street: A Brief History of Predicting the Unpredictable* (New York: Houghton Mifflin, 2013), chap. 4.
6. In developing the account of Thorp's shorting strategy, I have been guided by ibid., 100–102.
7. Ibid., 101.
8. Jenny Strasburg and Anupreeta Das, "NYSE to Sell Itself in $8.2 Billion Deal: Planned Takeover Highlights Rise in Electronic Trading," *Wall Street Journal,* updated December 2, 2012, available at http://online.wsj.com/news/articles/SB10001424127887324461604578191031432500980 (accessed February 23, 2014).
9. Sal Arnuk and Joseph Saluzzi, *Broken Markets: How High Frequency Trading and Predatory Practices on Wall Street Are Destroying Investor Confidence and Your Portfolio* (New York: Financial Times Press, 2012), 69.
10. For an explanation of the switch from fractions to decimals, see the Investopedia answer to a reader's question dated February 26, 2009, available at http://www.investopedia.com/ask/answers/04/073004.asp (accessed February 4, 2014).
11. Ibid., 83.
12. Ibid., 46–47.
13. Scott Patterson, *Dark Pools: High-Speed Traders, A. I. Bandits, and the Threat to the Global Financial System* (New York: Crown Business, 2012), 45.
14. Ibid., 7.

15. See the Bain Report "A World Awash in Money," November 14, 2012, available at http://www.bain.com/publications/articles/a-world-awash-in -money.aspx (accessed February 4, 2014).

16. Michael Lewitt, http://www.thecreditstrategist.com, January 1, 2013.

17. Ibid.

18. Patterson, *Dark Pools,* 63.

19. Rich Miller, "NYSE Opens Mahwah Data Center," available at http:// www.datacenterknowledge.com/archives/2010/08/09/nyse-opens-mah wah-data-center (accessed February 4, 2014).

20. Arnuk and Saluzzi, *Broken Markets,* 32.

21. Michael Crichton, *Prey* (New York: Harper, 2002), xi.

22. Didier Sornette, *Why Stock Markets Crash: Critical Events in Complex Financial Systems* (Princeton, NJ: Princeton University Press, 2003), 393–94.

23. Paul Krugman, *The Self-Organizing Economy* (Malden, MA: Blackwell, 1996), 2.

24. Brian Arthur, John Holland, Blake LeBaron, and Richard Palmer, "Asset Pricing under Endogenous Expectations in an Artificial Stock Market Model," *The Economy as an Evolving Complex System, II,* eds. W. Brian Arthur, Steven Durlaf, and David Lane (Reading, MA: Perseus, 1997), 15.

25. Friedrich Hayek, *The Fatal Conceit: The Errors of Socialism*, ed. W. W. Bradley (Chicago: University of Chicago Press, 1989), 76.

26. See "Flash Crash," a Wikipedia article available at http://en.wikipedia .org/wiki/Flash_crash (accessed February 4, 2014).

27. *Money and Speed: Inside the Black Box,* transcript, available through iTunes and in the author's possession.

28. Nathaniel Popper, "High-Speed Trading No Longer Hurtling Forward," *New York Times,* October 14, 2012.

29. Quoted in Patterson, *Dark Pools,* 274.

30. Nathaniel Popper, "Beyond Wall St., Curbs on High-Speed Trading Advance," *New York Times,* September 26, 2012.

31. Arthur Levitt, "Don't Set Speed Limits on Trading," *Wall Street Journal,* August 17, 2009.

32. Quoted in Nathaniel Potter and Peter Eavis, "Errant Trades Reveal a Risk Few Expected," *New York Times,* August 2, 2012.

33. Per Bak, *How Nature Works: The Science of Self-Organized Criticality* (New York: Springer-Verlag, 1996), 1–2.

34. See the Wikipedia articles "Bloomberg L.P." and "Bloomberg Terminal," available at http://en.wikipedia.org/wiki/Bloomberg_L.P.; and http:// en.wikipedia.org/wiki/Bloomberg_terminal, respectively (both accessed February 4, 2014).

Chapter 9. Reprogramming Life—Deprogramming Minds

1. Albert Robida, *Twentieth Century,* trans. Arthur B. Evans (Middletown, CT: Wesleyan University Press, 2004), xxvii–xxviii, 16.

2. Tony Dokoupil, "Is the Internet Making Us Crazy? What the Latest Research Says," *Newsweek,* July 9, 2012, available at http://www.newsweek.com/ internet-making-us-crazy-what-new-research-says-65593 (accessed February 5, 2014).

3. Nicholas Carr, *The Shallows: What the Internet Is Doing to Our Brains* (New York: Norton, 2011), 86

4. Quoted in Dokoupil, "Is the Internet Making Us Crazy?"

5. Edmund DeMarche, "Pennsylvania Hospital to Open Country's First In-patient Treatment Program for Internet Addiction," September 1, 2013, FoxNews.com, available at http://www.foxnews.com/tech/2013/09/01/ hospital-first-inpatient-treatment-internet-addiction (accessed February 5, 2014).

6. Larry Rosen, *iDisorder: Understanding Our Obsession with Technology and Overcoming Its Hold on Us* (New York: Palgrave, 2012), 69–70.

7. Jakob Nielsen, "F-Shaped Pattern for Reading Web Content," April 17, 2006, available at http://www.nngroup.com/articles/f-shaped-pattern -reading-web-content (accessed February 5, 2014).

8. Carr, *Shallows,* 90.

9. Ibid., 91.

10. Ken Auletta, "Business Outsider," *New Yorker,* April 8, 2013, 31.

11. Philip Boffey, "The Next Frontier Is Inside Your Brain," *New York Times,* February 23, 2013.

12. Quoted in Alan Schwarz and Sarah Cohen, "More Diagnoses of Hyperactivity in New C.D.C. Data," *New York Times,* March 31, 2013.

13. Roger Cohen, "The Competition Drug," *New York Times,* March 4, 2013.

14. "Braingate," a Wikipedia article available at http://en.wikipedia.org/wiki/ Braingate (accessed February 5, 2014).

15. For this quotation and more on the Kavli Foundation and its neurotechnology initiatives, see http://www.kavlifoundation.org/brain-initiative (accessed February 5, 2014).

16. Quoted in Nick Bilton, "Disruptions: Brian Computer Interfaces Inch Closer to Mainstream," *New York Times,* April 28, 2013, available at http:// bits.blogs.nytimes.com/2013/04/28/disruptions-no-words-no-gestures -just-your-brain-as-a-control-pad (accessed February 5, 2014).

17. Ibid.

18. Michael Hanger, "Toward a History of Attention in Culture and Science," *MLN* 118, no. 3 (April 2003): 670.

19. "Ad Men Use Brain Scanners to Probe Our Emotional Responses," *The Observer,* January 14, 2012.

20. Marco Iacoboni et al., "This Is Your Brain on Politics," *New York Times,* November 11, 2007.

21. "Is Your Brain on Politics?: Neuroscience Reveals Brain Differences between Republicans and Democrats," from an original article by Jeff Stensland, available at http://www.sciencedaily.com/releases/2012/11/1211011050 03.htm (accessed February 5, 2014).

22. Gary Small and Gigi Vorgan, *iBrain: Surviving the Technological Alteration of the Modern Mind* (New York: HarperCollins, 2008), 32–33.

23. Friedrich Schiller, *On the Aesthetic Education of Man in a Series of Letters,* trans. E. M. Wilkinson and L. A. Willoughby (New York: Oxford University Press, 1967), 35.

Chapter 10. Meltdowns

1. John Maynard Keynes, "Economic Possibilities for Our Grandchildren," *Essays in Persuasion* (New York: Norton, 1963), 358.

2. Thorstein Veblen, *The Theory of the Leisure Class* (Oxford, Eng.: Oxford University Press: 2009), 30, 33.

3. Bertrand Russell, *"In Praise of Idleness" and Other Essays* (New York: Norton, 1935), 11, 23, 32–33.

4. Carl Horne, *In Praise of Slowness: How a Worldwide Movement Is Challenging the Cult of Speed* (New York: HarperCollins, 2004), 188.

5. Juliet Schor, *The Overworked American: The Unexpected Decline of Leisure* (New York: Basic Books, 1991), 4, 2.

6. Keynes, "Economic Possibilities for Our Grandchildren," 562.

7. "More Work Goes 'Undercover': Bringing the Office to Bed for 3 a.m. Emails to China; Wi-Fi Mattress," *Wall Street Journal,* November 13, 2012.

8. Schor, *Overworked American,* 18.

9. Becket Adams, "U.S. CEO Goes Off on France's Work Ethic in Epic Letter: 'Lazy' Union Workers Who Talk Too Much," available at http://www.theblaze.com/stories/2013/02/20/u-s-ceo-goes-off-on-frances-work-ethic-in-epic-letter-lazy-workers-who-talk-too-much (accessed February 5, 2014).

10. Schor, *Overworked American,* 80.

11. Keynes, "Economic Possibilities for Our Grandchildren," 572.

12. Schor, *Overworked American,* 126.

13. Friedrich Nietzsche, *The Gay Science,* trans. Walter Kaufmann (New York: Random House, 1974), 329.

14. "Cittaslow," a Wikipedia article available at http://en.wikipedia.org/wiki/Cittaslow (accessed February 5, 2014).

15. For more on the Slow Movement, see http://slowdownnow.org (accessed February 5, 2014).

16. Mark Fischetti, "Did Climate Change Cause Hurricane Sandy?" *Scientific American,* October 30, 2012.

17. National Research Council, *Abrupt Climate Change: Inevitable Surprises* (Washington, D.C.: National Academies Press), 1.

18. Michael Lewis, *Boomerang: Travels in the New Third World* (New York: Norton, 2011), 13.

19. Ibid., 2.

20. Ibid., 3.

21. Andrew Higgins, "Teeing Off at the Edge of the Arctic? A Chinese Plan Baffles Iceland," *New York Times,* March 22, 2013.

22. Quoted in David J. Unger, "Arctic Council: China Looks North for Oil, Gas, and Fish," available at http://www.csmonitor.com/Environment/Energy-Voices/2013/0515/Arctic-Council-China-looks-north-for-oil-gas-and-fish (accessed February 5, 2014).

23. Andrew Blum, *Tubes: A Journey to the Center of the Internet* (New York: Ecco, 2012), 230.

24. James Glanz, "Power, Pollution and the Internet," *New York Times,* September 22, 2012.

25. Ibid.

26. Eli Pariser, *The Filter Bubble: How the New Personalized Web Is Changing What We Read and How We Think* (New York: Penguin Books, 2001), 11.

27. Glanz, "Power, Pollution and the Internet."

28. Ibid.

29. William J. Baumol, *The Free Market Innovation Machine: Analyzing the Growth Miracle of Capitalism* (Princeton, NJ: Princeton University Press, 2002), 1.

30. National Research Council, *Abrupt Climate Change,* 14.

31. James Hansen, "Can We Defuse the Global Warming Time Bomb?" available at http://naturalscience.com/ns/articles/01-16/ns_jeh.html (accessed February 5, 2014).

32. Kenneth Golden, Elizabeth Hunke, Cecelia Bitz, and Mark Holland, "Sea Ice in the Global Climate System," available at http://www.mathaware.org/mam/09/essays/Golden_etal_Sea_Ice.pdf (accessed February 5, 2014).

33. Kevin Schaefer et al., "Policy Implications of Warming Permafrost," available at http://www.unep.org/pdf/permafrost.pdf (accessed February 5, 2014).

34. Paul Voosen, "Geologists Chip Away at Mystery of Climate's Influence on Volcanoes," *Chronicle of Higher Education,* May 24, 2013.

35. Philip Conkling et al., *The Fate of Greenland: Lessons from Abrupt Climate Change* (Cambridge, MA: MIT Press, 2011), 102.

36. Quoted in Elizabeth Kolbert, "The Climate of Man—I," *New Yorker,* April 25, 2005, 14.

37. Quoted in Justin Gillis, "Heat-Trapping Gas Passes Milestone, Raising Fears," *New York Times,* May 10, 2013.

38. Edward Wong, "Cost of Environmental Degradation in China Is Growing," *New York Times,* March 29, 2013.

39. Naomi Oreskes and Erik M. Conway, *Merchants of Doubt: How a Handful of Scientists Obscured the Truth on Issues from Tobacco Smoke to Global Warming* (New York: Bloomsbury Press, 2010), 11, 248–49.

40. Ibid., 252, 254.

41. Mark Hertsgaard, "Harvesting a Climate Disaster," *New York Times,* September 12, 2012.

42. Geoffrey Parket, "The Inevitable Climate Catastrophe," *Chronicle of Higher Education,* May 28, 2013.

43. Milan Kundera, *Slowness,* trans. Linda Asher (New York: Harper, 1996), 39.

44. Quoted in Guy Clayton, *Hare Brain, Tortoise Mind: How Intelligence Increases When You Think Less* (New York: HarperCollins, 1999), 175–76.

Index

Page numbers in *italics* refer to illustrations.

Monetary Control Act (1980), 100
Monetary History of the United States (Friedman and Schwartz), 39
Money and Speed (Meerman), 256, 260
monotheism, 181
Montebourg, Arnaud, 307–8
Montgomery Ward, 98
Montulli, Lou, 190–91
Moore, Charles, 103
Moore's law, 1, 231
Morgan Stanley, 132, 190, 315
Morris, Errol, 164
Morse, Samuel F. B., 27–28, 117–18, 119, 122
Morse code, 122
mortgages, 100–101
Mosaic Communications, 189–90
MTV, 131
Muybridge, Eadweard, 28, 30–31, 33, 73, 75
MySpace, 206

Nanex (technology firm), 241
NanoSpeed Market Data Mesh, 239
National Academy of Sciences, 330
National Association of Securities Dealers (NASDAQ), 132, 133–34, 230–31, 233–34, 235, 239, 257
National BankAmerica, 99–100
National Banking Act (1863), 110
National Biscuit Company, 98
National Center for Atmospheric Research, 331
National Center for Supercomputing Applications, 189
National Environmental Policy Act (1970), 338
National Research Council, 319
National Retail Dry Goods Association, 99

National Science Foundation, 191
NBC (television network), 130
Negroponte, Nicholas, 186–87, 210
neoclassical economics, 246, 247, 247–48, 251–52
neoliberalism, 56, 157, 165, 237; antecedents of, 37, 40, 50; austerity stressed by, 167; debt reduction and, 167; individualism stressed by, 57, 251–52, 295; leisure mistrusted by, 306, 307–8; perils of, 91; triumph of, 144, 146, 172
Netscape, 189–91, 203
Network Nation (John), 117
networks: centralized vs. decentralized, 188–89; disruptions of, 10; emergent complex adaptive, 249–54, 255, 261, 262, 266, 330, 332, 334; financial markets and, 147, 150; Hayek's view of, 254; interdependency of, 18; origins of, 17; television vs. computer, 210–11
NeuroFocus, Inc., 293
neuroscience, 274, 288, 292–94
Neurotechnology Initiatives, 291
Newcastle, England, 19
New Deal, 179
New England, 20
Newman-Norlund, Roger, 294–95
newspapers, 97, 128, 186–87, 191, 208–10
Newton, Isaac, 247
New York, 20, 26, 127, 135
New York Stock Exchange (NYSE), 109, 235; data center of, 241–42; decline of, 228–30, 234; "Flash Crash" on, 256, 258; NASDAQ vs., 130, 132, 231; sale of, 227–28; share volume on, 134, 228, 232–33
New York Times, 209